The Story of Unity

By
James Dillet Freeman

UNITY® Books

Unity Village, Missouri

Fourth Edition 2000

For information, address Unity Books, Publishers, Unity School of Christianity, 1901 NW Blue Parkway, Unity Village, MO 64065-0001.

To receive a catalog of all Unity publications (books, cassettes, compact discs, and magazines) or to place an order, call the Customer Service Department: (816) 969-2069 or 1-800-669-0282.

Cover design by Gail Ishmael

Interior drawings of Unity Village by Liesa Goettel

Library of Congress Cataloging-in-Publication Data

Freeman, James Dillet.
    The story of Unity / by James Dillet Freeman.
        p.   cm.
    ISBN 0-87159-145-6 (hardcover)
    1. Unity School of Christianity—History. 2. Fillmore, Charles, 1854–1948. 3. Fillmore, Myrtle, 1845–1931. I. Title.
BX9890.U53 F74 2000
289.9'7'09—dc21   99-046337

ISBN 0-87159-145-6
Canada BN 13252 9033 RT

Publisher's Note

The Story of Unity was first published in 1951 with the title *The Household of Faith: The Story of Unity*. It included fifteen chapters on the growth of the Unity movement and a section of selections from the writings of cofounder Charles Fillmore. Later editions omitted this section.

In 1978 a revised edition updated the original fifteen chapters and included selections from the writings of *both* Charles and Myrtle Fillmore, the other cofounder of Unity. There have been many changes to Unity since then, but because this is a history of Unity, we ask that the reader understand that many "current" details have changed. For example, in 1999 Silent Unity, the international prayer ministry started by Myrtle and Charles, received about a million letters and more than one million phone calls from people requesting prayer support, all up considerably from the numbers in this book. To revise such details with every printing would be a daunting task and one best suited, perhaps, to another work.

However, to continue the story, we have added a new appendix that updates Unity chronology since the mid-'70s.

Foreword

Having been immersed in the Unity movement during my entire lifetime, it is difficult to be objective about this book. Also, adding to my dilemma is that the author, James Dillet Freeman, is a lifelong friend and valued associate. Nevertheless, I will say without hesitation or qualification that I find *The Story of Unity* both a factual and fascinating account of how a courageous American couple gave the world a new practical approach to Christianity at a time when it was badly needed.

I personally can bear witness to how this new viewpoint toward the Jesus Christ message has grown, flourished, and changed countless lives for the better. Beginning with a freshly inspired insight into a traditional concept, and precious little more, Charles and Myrtle Fillmore promoted ideas which have spread around the globe and have had a positive influence on religious thought both within and outside Christianity.

It has been my pleasant, interesting, and challenging duty to succeed my grandfather Charles Fillmore, the cofounder of Unity, and my uncle Lowell Fillmore, as the third president of the parent organization of our movement, the Unity School of Christianity. Our work has experienced a steady if unspectacular growth for almost a century, and I believe the best is yet to come. Although through the years strong individual personalities have risen to positions of influence within this movement, none has become dominant nor has altered our founders' course of adhering to God's Truth wherever or however it is progressively revealed. Today, as this book accurately relates, Unity's approach strives to be psychologically healthy, scientifically sound, intellectually challenging, and spiritually satisfying.

While we seek to adapt and innovate to meet the spiritual needs of a changing universe, I believe, as does every Unity leader described in this volume, that Unity will always be essentially a household of faith—faith in God as the source of all good, and faith in His Spirit as the one presence and power in all creation.

Charles R. Fillmore
1978

CONTENTS

Chapter I

The Faith of the Fillmores

"According to Your Faith"

IN THE MIDDLE OF THE SPEECH, the fire in the stove went out. When the speaker noticed this, he did not stop his speech—he went right on—but he came down from the platform and, picking up a stick of wood, took out a knife and began to whittle kindling. With this kindling he re-lighted the fire. As he worked, he kept on speaking calmly, occasionally emphasizing his remarks by gesturing with the stick of wood from which he was whittling. When he had the fire going once more to suit him, he remounted the platform, speaking all the while.

A boy in the congregation had attended other religious meetings but never had he been to one like this, where the minister built a fire and made a speech at the same time. The simple act seemed to light a fire inside the boy. He was so impressed that he volunteered, during the time that he was in Kansas City, to come to all the meetings that the man conducted and keep the fire going.

Many years later he wrote to Unity to tell about the incident, for the speaker had been Charles Fillmore, a cofounder of Unity School. The fire in the stove burned to ashes many years ago but the fire that was lighted in the boy's heart and mind is today still burning as brightly as ever.

Charles Fillmore lighted many fires in many minds. He was a fire-bringer, a carrier of the Promethean spark.

9

He was highly developed spiritually, yet his spirituality was salted by a sense of practicality. He was an original and creative thinker and moved boldly into new realms of thought, yet he never lost the common touch. He was always trying to light fires in people's minds, but if the fire in the stove that warmed their bodies went out, he attended to that also. His head was in the clouds, but his feet were on the ground. He was gifted with uncommon sense, but he had an uncommon lot of common sense. There was about him the divine simplicity that must have characterized Jesus and some of the great philosophers of ancient times. You might imagine Socrates lighting the fire, if it went out in the middle of one of his discourses with his students. Charles Fillmore was such a man.

Probably few persons have spent more hours in prayer than he. He lived for ninety-four years, and the last sixty of those years were for him almost a constant prayer. His life had one purpose—the unfoldment of his own spiritual qualities so that he might help others to find and unfold the Spirit within them.

Afflicted with a physical handicap that kept him more or less in pain, he might have settled for half a life. But he was not content to take life and half live it. He had the divine intuition that life is meant to be something grand and wonderful. He felt that life is good and that it should be full of joy, not suffering; that evil is only the result of human failure to understand and to apply the truth about self. He felt that people develop only a fraction of their inherent powers. He spent much of his lifetime praying and thinking and laboring to develop those powers within himself.

Perhaps it was because he himself needed physical help so much that he was not content with a religion that merely taught him to endure his pain. Religion to him was not an artist's subtle drawing to be hung up on the temple wall and occasionally admired, it was a set of working drawings that he could carry about with him in the back pocket of his mind and apply to any situation that might arise. He sought for a religion that would heal.

He felt that it is as right for us to have an alert mind, a healthy body, and prosperity in our affairs as it is for us to be spiritual. He felt that we are meant to live abundantly on all levels of our being; that it is God's will for all of us to be strong and vigorous and rich and successful and happy. He never had much sympathy with religions that emphasize the spiritual to the exclusion of our other needs. You might say of him, as Jesus said of Himself: "I came that they may have life, and have it abundantly."

Charles Fillmore came to men and women who had been taught that God is far away and hard to approach, that God is a stern judge, and this life is meant to be a trial and a vale of tears; and he proved to them by his own way of living that none of these things is true.

To Charles Fillmore, God was a personal friend. He spent many hours every day in simple conversation with Him. He loved God, and God loved him, and they met together frequently and talked matters over in prayer. Charles took his affairs and his needs to God. He wrote of God:

> Never be formal with God. He cares no more for forms and ceremonies than do the principles of mathematics for fine figures or elaborate blackboards.
>
> You cannot use God too often. He loves to be used, and the more you use Him the more easily you use Him and the more pleasant His help becomes. If you want a dress, a car, a house, or if you are thinking of driving a sharp bargain with your neighbor, going on a journey, giving a friend a present, running for office, or reforming a nation, ask God for guidance, in a moment of silent soul desire.

He did not believe that God gives us everything we ask for, good or bad; but he did believe that we should take everything to God in prayer. One time a saloonkeeper came to him for prayers for healing and was helped. The saloonkeeper then said: "I also need prayers for prosperity, but of course you could not pray for a man in my business to prosper."

Charles Fillmore replied: "Certainly. God will help

you to prosper. 'If ye shall ask anything of the Father, he will give it you in my name,' does not exclude saloon-keepers." He prayed for prosperity for the man, just as he would have prayed for anyone else, and learned afterward that the man had gotten out of the saloon business and had found prosperity in other lines of work.

Because Charles Fillmore was a man of prayer, but a practical man as well, thousands of people today have health of body, success in their affairs, and happiness in their lives that they would never have had except for him.

Never an issue of *Unity* magazine appears that does not contain the stories of those who have changed their life by the application of the ideas taught by the Fillmores. Never a day goes by that letters do not come to Unity School of Christianity telling how someone prayed and prayer was answered. (Unity School never prints a letter from a correspondent without first receiving permission to do so.) One person writes:

> *Dear Silent Unity:* Please accept our thank you's for your prayers for my father for the past days and weeks.
>
> The blessings which have come our way have been tremendous. First of all, the ulcers on the legs are almost completely healed. The doctor was considering amputating one leg at the time of admission, he was so certain the infection was that severe. We were advised the hospital stay would be about six months if the leg could be saved.
>
> In the past week, the doctor was advising a nursing home, which upset all of us so much. My father just dreaded going into a nursing home. This is no longer even a consideration. He will be coming home soon. Praise God.
>
> Another miracle—because of my mother's feeling toward my father (she is now deceased), I didn't think he was worth bothering with. I had been acting out all of the things she had told me about my dad, that he was stupid, slow, etc. I had dreaded the hos-

pital visits, I hated sitting down and being forced to talk with this man.

I became aware of my feelings, then made a decision—I was going to do the loving thing, no matter what. I would take care of this old man in a loving way regardless of how I thought l felt. The miracle then happened, I really began to feel loving. I really believe I found God through him. He's a sweet man, not at all like my mother had pictured him for me.

There have been so many other people who have touched me, and that I have touched in the hospital, it has been a beautiful and needed experience for all of us. I am so grateful.

And another writes:

Dear Friends: To capture on paper my feelings at this moment is difficult. How do you paint rainbows, light, and love on a letter? Encouraged by the thoughts and meditations received from *Daily Word* and *Unity* magazine, I recently just turned my life around. I quit my job of eleven years, moved my home, lost 45 pounds, and cut my hair. I have returned to junior college on a full-time basis, found a new place to live (completely furnished—includes an 86-year-old grandmother whose eyes still sparkle), and start a new job on the 17th of this month.

It was so easy, everything just sort of fell into my lap.

In *Daily Word* you said: "There is a wonderful, beautiful plan for your life." Perhaps that sentence can convey how I feel. I'm not sure exactly where I'm going—don't even care, because inside of me a little voice is reading a map and I know it's right for me.

Thank you for helping. You're God's partner, as well as His publisher.

And yet another:

Dear Friends: On Wednesday morning I called requesting you pray with me in a difficult financial situation.

Within an hour dramatic changes began taking place. During that day I was paid two fees from

wholly unexpected sources and the dire emergency
was over.

What happened cannot be explained in any other
way except as an answer to prayer.

I am so grateful.

Through the years thousands and thousands of letters like these have come to Unity School of Christianity
telling of people helped, people healed, people lifted up,
people transformed—because they prayed! Because
Charles Fillmore prayed and taught others to pray! Because he and his wife Myrtle Fillmore dedicated their
lives to prayer, and to the service of their fellow human
beings!

Charles and Myrtle Fillmore worked together to
build Unity. It was Myrtle Fillmore who first accepted the
idea of divine healing; it was Charles Fillmore who edited the first magazine. It was Myrtle Fillmore who first
led Silent Unity; it was Charles Fillmore who named the
work Unity and developed it into the worldwide organization it is today. It was Myrtle Fillmore who led the
people in meditation and prayer; it was Charles Fillmore
who made speeches and wrote books. They worked together as heart and head work together, and from their
united efforts grew the great movement that is Unity. If
Mrs. Fillmore supplied the original impetus, it was her
husband who supplied the greater part of the energy that
carried it forward.

Charles and Myrtle Fillmore had a simplicity about
them that endeared them to all who knew them. They
soared, but they lived simply. They founded a faith that
reaches around the world, yet their humility was as great
as their accomplishments. It was Unity, not Charles and
Myrtle Fillmore, whose success they worked to forward.
There was no pretense about these two. They never took
a title to themselves and they were such unassuming
people that no one else felt like calling them by a title
either. Among their workers and close friends, there was
almost a family feeling, and many of these called them

"Papa Charley" and "Mama Myrtle." They were the kind of people who, when they went to the vegetarian cafeteria that Unity once had on the corner of Ninth and Tracy in Kansas City, stood in line, took their turn, and paid for their meals just as everyone else did.

Charles and Myrtle Fillmore believed that the most important things in their lives were their ideas and their works, the good they did for others; they were teachers. Those who came to Kansas City after 1906 and studied under them remember them always as they appeared on the platform at 913 Tracy Avenue before the congregation of the Unity Society of Practical Christianity on a Sunday morning. Myrtle Fillmore, wearing her white hair like a crown, gentle, smiling, sitting silent with a look not wholly of this world, and Charles Fillmore standing at the rostrum leaning slightly to one side with his hands braced before him and making in his calm, deliberate style some observation like the following:

> God is the health of His people. God is infinite life. Let us hold to the Spirit of God, demonstrating itself in life everywhere. That is what the scientific world is preaching today, and we cannot get away from this proposition of the omnipresence of the one life. There is nothing else to come but the Spirit of Truth. We do not look for another. We know that the Spirit of Truth is here. It has always been here, but we have turned our face in another direction. We have looked somewhere else rather than to the Spirit of Truth. The Spirit of Truth is in the midst of you. It is in you, and you will never have peace of mind, you will never have success in any way, you will never have health of body, you will never have anything satisfactory until you demonstrate its presence and its power in your life.

Charles Fillmore was always a student and a teacher, seeking, always seeking, for further insight into the mysteries of life. He spent years poring over the Bible, working out his volumes of interpretation, trying to uncover the hidden meaning of the Scriptures in terms of human life and affairs. He spent years on years in prayer and thought, seeking a knowledge of the mysteries wrapped up in his own being, slowly working out his concept of the twelve powers of man, seeking in the silence to unfold and quicken these powers in his own body, working night after night into the early morning hours to send his word down into the cells of his body, to quicken and regenerate them to eternal life.

Charles and Myrtle Fillmore were more than teachers. They were healers. They were not content merely to have ideas or even to tell others of the ideas. They took the ideas and worked to demonstrate them in their own lives and bodies. The very heart of the Unity teaching has to do with healing the ills of mind, body, and affairs. Unity began with the healing of Myrtle Fillmore. Its first fruits were the healing of her friends and neighbors, accomplished by her realization of the Christ power within. The heart of Unity today is Silent Unity, which sends its message of healing to millions of persons throughout the world each year. In the anteroom outside the Fillmores' offices, each day people waited their turn to have these two teachers, who had touched God's power and whom God's power had touched, utter a healing prayer for them.

Charles and Myrtle Fillmore were builders, too. Go out to Unity School today and walk down the shady lanes or stand and gaze at the buildings that house Unity and you get a sense of what they built. It was their son Rickert who erected most of the buildings at Unity Farm, but it was they who envisioned such a spiritual center; and it was they who from nothing but an idea and faith in that idea, built the Unity work of which the buildings are but a visible expression.

Today printed materials in a dozen languages pour out of the buildings to be sent to millions of people in most of the countries of the earth. Inspirational Unity pieces are broadcast from radio and television stations across the nation. Every day teachers and Truth lecturers in hundreds of Unity centers expound to thousands of eager students the Jesus Christ message as it was interpreted by Charles and Myrtle Fillmore. And thousands come every year to Unity Village to absorb the ideas of these two pioneers and to bask in the tranquil atmosphere of the spiritual community they left behind them.

Charles and Myrtle Fillmore had many abilities. They were practical people: teachers, ministers, healers, builders. But they had vision, too. They worked to turn their ideas into magazines and buildings, into restored bodies and renewed minds and illumined lives. But their ideas soared even beyond their accomplishments. They had the vision of the perfect person in God, and this perfection was their goal. They aimed at the highest, and how high they mounted! They aimed at eternal life, and how much of life they won, not only for themselves but for how many others! Because they lived close in thought and aspiration to God, there was about them an atmosphere of spirituality that those who were near them felt.

About Myrtle Fillmore, there was always an unworldly quality that once made her husband say of her, "Myrtle belongs on another planet." She was not much concerned with worldliness. Almost all the writing that she did was in private letters, most of which have disappeared. Her speaking rarely consisted of formal addresses, but was more likely to consist of the inspiration that came to her at the moment. When she spoke, thought moved through her as a butterfly moves through a field of summer flowers, lighting on an idea, hovering for a moment, tasting its sweetness, then moving on to another. Little that she said was ever written down. Yet though most of the words she uttered have vanished, their effect has not vanished from the hearts and minds of those who heard them and were lifted up, nor from the flesh of those who heard them and were healed. Unity itself is the ever-living, ever-growing expression of her spirit.

About Charles Fillmore, there was something of the prophet. He lived simply and he lived very close to God and he felt very strongly that God was speaking to him, using him to convey divine ideas. Like Joseph and Daniel, he felt that God came to him in dreams and visions of the night and revealed to him much of the Truth about which he wrote and spoke. He was always looking forward. He foresaw radio and talked about it in sermons and articles. He foresaw that the atom would be split and become a source of power. His mind was always ranging far ahead of most persons, even ahead of his fellow workers.

The mother of one of the editors at Unity School recalled that the first time she ever went to hear Charles Fillmore speak she thought he talked about "crazy things, such as talking through the ethers and harnessing the ethers to do our work for us"; she almost never went back.

Once one of his editors questioned an article Mr. Fillmore had written about atomic energy. Years later the first atomic bomb was detonated in New Mexico.

Charles and Myrtle Fillmore followed the "visionary gleam." They were pioneers of mind and spirit. They were never bound by limited concepts about life but were always striking out into the new. They were people with the courage to step out on faith. "Do not judge according to appearances," said Jesus, and Charles and Myrtle Fillmore took Him at His word. Appearances might say, "You cannot do it," but Charles and Myrtle Fillmore did not believe in appearances. "If you need something," said Mr. Fillmore, "go ahead and get it, do something about it."

Charles and Myrtle Fillmore were a man and a woman of faith. In the word *faith* is summed up the story of their life and works—and the story of Unity. They did their works through faith. They soared beyond their works through faith. They were teachers through faith. They were healers through faith. They were builders through faith. They were overcomers through faith.

Many, many times in the history of Unity they came to a place where it seemed that they could not go on, yet they went on through faith.

They taught that God is a help in every need and they prayed in this simple faith. Over and over when they were in need, they went to God to prove that what they taught is true. All that they thought and wrote and did they wrought through faith. Through faith, they turned to God in the beginning. Through faith, they healed their bodies. Through faith, they brought healing to others. Through faith, they founded Unity. Through faith, they persevered in their idea when everything seemed to say that they were destined for failure. Through faith, they built a work that rings the world around with faith and prayer.

They never lost faith.

Once Unity was in serious financial straits. Bills that had to be paid were piling up, and there did not seem to be money enough to meet the payroll. The Fillmores called their staff together to pray about the matter. One of the staff said, "Let us pray that the money holds out."

"Oh, no," whispered Myrtle Fillmore, "let us pray that our faith holds out."

Chapter II

Charles Fillmore's Early Years

"Youth and the Dawn of Life"

CHARLES FILLMORE was born into this present itinerary on August 22, 1854, at 4 a.m., on an Indian reservation just outside the little town of St. Cloud, Minnesota, in a log cabin that his father Henry had built by a ford over the Sauk River. He was christened Charles Sherlock Fillmore. He never used his middle name.

Charles Fillmore once wrote about one of his ancestors, John Fillmore: "As a boy of thirteen he was kidnapped on the coast of England by pirates. He was on the pirate ship for eighteen years. Finally he and a companion tied the pirates while they were under the influence of liquor and sailed the ship into Boston harbor, where the pirates were executed. This little incident in my family history has often reminded me of what a lecturer on heraldry once said about his family tree: that he was somewhat timid about looking it up because he might find something hanging to it. A facetious member of the audience queried, 'By the neck or the tail?'"

Millard Fillmore, thirteenth President of the United States, was Henry Fillmore's second cousin. An uncle of Henry's, Glezen Fillmore, was the first ordained Methodist Episcopal Minister in New York State and established the first Methodist Episcopal Church in Buffalo, New York.

Charles' father Henry was born and reared in Buffalo. After receiving a common school education, he left the city for the wilderness of Minnesota. In Minnesota, he became a trader with the Chippewa Indians and settled on a small reservation located just north of St. Cloud.

Young Fillmore, the Indian trader, had been in Minnesota only a few months when he met and married Mary Georgiana Stone, the eighteen-year-old daughter of a millwright. Born in Nova Scotia of Welsh and English ancestry, she had been brought West by her father when she was a child.

Charles Fillmore was born in a log cabin where the only protection against the forty-degree-below-zero cold of the Minnesota winters was the huge fireplace, which devoured logs at a rate that kept Charles and his younger brother Norton busy throughout the winter.

When Charles was seven, his father Henry left home. He had managed to acquire some land about ten miles north of the cabin where the boys lived with their mother and there he built another cabin for himself. From then on, the boys spent part of their time with their mother and part with their father.

As Charles Fillmore later wrote, his childhood was "romantic but crude and unprofitable." It was a kind of Huckleberry Finn existence. Hunters and trappers came and went, roving bands of Chippewa and Sioux Indians passed by the cabin. Charles spent a great deal of time wandering in and out of the Indian lodges and tepees as freely as did the Indian children. In this way, he and his mother learned some words of the Chippewa tongue, and years later Grandma Fillmore taught these to Rickert and Lowell. When a member of that tribe visited Unity long afterward, one of the boys was able to repeat a few words in the Chippewa language, which the Indian seemed to understand.

Peaceful relations, however, were never to be taken for granted, and misunderstanding was commonplace. When Charles was less than two years old and he and his mother were alone in their cabin, a band of painted Sioux rushed up. The leader, a towering medicine man fantastically painted and decked in the full regalia of his profession, strode into the cabin, tore little Charles out of his mother's arms, and rode away with him. It was evening before the warriors brought him back to his distracted mother. Where they had taken him and what they had done with him, Charles could not remember, but he always had a feeling that they had used him in some mystical ceremony.

Charles attended a log-cabin school where there was one schoolmaster for all the students and the school term was only for the three mid-winter months of the year. He went to this school for only a few years, so he did not have much formal education. Neither did he have many opportunities to go to church.

Though the family was not rich, there was never any dire lack of food in the house. Food in Minnesota in the 1850s was easy to obtain. Wild game and berries of all kinds were plentiful. Many times in the winter and early spring, Charles and his brother would go down to a nearby creek or pond and break the ice to find cranberries frozen under it, or perhaps to fish. In the fall, there was an abundance of wild rice and Charles would go out in a canoe, just as the Indians did, and bending the rice blades into his canoe, he would beat off the grain with a stick and bring it home to dry and store.

It was the mother, Mary Georgiana Fillmore, who was to be the chief force in shaping Charles' destiny. Life had never been easy for Mary Fillmore—or "Grandma Fillmore," as she came to be known to the Unity workers —but she had never asked for ease. Like her son Charles, she was one of those persons who have a rich zest for life. She was not afraid to live. Neither the natural wilderness in which she was reared nor the economic wilderness in which she found herself by the necessity of having to single-handedly raise a family ever daunted her.

Mary Fillmore was a strong character. She wrapped herself in an imperious manner and developed a tenacity of will with which she could press forward through poverty or inharmony or whatever obstacle she faced, until her goal was reached.

Mary Fillmore needed her tenacity of purpose to raise her family in the wilderness. At twenty-five, she found herself alone with two children to feed and care for; the oldest, seven; the youngest, five. She lived in a crude cabin four miles outside the nearest town, surrounded by half-savage Indians and half-civilized whites, mostly French traders and trappers who spoke a foreign tongue. The people were hospitable, however, and she managed to make enough money as a dressmaker to keep the three of them clothed and fed. The food was simple, but with the magic known only to those who have to do it, Mary Fillmore had learned how to take a small bag of beans and a soupbone and turn them into a week's meals for three.

After five years of this struggle, one of the members of the little family, Norton, ran away from home and never returned to live with them. He disappeared into the West and out of the life of Charles Fillmore, except for occasional contacts.

It was a short time after his brother left that Charles Fillmore met with the accident that was probably the determining incident of his life. His hip was dislocated in a skating accident. A doctor decided that rheumatism had set in and treated the boy for that. There was no improvement; instead the leg grew steadily worse. A succession of doctors produced a succession of diagnoses, but no improvement in the patient. In the words of Charles Fillmore, himself, "I was bled, leached, cupped, lanced, seasoned, blistered, and roweled. Six running sores were artificially produced on my leg to draw out the diseased condition that was presumed to be within. Physicians of different schools were employed, and the last one always wondered how I ever pulled through alive under the treatment of the 'quack' that preceded him; and as I look back at it now it's a miracle to me how I ever got away from them all with the little bundle of bones and sinews that I found in my possession after they had finished their experiments."

By that time, the hip socket had been destroyed, the

leg had stopped growing and could not be moved. For more than two years, the disease ran its course in the leg, sometimes seeming to disappear only to return with increased violence. Many times during the course of the sickness, Charles did not believe that he was going to come through. Often he must have wondered why he was making the struggle. It was a titanic struggle. But there was a titan in the little body, and the struggle was made. Whenever he could be, he would be up and about on a pair of handmade crutches, hopping around the cabin, doing what he could to help. When the disease would bring his body down again, it did not bring him down in spirit. He never gave up.

This boy did not know what it meant to give up—to sickness, to poverty, to discouragement. Probably the spirit of the mother, by this time a veteran of hardship, helped him more than anything else, for she fired the son with her courage, which, if it had no power to stop the infection in the leg, did have power to stop the infection from spreading to the boy's spirit. The spirit remained whole, and as is very often the case under such conditions, even grew stronger.

Qualities of the heart and mind are like physical qualities, they are developed by exercise. Often we make no effort to acquire them unless life forces demands for them upon us; but once we have them, they are ours to use. For two years, merely to keep the thin flame of life flickering in his body, Charles Fillmore had to call on all the energy he could command; he had to build the will to live, or die. He had to build courage. He had to build resourcefulness. When the struggle ended in victory, these qualities remained and were his to put to other purposes.

When after two years the disease had run its course, it left a withered leg. But it left something else, too—a spirit that would not give up, a spirit that was not daunted by pain, a vital, determined, courageous spirit. It was this robust spirit that was to shape the life of the man.

Youth is the time of life when men engage most ac-
tively in physical pursuits, but this activity was denied
Charles Fillmore. Here were an alert, swift, vital mind
and a bold, self-reliant, enterprising spirit lodged in a
body incapable of much physical activity. This mind and
this spirit had to find an outlet for their energy. Charles
Fillmore did not have less energy than others; he had
more. The two-year struggle he had made against disease had released tremendous quantities of energy
within him. Now he had to put this energy to use.

He started back to the one-room schoolhouse, but his
difficulty in getting about made it hard for him to go to
school; moreover, in a short time he had to go to work to
help his mother.

His first job was as a printer's devil in St. Cloud.
Here he learned some of the printer's trade that was to be
of use to him thirty years later when he came to publish
the magazine *Unity*. After that, he worked in a grocery
store and in a bank.

Charles worked hard in the grocery store and the
bank, but his work could not begin to absorb his energies. He had a mind that demanded more vigorous use
than he could put it to in his work.

At this time, an army officer named Edgar Taylor
happened to be stationed in St. Cloud. His wife Caroline
had gone through college, a rare attainment for women of
that time. This woman had a genuine love for classical
literature. They had a son, Edgar, a boy of Charles' age,
to whom she was devoted, and she was determined that
this boy should amount to something. At the time when
young Charles met her and was drawn to her, she happened to be busy teaching her son, much against his will,
the classical literature that she herself loved so much.

Here was a woman who had read and thought; her
mind was full of knowledge. She was familiar with many
books, most of which the young son of an Indian trader
probably had never even heard about. But Charles had a
curious and avid mind, a spirit ready for books and learning, and however Edgar reacted to literature, Charles

was happy to make its acquaintance. Shakespeare, Tennyson, Emerson, Lowell, and we do not know how many others, were poured one after another into the active ferment of his imagination. Edgar Taylor might have preferred to be out running around with other boys, but Charles, who was unable to do this, reveled in the books that Mrs. Taylor introduced him to. He learned to love the beautiful language and exalted ideas of Shakespeare and Tennyson. They made such a deep impression on the boy's mind that all his life his writings were embellished with quotations from their works. So much did the American writers James Russell Lowell and Ralph Waldo Emerson come to mean to him, that later he and his wife Myrtle, who was also a great admirer of the writers, gave each of their first two sons Lowell Page and Waldo Rickert, the name of one of those two great New England transcendentalists. Later Charles Fillmore was to write an article on the metaphysics of Shakespeare, and numerous quotations by Emerson were to appear in the pages of *Unity.*

Not only did Mrs. Taylor teach him to read great literature, but she also taught him the rules of grammar and gave him writing exercises to perform. Many an evening when he came home from the grocery store or the bank, he and she together would pore over something he had written while she pointed out mistakes and assisted him with his rhetoric. Besides her interest in literary matters, she was interested in the new ideas that, seeping out of New England, were making people here and there question the concepts of orthodox theology, and she helped to stimulate an interest in those new ideas in the young man who had turned to her for learning.

Above all, however, by teaching him grammar and acquainting him with the beautiful phrasing and noble ideas of the great English and American poets and essayists, she was helping him to prepare to express ideas of his own when at last they should come to him. When, three decades later, he felt the urge to express the new thoughts that were unfolding in his mind, the small amount of formal schooling he had obtained would have equipped him but poorly for the task that was his; but thanks to Mrs. Taylor, when at last he found something to say, he had the skill with which to say it so that people would stop and pay attention to it.

Meanwhile St. Cloud was growing up. By 1870 it had a population of 3,000. Had Charles Fillmore stayed there, he might have become in time a prosperous merchant or a banker, for he was to prove later that he had a shrewd business sense; but such a prospect could never have held much allure for a man as imaginative of mind and adventurous of spirit as Charles Fillmore. Among the books he read there were many about the West. Out West, there were marvelous opportunities. There fortunes were being made, mines being discovered, cities being built. It was a young land exploited by young men and it beckoned to the young with hands dripping gold and adventure.

Charles Fillmore had a cousin who lived in the little town of Caddo, located just north of the Texas border in the Indian Territory that is now Oklahoma. One day in the spring of 1874, when Charles was nineteen years old, he packed his clothes, went down to the railroad station in St. Cloud, bought a one-way ticket to Caddo, and got on the train.

Caddo was located in what was probably the wildest district in the United States, and Charles Fillmore did not stay there long. He went on to the end of the Missouri, Kansas & Texas Railroad, which had its terminus twenty miles south, across the Red River in Denison, Texas. In Denison he managed to make a friend of the chief clerk in the freight office and was hired to check cars in the yard. With a sheet of paper and a pencil, he would go out each day to write down the numbers of all freight cars that were in the vicinity of Denison. All his spare time was spent in the freight office helping his friend the clerk do his work. His other friends laughed at him for this diligence, but it proved ultimately not to be without profit, for one day the clerk became ill and Charles was the only person who knew how to perform his duties. For the next five years, Charles Fillmore worked as chief clerk in the freight office of Missouri, Kansas & Texas Railroad in Denison.

As soon as he was able, he sent for his mother. Charles and his mother were unusually close all their lives. She had reared him and supported him. When he had been sick, she had inspired him to live. Later when he and his wife Myrtle were busy founding Unity, she was to take care of the family, cooking the meals, keeping house, making and mending clothes, washing, feeding, and tending the three boys through illness and health, getting them off to school and welcoming them home again, and stretching the few dollars that the founders of Unity were able to provide into food and clothing enough for all. All her life, with doting eyes and loving heart, she was to stand by and look after the needs of the one she called "my boy Charles." Now when he sent for her, she was quick to come to Denison to make a home for him. To help support the home, she once more went to work as a dressmaker.

Among all American pioneers were many of education and refinement. Denison had no small number of these. It was inevitable that they should gravitate together to discuss the literary and philosophic matters that interested them. Charles attached himself to such a group. They were young people who met at one another's homes in the evening, often to read poetry, or if the urge should strike them, to write a few lines.

We know that Charles joined this group, because it was as a member of it in 1876 that he met a red-haired schoolteacher who had come down from Clinton, Missouri, two years before. The name of this teacher was Myrtle Page.

Chapter III

Truth Comes to Myrtle Fillmore

"The Two Shall Become One"

MYRTLE PAGE was next to the youngest of the nine children of Marcus and Lucy Page. She was born in Page-town, Ohio, August 6, 1845. Her family had been early settlers of the town and were influential citizens. They were members of the Methodist Episcopal Church. Her religious training was strict. The family frowned upon most forms of amusement, and the children were not permitted even such diversions as playing cards or danc-ing. Myrtle, however, was the favorite of her father, and in lighthearted moments, when the rest of the family were not around, he taught her how to dance the High-land fling, which she loved to do.

Myrtle had been christened with the name Mary Caroline but she never liked it. From her infancy she could remember her father calling her by the pet name, "Myrtilee, Myrtilee." As a little girl, she adopted the name Myrtle.

She had a better-than-ordinary education for young women of her time, for when she was twenty-two, she enrolled at Oberlin College where she took the "Literary Course for Ladies." After she left college, she went to Clinton, Missouri, a small town about seventy miles southeast of Kansas City, where her brother David Page had moved his family. Here she secured a position teach-ing in the village school.

Myrtle was not a robust person, for she had been

brought up in the belief that she was an invalid and had
inherited a tendency to tuberculosis. She did not, however, let this belief interfere with her life. She lived an
active life, working hard as a teacher and entering enthu-
siastically into many of the activities of the local Methodist church. When she was about thirty years of age, seriously ill with tuberculosis and malaria and hoping to find
health in a warmer, drier climate, she went to Denison,
Texas. Here, as soon as she felt well enough, she opened
a small private school. It was while she was teaching in
this school that she and Charles met.

Myrtle had the same literary interests that Charles
had. She loved to read poetry and philosophy and she
loved to recite. It was through a recitation she gave that
Charles Fillmore first took notice of her. He had gone to
spend a literary evening at the home of some friends, and
there a good-looking, vivacious, red-haired young
woman got up and recited a poem for the group. Charles
later told friends that at that first moment, as he watched
her and listened to her, something inside him said:
"There's your wife, Charles."

In a short time, the two were exchanging books and
ideas; and since they were also interested in scientific
matters, they often went out into the countryside together, searching for fossils. When, in 1878, Myrtle left Denison and returned to Clinton to teach school there again,
Charles wrote to her asking if they could carry on their
acquaintance by correspondence. She replied:

> I was truly pleased to find, when I returned from
> my visit in the country Thursday, among my other
> mail, a letter from you. Such a correspondence would
> prove rather a treat than a burden to me. I shall ever
> feel grateful to you for contributing so much to my
> literary enjoyments and for new thoughts and
> suggestions, yes, and for a kind of sympathy I seldom
> meet.
>
> I have learned many lessons in the past year.
>
> > "What the world teaches profits to the world.
> > What the soul teaches profits to the soul.

Which then first stands erect with Godward face,
When she lets fall her pack of withered facts,
The gleanings of the outward eye and ear,
And looks and listens with her finer sense;
Nor Truth nor knowledge cometh from without."

You question my orthodoxy? Well, if I were called upon to write out my creed it would be rather a strange mixture. I am decidedly eclectic in my theology. Is it not my right to be? Over all is a grand ideal God but full of love and mercy. And dear to my heart is Christ, the perfect man, who shared our earthly sorrows, yet ever lived blameless, and taught such sweet lessons of patience, forgiveness, and tolerance. Outside of ourselves must we go for a strength to trust and rely on. Trusted, that strength proves a help. Call it by what name you choose, the soul understands it.

Last Sabbath I had a glorious time. They sent for me to visit down in the country among my old Fairview friends, and Sunday there was a "basket meeting way off in the woods." I went. The sermons were quite good, and the spot was divine. Near the preacher's stand rose a great ledge of rock that overhung a small stream. It stretched for a half mile or more. Oh, it was grand! I went up on the top, gathered ferns and mosses—the most beautiful mosses! One's foot sunk down among them, green and silver gray they were. And the most picturesque nooks and grottoes. Oh, to me came the messages then, from the divine Spirit, more direct than through His human messengers!

The good, simple-hearted country folk enjoyed seeing me enjoy it so and confessed, "It was mighty nice." They saw rock and moss, listened decorously to the man of God, while I, in a kind of charmed life, was a part of all I saw—and a part of God. What have I said? But you understand me, you know there are times when we go out and seem to become a part of this great Spirit of the universe. Now, I seldom dare confess to this foolish (?) other life I keep within myself, but I couldn't live without it. And when I try

to choke it out, I am the most miserable creature on
earth.

Meanwhile Charles continued to work in Denison,
but a year later, in 1879, he lost his job with the railroad.
This came about over a friend who also worked in the
freight office. When a visiting dignitary on the railroad
came through Denison and in the presence of Charles
made a false accusation against this friend, Charles'
sense of fair play and loyalty sprang vigorously to his
friend's defense. After a furious argument in which he
told the official in no uncertain terms that the accusation
was untrue, he was dismissed.

However, for some time before this, Charles had
been thinking of leaving Denison. His being a clerk in a
freight office had proved to be no more satisfying than
his working in a bank or a grocery store had been. His
mind was reaching out for something more. He was restless for new enterprises. He did not know just what it was
that he wanted to do but he knew that he was not content
with the sort of thing that he had found. Out in Colorado,
gold and silver had been discovered and people were
making fortunes over night, so out to Colorado went
Charles Fillmore.

The first work that he secured there was as a mule-
team driver. The work was extremely hazardous and required so much stamina that it is difficult to believe that
a man with his physical handicap could have done it, but
he did. The life of a mule-team driver was the crudest
sort of life imaginable and exposed to all kinds of peril.
At night, Charles slept under his wagon, the only shelter
he had against the mountain weather. The trails through
the passes were scarcely trails at all, and it was sometimes all that he and the six mules he drove could do to
get the wagonload of freight to its destination. "Once,"
he told a friend, "mules, wagon, and all went off the edge
of a precipice." But he was able to fling himself from the
wagon seat to safety.

One of the towns to which Charles drove his team

was Gunnison, Colorado. This was a brand-new boom town when he went there in 1879. Buildings were going up on every side as fast as men and materials could be brought in to build them, and new mines were being discovered every day. Charles looked about him, discovered that Gunnison held much better prospects than driving a mule team over the mountain trails, and stayed. Here he learned to be an assayer and for the next two years engaged in the mining and the real estate businesses. Some of the partners that Charles had at this time became important figures in the early development of Colorado.

With all his arduous activities, however, he did not forget the titian-haired schoolmistress in Clinton, Missouri, with whom he had so many ideas and interests in common. His correspondence with her continued and increased in ardor. In the spring of 1881, he took a trip back to Clinton, and there, on March 29, he and Myrtle were married.

That night, Charles and his bride got on the train for Colorado and set out on the great adventure of their life together. Three weeks later, Myrtle was writing excitedly back to her sister:

> This is the first work my pen has done since I crossed the "delectable mountains." (Charles smiles at my name for the Continental Divide.)
>
> Of the three weeks since *the day,* one was spent on the road, one in resting, and this last one in taking in the situation. Gunnison, like all rapid growths, has not stopped for the extras. We all live in one dooryard fenced in by the mountains. Children and burros seem to have spontaneous growth here and belong to no one in particular but rove round over the unfenced wastes, creating a melody that makes one unconsciously shield his ears.
>
> Three weeks ago, we left you. I seem to have an unsorted jumble of mountains, snow, and strange experiences in my mind to fill up this space between now and then. Our journey was delightful—I might

fib a little to include our trip over the range. We
remained at Poncha Springs, the end of the rails, two
days, resting for our stagecoach trip. We left Poncha
in a stagecoach at 7 in the morning (Monday). At 11
we had a layover at a ranch till 8 o'clock at night,
waiting for the snow to freeze on the mountains. We
had Mark Twain's typical driver, by name "Jack."
When we were finally transferred to sleigh runners,
such an experience as we had. There were eleven
men, I the only lady.

The roads or passes were in such fearful condition
that the men were obliged to walk the greater part of
the way up. It was grand. The moon hung above, the
stars seemed to crown the higher peaks. Constant
changes seemed taking place, mountain on mountain piled on one side, water pouring down in cataracts among the pines far, far below. Again fields of
snow would rise till the stars seemed to have them
for background. On the other hand one misstep
would have landed us hundreds of feet below where
the snow was pierced by the dark needles of the
pines.

It was a very dangerous ride. We were two days
and one night getting through and had to contrive all
manner of ways to get through at all. We had several
breakdowns. Sometimes the men had to use all their
strength to steer the sled clear of some steep precipice.

I enjoyed it the first day and night, it was all so
new and sublime. We reached the summit at midnight. Old Mount Ouray lay at our right covered with
snow and crowned with stars. The moon, that had
seemed to us to set two or three times, rose again and
gave us light. We commenced our descent. The roar
of the waters that seemed to make the road their bed
gave a new touch to the sublime.

I wasn't aware at the time that I was doing anything remarkable by keeping cool during all this
journey of hairbreadth escapes, but "Jack" seemed
to have conceived a great respect for me and laid
aside all his adjectives and even compromised himself enough to enquire after the comfort of "the

lady." I learned that I gained quite a reputation for bravery among the masculine part of our adventurers, who seemed to have discussed the subject and agreed "that not one lady in a thousand would have shown such coolness and bravery."

We got into Gunnison about 6 o'clock Tuesday afternoon. The Halls had been worrying about us, having heard fearful reports of the treacherous mountain roads. And it was fortunate we got through when we did, for almost a week passed before the next coach got through.

The two adventurers did not stay in Gunnison long. Charles' enterprises there did not turn out favorably. Pueblo, Colorado, was in the midst of a real estate boom, so it was there that the enterprising young man took his bride.

When he arrived in Pueblo, Charles had exactly ten cents in his pocket, but he had in his head and heart that which made up for his lack of money—he had courage, self-reliance, and intelligence. The first thing he did was go to a grocery store and order some groceries to be sent to the rooms where he had left Myrtle. Since he had no money, he told the grocer to send the order C.O.D.; but when the food was delivered and Myrtle had no money to pay for it, the delivery boy took it back. In the meantime, Charles had met a friend on the street and borrowed ten dollars with which he returned to the grocery store to pay for the groceries, giving the grocer the impression that he was outraged at having been embarrassed over such a trifling sum. He had observed that the grocer was not using all the space of the store and he talked the man into letting him use part of this space to open up a real estate office for himself.

In the real estate business in Pueblo, Charles Fillmore prospered. He was always a person of original ideas and he had ideas about how to sell real estate. An early-day historian of Kansas City was to write about him in regard to his real estate activities there a few years later: "Fillmore & Company have always been governed by

ideas original with themselves and have been eminently
successful." Among the things he did in Pueblo to attract
business—this was at a time before such methods of advertising became common—he fitted out a pony and
wagon with huge signs made out of red letters on yellow
cloth to advertise his business and drove the pony and
wagon around the streets of Pueblo.

In Pueblo, two sons were born to the Fillmores, Lowell Page in 1882 and Waldo Rickert in 1884. Shortly after
the birth of this second son, the real estate boom ended.
Charles' partner at that time was Charles Small, brother-
in-law of Nona Brooks, who later founded Divine Science. The two men struggled along for a time to make a
living, but their income grew less and less and at last
they decided to break up the business.

Charles Fillmore was never one to be content with
mediocre success. Since, at the moment, he could see no
place in Colorado where there was much prospect of
immediate prosperity, he decided to move on. He paused
briefly in Omaha, Nebraska, but in the winter of 1884,
went on with his family to Kansas City and opened up a
real estate business there.

In 1884, there was no better spot in the nation than
Kansas City for an enterprising real estate operator. The
town at the confluence of the Kaw and Missouri Rivers
was just beginning to grow, and in the next four years an
extraordinary real estate boom was to take place there.
The whole community was seized with the spirit of expansion. Real estate values doubled, tripled, soared out
of sight. Office building were sold, re-sold, and re-sold
again in a single day, each time at a profit. When new
subdivisions were opened up, people stood in line waiting for an opportunity to invest their money in a lot. It
was a great period of growth. Downtown values rose and
rocketed. Outlying farms sold at downtown prices. Population swelled. By 1887, the real estate transactions of
Kansas City were exceeding in value those of Chicago.

In the midst of this boom, Charles Fillmore brought
his family and opened up his business. His experience in

Pueblo had equipped him to move capably in conditions like these and, in a short time, he was more prosperous than he had ever been before. He acquired some land in the northeast section of the city and laid out a real estate subdivision that he named Gladstone Heights, the name it still bears.

Charles Fillmore was a shrewd businessman. He had abundant energy and original ideas and he put them to work for him. He bought and sold, and sold and bought, and he made money. Once he even sold the building in which he had his offices and made $10,000 on the deal. In a short time, he had accumulated a nice sum and had played a part in the development of Kansas City. To this day, some of the streets of that city still bear the names he gave them, among them, Myrtle Avenue, which he named for his wife, and Norton Avenue, which he named for his brother.

During this time, Charles continued his interests in mining. He was a partner in a silver mine outside Silverton, Colorado, and one summer took his wife and oldest son there, leaving Rickert with "Grandma" Fillmore in Kansas City. For three months, Charles and Myrtle and Lowell lived in a tent high up on Red Mountain, with some crude furnishings that they had managed to contrive and one or two items that they had brought in on the backs of burros. Nearly every night, even in midsummer, snow would fall and cover the tent. In the morning, they would beat the snow off the tent. It would melt as the sun rose in the heavens, but the next night everything might be covered by snow again. The boy Lowell played about the camp, and all three of them roamed among the mountains while Charles prospected for silver. The simple life and healthful mountain air must have been especially beneficial to Myrtle, who had been suffering from tuberculosis. The family was able to remain there for only a few months, for although at first it had appeared that the mine was going to be a rich one, the vein of silver failed unexpectedly, and in the fall the three went back to Kansas City.

A period of depression now settled in the affairs of the Fillmores. The failure of the mine was followed shortly by the collapse of the real estate boom in Kansas City. Charles and his family were left with no financial resources at all and were actually in debt. In the meantime, Myrtle underwent a spell of severe sickness. From her earliest childhood, she had been taught to think of herself as an invalid. In her early years, tuberculosis that she had been brought up to fear had developed in her, and in Clinton she had also contracted malaria. In the mountains, her condition had improved, but now, when the family was having its hardest financial struggle, the tuberculosis returned more virulently than ever.

At that time, Myrtle had great faith in medicine and tried all sorts of medical remedies. Her son Lowell recalls that the medicine cabinet was always full to overflowing with pills and nostrums with which she was continually dosing herself and all the other members of the family. But doctors told her that if she remained in Kansas City she would probably have only a short time to live; there was nothing that they could do for her.

The Fillmores considered returning to Colorado. There seemed to be many reasons why they should make such a move. The mountain climate might alleviate Myrtle's condition. They had many friends in Colorado. Charles had excellent business connections there. It would be easy for him to re-establish himself. Yet in spite of all these reasons, they stayed in Kansas City. For at this time, Charles Fillmore had an unusual experience:

> I had a strange dream. An unseen voice said, "Follow me." I was led up and down the hilly streets of Kansas City and my attention called to localities I was familiar with. The Presence stopped and said: "You will remember having had a dream some years ago in which you were shown this city and told you had a work to do here. Now you are being reminded of that dream and also informed that the invisible power that has located you will continue to be with you and aid you in the appointed work." When I

awoke, I remembered that I had had such a dream and forgotten it.

Charles Fillmore had always been interested in religion, though his approach to it was an unorthodox one. He had occasionally gone to church with his mother, who had been reared as an Episcopalian and knew the litanies by heart. But it was not from the standpoint of one who has been reared in a doctrine from childhood and simply accepts it as part of his life that Charles approached religion. His approach was from a philosophic standpoint. Charles Fillmore was born to yearn after God, to seek Him with all his heart. He had an instinctive urge to seek out the meaning of life and he was the kind of person who had to find the meaning in his own soul. He had to find God for himself. Other persons might point the way, others might give him hints and clues, but he would have to test their ideas for himself and prove them in his own mind and his own life before they would have validity for him.

It is easy to imagine him as a young man poring by candlelight over the lines of masters like Shakespeare and Emerson, reading them over and over to himself, but he was not passively accepting what they said. He had his own thoughts about their conclusions. Charles Fillmore was innately religious in the highest sense. He was born with a curious and capable mind that was intended to inquire into Truth and into the nature of many things. His was a mind on fire to know the Truth, and he sought for it everywhere. The statement that Myrtle Page had written of herself, "I am decidedly eclectic in my theology" could be aptly applied to Charles Fillmore. If he rejected anything, it was never arbitrarily; he had examined it, tested it, and decided that it was wanting in value. He studied many philosophies and religions.

As a young man, one of Charles' first interests had been spiritualism. He had a friend who felt that he had the powers of a medium, and the two of them had spent many evenings together in the dark facing each other

silently across the table, their fingers pressed lightly
against the table top to see if they could not waft it mys-
teriously into the air. Later Charles Fillmore repudiated
spiritualism, but only after having thoroughly looked into
it.

From the first issues of his magazine *Modern
Thought,* we know that Charles Fillmore also had a
knowledge of such teachings as Buddhism, Brahmanism,
Theosophy, and Rosicrucianism, as well as Christianity.
In one of the early issues of the magazine, he wrote of
himself and his wife: "We have taken more than forty
courses (in metaphysical subjects), some of them costing
as much as $100." Besides all this, he had a considerable
understanding of the teachings of many Christian de-
nominations.

Many years later, a Catholic friend was visiting him.
The friend expressed a desire to go to Mass but had no
means of getting to church from Charles' home. Charles
said that he would take her. So they drove to the little
Catholic church in Lee's Summit. Afterward Charles as-
tonished his friend by explaining to her the symbolical
meaning of every part of the ritual of the Mass.

Charles and Myrtle Fillmore sought Truth freely
wherever they could find it. They were not limited in
their beliefs and were no respecters of labels. Perhaps it
is their early eclecticism that is responsible for Unity's
love for and appreciation of all religious teachings. To
this day when Unity School receives a letter from someone who wants to argue about his belief, there is still
only one answer:

"We see the good in all religions and we want
everyone to feel free to find the Truth for himself wherever he may be led to find it." Unity does not stress the
differences, but the points of agreement.

At any rate, when Charles Fillmore had this dream
in which he was shown that Kansas City was the town
where he should remain because he had a work to do
there, the dream did not fall on unfertile soil. Years of
study and meditation and an inquiring and receptive

mind had prepared him to obey the promptings of the Spirit in him.

At about this same time, another important event happened. A lecturer named Dr. E. B. Weeks came to Kansas City and delivered a series of talks on a subject that was then being referred to by names such as, "New Thought," "Christian Science," and "Divine Science." Dr. Weeks was sent to Kansas City from Chicago as a representative of the Illinois Metaphysical College, which had been founded shortly before by Emma Curtis Hopkins.

Emma Curtis Hopkins was one of the most unusual figures that have appeared in the whole metaphysical movement. Originally she had been associated with Mary Baker Eddy as an editor of the "Christian Science Journal," but as the two had not seen eye to eye on many questions, Mrs. Hopkins left the Eddy School of Christian Science. From Boston, she went to Chicago where she founded a school of her own, which was probably the most influential school of its kind at the time. Emma Curtis Hopkins was a teacher of teachers. Many founders of metaphysical movements learned their fundamental principles from her. Besides Charles and Myrtle Fillmore there were: Charles and Josephine Barton, who published the magazine "The Life" in Kansas City and had a Truth movement of their own; Melinda Cramer, the first president of the International Divine Science Association; Dr. D. L. Sullivan, who taught Truth classes in St. Louis and Kansas City; Helen Wilmans, editor of "Wilmans Express" and a very influential New Thought teacher at the turn of the century; the popular writer, Ella Wheeler Wilcox; Paul Militz and Annie Rix Militz, who founded the Homes of Truth on the West Coast; Mrs. Bingham, who taught Nona Brooks, founder of the Divine Science movement in Denver; C. E. Burnell, a popular lecturer throughout the country for many years; H. Emilie Cady, who studied under Mrs. Hopkins on one of her trips to New York; and many others.

Charles and Myrtle Fillmore took several courses of

study under Mrs. Hopkins and became her fast friends. They were among her favorite pupils. Later she was often to write to them when she had cases for healing that seemed unusually difficult to her, for she felt that the Fillmores had superior ability as healers. Once she wrote to them from New York: "Please, please keep on praying for John. I cannot believe that it is merely a coincidence that he always rallies at the times when I know you are praying for him." It was this teacher who had sent Dr. Weeks to Kansas City.

The Fillmores went to the lecture by Dr. Weeks out of curiosity and need. How closely their experience in finding Truth parallels the experience of thousands since then in finding Unity! For over and over the letters that come to Unity declare: "We had tried everything. We had given up hope. We did not know where to turn, and a friend told us about you, so now we are writing to you."

That was the way it was with Charles and Myrtle Fillmore. One evening in the spring of 1886, when Myrtle was desperately sick and they did not know where to turn, they went to hear Dr. Weeks, who had been recommended by a friend who had been studying this "New Thought," as it was called, and felt that Myrtle might get help from it for her physical condition. They did not know much about the subject but they had tried everything else that they knew about, and all had failed. They had reached the place where they were willing to try anything. Charles Fillmore came away from that lecture long ago feeling no different than when he had gone in, but the woman who walked out of the hall on his arm was not the same woman who had entered it. A new, a different, a liberating, a transforming conviction was blazing in her heart and mind. Everyone has gone to hear a lecture and had the experience of having some statement of the lecturer's stand out so vividly in his mind that he has felt, "He said that especially for me." That is the way it was with Myrtle Fillmore that night. As she walked from the hall, one statement repeated itself over and over in her mind:

I am a child of God and therefore I do not inherit sickness.

Over and over in her mind the words tolled like a bell:

I am a child of God and therefore I do not inherit sickness.

In one hour Myrtle Fillmore's whole outlook toward herself and her life had been changed. Like a revelation —and surely such it was—this simple and divine idea that she was a beloved child of God, that God's will for her could only be perfect life and wholeness filled her mind and possessed her being. The old belief that she was an invalid, that she had been born to be an invalid, was as waters that have passed away. Even as she stepped out of the doors of the hall, this new, this divine realization was working in her, not only in her mind but in the very cells of her body:

I am a child of God and therefore I do not inherit sickness.

Like the little leaven that leavens the whole loaf, this thought was to work in her until it had made her every whit whole. It was not to let her go until through her thousands of persons had been made whole, too. It was not to let her go until she and her husband, who was soon set afire with it too, had founded a faith that reached around the world and blessed the lives of millions of persons who with her would joyously declare:

I am a child of God and therefore I do not inherit sickness.

Chapter IV

The Founding of Unity

"In the Beginning"

A FEW YEARS LATER, Myrtle Fillmore wrote one of the most popular articles that have ever appeared in *Unity* magazine—the story of her healing.

> I have made what seems to me a discovery. I was fearfully sick; I had all the ills of mind and body that I could bear. Medicine and doctors ceased to give me relief, and I was in despair when I found practical Christianity. I took it up and I was healed. I did most of the healing myself, because I wanted the understanding for future use. This is how I made what I call my discovery.
>
> I was thinking about life. Life is everywhere—in worm and in man. "Then why does not the life in the worm make a body like man's?" I asked. Then I thought, "The worm has not as much sense as man." Ah! intelligence, as well as life, is needed to make a body. Here is the key to my discovery. Life has to be guided by intelligence in making all forms. The same law works in my own body. Life is simply a form of energy, and has to be guided and directed in man's body by his intelligence. How do we communicate intelligence? By thinking and talking, of course. Then it flashed upon me that I might talk to the life in every part of my body and have it do just what I wanted. I began to teach my body and got marvelous results.
>
> I told the life in my liver that it was not torpid or

inert, but full of vigor and energy. I told the life in my stomach that it was not weak or inefficient, but energetic, strong, and intelligent. I told the life in my abdomen that it was no longer infested with ignorant thoughts or disease, put there by myself and by doctors, but that it was all athrill with the sweet, pure, wholesome energy of God. I told my limbs that they were active and strong. I told my eyes that they did not see of themselves but that they expressed the sight of Spirit, and that they were drawing on an unlimited source. I told them that they were young eyes, clear, bright eyes, because the light of God shone right through them. I told my heart that the pure love of Jesus Christ flowed in and out through its beatings and that all the world felt its joyous pulsation.

I went to all the life centers in my body and spoke words of Truth to them—words of strength and power. I asked their forgiveness for the foolish, ignorant course that I had pursued in the past, when I had condemned them and called them weak, inefficient, and diseased. I did not become discouraged at their being slow to wake up, but kept right on, both silently and aloud, declaring the words of Truth, until the organs responded. And neither did I forget to tell them that they were free, unlimited Spirit. I told them that they were no longer in bondage to the carnal mind; that they were not corruptible flesh, but centers of life and energy omnipresent.

Then I asked the Father to forgive me for taking His life into my organism and there using it so meanly. I promised Him that I would never, never again retard the free flow of that life through my mind and my body by any false word or thought; that I would always bless it and encourage it with true thoughts and words in its wise work of building up my body temple; that I would use all diligence and wisdom in telling it just what I wanted it to do.

I also saw that I was using the life of the Father in thinking thoughts and speaking words, and I became very watchful as to what I thought and said.

I did not let any worried or anxious thoughts into

my mind and I stopped speaking gossipy, frivolous, petulant, angry words. I let a little prayer go up every hour that Jesus Christ would be with me and help me to think and speak only kind, loving, true words. I am sure that He is with me because I am so peaceful and happy now. . . .

I want everybody to know about this beautiful, true law, and to use it. It is not a new discovery, but when you use it and get the fruits of health and harmony, it will seem new to you, and you will feel that it is your own discovery.

In two years, Myrtle Fillmore was no longer an invalid. Through her prayers she was made absolutely whole.

"I want everybody to know about this beautiful, true law, and to use it," she wrote; and as she became well, many did come to know about it, for her neighbors who knew how sick she had been saw the change that was wrought in her and became curious as to what she had done to bring about such a miracle. People began to come to her for help.

The Fillmores did not deliberately set out to found an organization. Mrs. Fillmore set out first to find healing for herself. Having found that, she wanted to share her discovery with others and she found that people wanted that discovery as much as she wanted to give it to them. People, hearing of the change in her, came to her and asked her for help.

Mr. and Mrs. Fillmore were then living in a house on Wabash Avenue in Kansas City, and one of the first persons who came to Mrs. Fillmore was an Irishman named Caskey who lived across the street. He was crippled and had to walk on crutches. It took him a long while to comprehend the idea she was trying to get across to him, for at first he did not believe that he could be healed. The two would discuss her ideas and pray together; then she would tell him to put down his crutches and walk. He would often say, "How do I know I can walk?" But again and again she would give him affirmative statements of prayer and have him repeat them with her. However much he might question and doubt, she knew that he could walk. So one day when she told him to put down his crutches and walk, that is what he did. He laid his crutches down and walked across the room. The crippled condition completely disappeared.

Years later, Lowell Fillmore was walking down a street when an express wagon drove up beside him and the driver jumped down from the seat. "Aren't you Lowell Fillmore?" the man inquired, and he went on to say that he was Mr. Caskey, whom Myrtle Fillmore had prayed with many years before.

Other persons began to hear about this woman on Wabash Avenue whose prayers were able to bring about healing.

The Fillmores' laundress had asthma. To her, too, Myrtle Fillmore suggested prayer, and in a short time she was whole again.

One day a salesman came to the door. He was selling picture frames and molding. He had a suitcase filled with samples of frames to show. Myrtle Fillmore was the kind of person who never turned people away. In a few minutes, he was inside the house and had his things spread out on the floor. Her son Lowell was there, and he crowded forward to see what the salesman had.

"This is my little boy," said Mrs. Fillmore to the salesman.

"Well," said the latter, "my little boy will never see again." This, of course, she immediately and vigorously denied. She told him of her own experience with prayer, and after a while he asked her if she would come to see his son who had advanced cataracts on both of his eyes.

When she first saw the boy, Myrtle Fillmore said his eyes looked as though they were covered with something like the white of an egg, but she was not dismayed by these appearances. She worked with him as she had with the others, helping him to realize that he was the beloved child of God, that God loved him, that God's will for him was perfect sight.

The second time she went to see him, he had improved so much that he could come to the door and let her in. In a short time his eyes were completely healed.

Her fame spread beyond her own neighborhood. People from other parts of Kansas City and even from nearby towns started coming to ask for help. To all of them, she gave the same response: that they were God's beloved children and His will for them was health, that the healing power of the Christ was in them and they too could have perfect wholeness by realizing this Truth.

In the meantime, Charles Fillmore had come but slowly to accept what to his wife had been an instant and overwhelming revelation.

"Although I was a chronic invalid and seldom free from pain, the doctrine did not at first appeal to me," he later wrote.

To Myrtle Fillmore, the realization of the Truth about herself and her relationship to God had come suddenly, in a flash of inspiration. She had a new conviction, a burning flame of faith. Charles Fillmore had a different kind of mind. He thought of himself as a hardheaded businessman, and he had a family to provide for. He was reluctant to let his business friends and associates know that he was interested in a newfangled religious idea such as his wife had. Still, because he was a practical man, when he saw the living, tangible results of his wife's faith, saw bodies rebuilt, crippled limbs renewed, and sight restored, he could not help but become interested.

Charles Fillmore was not one to take things on blind faith. He had an inquiring, scientific turn of mind. When he saw the healings that were coming as a result of his wife's prayers, he began to question why they should come to pass. If people were being healed, there was a reason for the healings. He commenced to inquire into this reason. He read all the books that he could find on the subject; and where courses were available, he took them. When he came to Kansas City, the Fillmores studied with Joseph Adams, who published a metaphysical journal called "The Truth Gleaner" in Chicago. They went to Chicago to study under Emma Curtis Hopkins.

At first Mr. Fillmore was disturbed by the many conflicting statements about Truth made by various teachers. He could not understand why there should be so many divisions and schools and such an assortment of opinions about an exact science. "The muddle was so deep," he wrote, "that for a time I was inclined to ridicule, yet I couldn't get away from the evidence of a great power back of the flood of contradictory statements."

There might be a doubt as to which one of the teachers was right, but as to the results there could be no doubt whatever. His eyes could see the results. About his doubt he wrote:

> I noticed, however, that all the teachers and writers talked a great deal about the omnipresent, omniscient God, who is Spirit and accessible to everyone. I said to myself, "In this babel I will go to headquarters. If I am Spirit and this God they talk so much about is Spirit, we can somehow communicate, or the whole thing is a fraud."
>
> I then commenced sitting in the silence every night at a certain hour and tried to get in touch with God. There was no enthusiasm about it; no soul desire, but a cold calculating business method. I was there on time every night and tried in all conceivable ways to realize that my mind was in touch with the Supreme Mind.
>
> In this cold, intellectual attitude one can easily understand why I did not seem to get any conscious result, but I kept at it month after month, mentally affirming words that others told me would open the way, until it got to be a habit and I rather enjoyed it.
>
> However, a time came when I began to observe that I was having exceedingly realistic dreams. For months I paid no attention to them, my business at that time being of the earth earthy—buying and selling real estate. The first connection that I observed between the dreams and my affairs was after closing the purchase of a piece of property I remembered

that I had dreamed about the whole transaction some months before.

After that I watched my dreams closely and found that there was a wider intelligence manifesting in my sleep than I seemed to possess in the waking state, and it flashed over me one day that this was the mode of communication that had been established in response to my desire for information from headquarters. This has been kept up ever since with growing interest on my part, and I could fill a large book with my experiences.

Everything which it is necessary for me to know is shown to me, and I have times without number been saved from false steps by this monitor. Again and again, I have had mapped out the future along certain lines for months and years ahead, and the prophecies have so far never failed, although I have sometimes misinterpreted the symbols which are used.

This was the way in which Charles Fillmore came into Truth. Being practical, he sought for something that was an exact science. Being a student, he studied under many teachers. In the end he turned, as must all who seek Truth, to the one true Source.

Perhaps it was because of this experience of his own that he was able to help so many others later on who, just as he had done, set out without much faith to go on— persons who could not accept simple statements simply because their intellect was continually raising doubts. To all these, Charles Fillmore could say because he had proved it by his own experience:

"Belief *cometh* by hearing, and hearing by the word of Christ." Set aside a time every day, a definite time, and pray whether you believe or not. Take a Truth statement and repeat it over and over. It does not matter that at first you do not believe it to be true. If you will persistently affirm Truth, even though you do not believe it at first, you will find that your prayers have power. Faith is like a mustard seed and it will grow. Pray, pray, and keep praying;

affirm, and yet affirm once more. Your persistent
prayers will succeed.

Charles Fillmore was never a half-way sort of person. Once he became convinced that he was on the track
of Truth, he threw all his mind and energies into its pur-
suit.

Although he did not immediately discontinue his
interests in real estate and mining, his absorption in spiritual matters became greater and greater. "My interest,"
he wrote, "became so pronounced that I neglected my
real estate for the furtherance of what my commercial
friends denounced as a fanatical delusion."

At this time Charles Fillmore took the most important step of his life.

His income was the lowest it had been in years, for a
depression was sweeping Kansas City, following the collapse of the real estate boom. The needs of his family
were the greatest they had ever been; in 1889 a third
child, Royal, was born. Charles had had no great amount
of formal schooling. He had had very little experience in
the publishing business. Nevertheless, he decided to
publish a magazine.

Charles Fillmore had come to believe in the ideas
that he had first learned from his wife. He had studied
them and probed them as thoroughly as he was able. He
had come to see that they made sense and presented a
scientific view of life. He had seen them actually demonstrated as true, for he had seen his wife and others healed
by them. "I had applied the healing principle to my own
case with gratifying results," he stated. "My chronic
pains ceased. My hip healed and grew stronger, and my
leg lengthened until in a few years I dispensed with the
steel extension that I had worn since I was a child."

Here was something of which he could say without
reservations, "This is Truth." Here was something that he
could believe in, live by. A timid man might have held
back, but Charles Fillmore had the courage of his convictions. Having found a faith, he dared to step out on that

faith. Having found something that he felt was worth saying, he said it.

In April 1889, he brought out the first issue of a magazine that he called *Modern Thought.* It contained sixteen pages. The pages, which were divided into three columns, were about 9×12 inches. Immediately under the name of the magazine appeared the motto: "Devoted to the Spiritualization of Humanity from an Independent Standpoint." The price was ten cents an issue, one dollar for a year's subscription. In the first number Charles wrote:

> The wave of spiritual thought that is sweeping over the land has created a demand in this vicinity for a publication devoted to its discussion and dissemination. With this object in view, *Modern Thought* had its birth. It is not the organ of any school of thought, but the mouthpiece of all honest souls earnestly seeking for spiritual light.

When Charles Fillmore began *Modern Thought,* he had come to the place where he was sure that there was a divine Principle and a science of Being; he had gained an insight into the nature of Truth; but he had not yet come to the place where he was certain as to the exact terms to be used in this science nor as to the exact approach that should be made to the Principle. He knew absolutely that the secret was hidden in himself, and it was clear from the first issue of *Modern Thought* that he thought of the Bible as a necessary guidebook to the Principle:

> Those who base their forms of worship on the Bible find that the fundamental truths are one. . . . Modern research . . . has thrown such additional light upon the original meaning of the Scriptures that it is not safe to assert positively that a single paragraph of the Bible is understood in our day as it was intended at the time it was written. It is the spirit, rather than the letter of the text, that those worship who have within them the true Christ principle.

In the first number, he had articles by Christian Scientists, Theosophists, and Spiritualists. He also had articles reprinted from occult magazines about the development of psychic power. The Modern Thought Publishing Company advertised and sold books of many kinds. In ensuing issues, there were articles about Buddhism and Brahmanism, and advertisements of periodicals and books written by all the schools of metaphysical thought. Charles Fillmore wrote: "We want the address of every lecturer and healer working on the Spiritual plane. Our aim is to spread all over this great West the good which we know lies in wait for those who are willing to receive it. We are not wedded to any school of metaphysics, hence shall be strictly impartial in our efforts."

The pages of *Modern Thought* were at first not even limited to metaphysical subjects, but contained articles on cheaper houses for working men, the Haymarket riots that had just taken place in Chicago, and excerpts from such works as Edward Bellamy's "Looking Backward."

This state of affairs did not last long, however. *Modern Thought* soon began to take a direction of its own. Charles Fillmore wrote:

> *Modern Thought* aims to occupy a broad platform, and to sympathize with reform movements of every kind, as we believe them all to be parts of a great forward movement of humanity under the direction of unseen intelligence, but it is not our province to become identified with them all, nor to give them a hearing in these columns.

In a few months, he felt called on to write an editorial divorcing himself and his magazine from spiritualism. Still later he repudiated occultism.

The Fillmores were moving steadily toward the teaching of practical Christianity that is today put forth by Unity School. They were moving away from the isms and the cults that had influenced them. In a short time, they were to write:

> These columns are open to teachers and healers

who advocate and practice Pure Mind Healing only. This does not mean magnetism, hypnotism, mesmerism, psychometry, palmistry, nor astrology. Not that we condemn any system, but . . . we find by experience that concentration is necessary to success and we wish to confine these pages to that specific doctrine, and Holy Ghost power, taught and demonstrated by Jesus Christ.

In April 1890, a year after the publication was begun, the name of the magazine was changed from *Modern Thought* to *Christian Science Thought.* Many persons have wondered if Unity was an offshoot of Christian Science. It was not. The Fillmores had many teachers; they read widely of the transcendentalism of the times and the new ideas in religion that were being advanced; but above all, as Charles Fillmore wrote, in this babel they went to headquarters. The Fillmores turned within themselves; they turned to God. The inspiration of the Almighty was their principal source and resource.

Charles Fillmore declared in the second issue of *Modern Thought:*

We are asked if the ideas set forth in these columns are endorsed by Christian Science. In order that persons who are ignorant of the teachings of the new philosophy may not be misled by statements made herein, we deem it a duty to inform them that our views are not those of orthodox Christian Science.

There are, however, many schools of metaphysical thought sailing under the general name of Christian Science. The initial impetus to the movement is attributed to Mrs. Eddy, of Boston, the author of "Science and Health."

As yet we know but little about this hidden force that is so potent in bringing health and happiness to mankind. Like all powerful agents, it is unseen, and thus affords scope for a universe of theories as to its character and modes. Any and all claims of exact knowledge of its nature are beyond the horizon of proof. However, it is enough to know, in our present

condition of ignorance of spiritual things, that such a
power for good to the human race is within our
grasp, and the momentous question is, through
which of the present schools can the people best be
reached. Experience proves that Christian Science
has outstripped all its competitors in spreading the
Truth. It is better organized and reaches the masses
more readily than any other movement for the benefit of mankind. A wise mechanic uses the tools at
hand best adapted to the work he has to do. He may
often wish that they were not quite so cumbersome,
but he finds it expedient to throw his energy into the
work, rather than stand around and growl at the
tools. On this ground, we are partial to and endorse
Christian Science, and *by Christian Science, we
mean all the metaphysical schools.* It is doing a wonderful work for humanity; has spread with a rapidity
that has no parallel in history. It has kindled a fire in
the hearts of men that cannot be extinguished, and is
silently finding its way into every household in the
land.

In 1890, the name *Christian Science* was used not
only by Mary Baker Eddy, but also by many others who
were teaching what we today call Truth or Christian
metaphysics. The Fillmores were never students of Mary
Baker Eddy. For their inspiration, the Fillmores had gone,
as all great teachers do, direct to God. Charles and Myrtle never thought of Truth as something to be learned out
of books alone or to be absorbed wholly from teachers.
They thought of Truth as something that each individual
must finally discover for himself in himself. Charles
wrote:

> The impression is abroad that each school of Chris-
> tian Science, mind-healing, mental science, meta-
> physical healing, psycho-therapeutics, mental cure,
> spiritual science, pneumatophony, old theology, on-
> tology, Christian metaphysics, mental healing, and
> so forth, has the power to confer upon the individual
> certain distinctive qualities not possessed by the
> other schools, and which qualities are exclusive,

God-given and attainable only at denominated
shrines. . . .

Many people are also blinded by a name, and labor under the delusion that because they have taken
lessons in Christian Science they are in possession of
truths that cannot be obtained anywhere in the universe, unless that magic name is over the door. . . .
People of limited spiritual unfoldment are sticklers
for names and creeds, and are thus worshipers of
idols. . . . They quarrel over names, names, names,
vapid, unmeaning names, that never were anything
of themselves and do not even represent that which
they allege to represent.

There had been a tendency for some time for the
leaders of all metaphysical movements, even those most
violently opposed to Mrs. Eddy's methods, to include
Christian Science in their name; thus it was after Mrs.
Hopkins changed the name of her school from the Hopkins Metaphysical Institute to Christian Science Theolog-
ical Seminary that the Fillmores changed the name of
their magazine to *Christian Science Thought.* Neither
Mrs. Hopkins nor the Fillmores meant, however, that
they were teaching the doctrine taught by Mrs. Eddy. As
Charles Fillmore wrote in 1890:

To the public understanding the name *"Christian
Science"* stands for all the different schools of metaphysics regardless of the technical differences by
which their leaders try to distinguish them . . . we
believe that the word Christ as applied to Truth represents an idea that has behind it the occult power
necessary to make it the dominant tone in the great
symphony which is to harmonize all the discords of
earth.

The name *Christian Science Thought* was retained
only for a year. Mrs. Eddy made it known that she felt
that the name *Christian Science* was her exclusive property and if the Fillmores wanted to use it they must also
follow her teaching. This, of course, they had never done.
They and other independent metaphysical leaders de-

cided that it was right that Mrs. Eddy should have exclusive use of the name and since their teaching was not the same as hers, they gave up the name. For the next few years the magazine was called simply *Thought.* Charles Fillmore said many years later:

> We have studied many isms, many cults. People of every religion under the sun claim that we either belong to them or have borrowed the best part of our teaching from them. We have borrowed the best from all religions, that is the reason we are called Unity. . . . We studied Christian Science. [They studied all the religions.] We were also classed as New Thought people, Mental Scientists, Theosophists, and so on, but none of these sufficiently emphasized the higher attributes of man, and we avoided any close affiliation with them . . . Unity is not a sect, not a separation of people into an exclusive group of know-it-alls. Unity is the Truth that is taught in all religions, simplified and systemized so that anyone can understand and apply it. Students of Unity do not find it necessary to sever their church affiliations. The church needs the vitalization that this renaissance of primitive Christianity gives it.

The name *Thought,* however, was also of brief duration. The Fillmores were not satisfied with this name. It was too general a term and did not exactly describe the movement. As Charles Fillmore had said of *Modern Thought:*

> The name was not an index to the principles which the paper advocated, and we were in consequence inundated by communications of a nature we did not care to publish, and were also constantly obliged to explain our exact place in the great maelstrom of modern thought.

In the spring of 1891, he and his wife and a few students met together one evening to pray. As they were sitting in the silence, suddenly into the mind of Charles Fillmore flashed the name *Unity.* At the moment, he had not even been thinking about a name and when it came to him it startled him.

"That's it!" he cried out. *"Unity!"* He told the others. *"Unity!* That's the name for our work, the name we've been looking for."

Later he told friends the name came right out of the ether, just as the voice of Jesus was heard by Paul in the heavens. "No one else heard it, but it was as clear to me as though somebody had spoken to me."

Then and there the name *Unity* was adopted. It was an apt and fortunate choice. The Fillmores had borrowed the best from all the religions. Where the churches had put the emphasis on controversial doctrinal points that had caused division after division in the Christian world, Charles and Myrtle Fillmore were to put their emphasis on the things that are practical, the things that apply to everyday thinking and living. They were not to found a new religion but were to work within the framework of existing religions and appeal to church members without causing them to divorce themselves from their church. They were to propound a teaching that people of all faiths could study and apply to their lives. They were to be a force for unity in the world. The movement that Charles and Myrtle Fillmore had founded was to live and grow under the name *Unity*.

Chapter V

The Early Publications

"And He Saith unto Me, Write"

WHERE TODAY the Unity publications encircle the earth, in April 1889 there was only one small magazine of sixteen pages called *Modern Thought,* read by a handful of subscribers. At the end of its first year of publication, there were only a few hundred readers. Today there are hundreds of workers employed in the production and circulation of the magazines. In 1889, all the work was done by one couple, Charles and Myrtle Fillmore. They had had no experience in the publishing business but they had an idea, an idea that they felt it was important for other persons to know about, and they were willing to work as hard and as long as they had to in order to get this idea before the world.

To publish a magazine presenting new religious beliefs was not easy. To support his family, Charles Fillmore had to continue in the real estate business and to keep as quiet as possible about the writing that he was doing in connection with the magazine. For many years, he wrote under the pen name of Leo Virgo. Myrtle Fillmore merely signed her articles M. or M.F.

Charles Fillmore published the magazine from his real estate office in the old Journal Building (which has since been torn down) located at the northwest corner of Tenth and Walnut streets in downtown Kansas City. As the real estate boom had collapsed in 1888 and business was slow, there was not at first much money to spend on

the magazine. Mr. Fillmore had to buy a little at a time
the paper on which it was printed, so that today the paper
in the bound files of the early issues is not always uni-
form in color and texture. He would go down to the paper
house, pick up the best value he could find for the
money, and carry it home with him.

When the magazine was five months old, the office
of *Modern Thought* was moved to the Deardorff Building
at Eleventh and Main.

In the September-October issue a want ad was inserted:

> WANTED—We want the services on this paper of a
> young man or woman who can set type and who is
> interested in the reforms we advocate. To such a one
> we will give a home and small wages. Address Chas.
> Fillmore, Kansas City, Mo., care of *Modern Thought.*

The ad produced no results, for in December Charles
wrote:

> We beg the pardon of our contributors and readers
> for the typographical and other errors that appear in
> these pages. Could they understand that everything
> but the typesetting is done by one man, and that that
> one man also labors in another field for the support
> of himself and family, they would certainly judge
> leniently. Our correspondents should also be charita-
> ble and not expect prompt responses to their letters—
> in fact they should consider themselves fortunate if
> they get any response whatever.

Charles and Myrtle Fillmore were indefatigable
workers. There was no limit to the amount of time the
two were willing to spend to promote the teaching of
Truth. In the early days, however, the magazine was not
always published on time. Once it did not appear at all.
Charles Fillmore merely inserted this terse, self-explana-
tory notice:

> Our typographical force is bent on taking a holi-
> day, and the editor having urgent business of a per-
> sonal nature, we have decided to omit the September
> number of *Modern Thought.*

The typographical force at that time consisted of a Mr. Palmer who owned some fonts of type and set the type for the magazine in his own home, where Mr. Fillmore would take the copy to him. It was several years before the Fillmores were able to buy type and hire their own typographers. This was some years after they had moved into the Hall Building at Ninth and Walnut streets, a move that was made in September 1890. Here Unity rented three rooms, in one of which type cases were later set up. In this room Harry Church, Unity's first hired printer, set the type for the magazine. He had a long brown beard, was a Seventh Day Adventist and a vegetarian.

On Saturdays, the oldest son Lowell Fillmore, who was then in grade school, would go down to the rooms in the Hall Building and help wrap the magazines, for which his father would pay him ten cents.

Charles and Myrtle Fillmore did almost all the work. They wrote most of the articles, edited all of them, wrote and addressed the letters, and took care of the details relating to the handling of subscriptions.

In 1898, the Unity offices were moved to a house on McGee Street. Here the composing room force consisted of two women.

When he finished high school, Lowell went to work for Unity at five dollars a week. He ran the small job press, printed the envelopes and stationery, and helped write letters. The forms were sent out to a printing shop where the magazines were printed. Lowell would hire an express wagon, carry the heavy forms down to it, careful not to spill one and "pie" a page, which would mean that it would have to be reset, lift them onto the wagon, inserting quilts between the forms so that they would not be damaged by the jolting ride, accompany them to the building where the printing shop was located, load them onto the elevator, and carry them into the pressroom. After the magazine was printed, he would take the type back to 1315 McGee. Also Lowell helped mail the printed magazines. The wrapping paper was bought in

big sheets, and Lowell cut it into wrappers of the proper
length with a hand cutter that was in the back room of
the house.

"Many things," wrote Lowell Fillmore, describing
the work as it was then carried on, "that I did as a part of
the daily routine and that took me just a few minutes to
do alone constitute whole departments now."

There were still only a few thousand subscribers.
Copies of the mailing list were hung on an upstairs closet
door. Every time a new subscription came in the name
was written on the bottom of the list.

Only a small stock of bound books ready for sale was
kept on hand. Lowell was the order-filling department. "I
often found," he said, "that we were out of some of our
books, which had been printed but not yet folded or
bound. So I would go and get the printed sheets of paper,
fold them by hand, get them ready, and stitch them and
trim them. We kept our finished stock in the office in the
front room; the printed pages, covers, binding materials,
and other things, in the pantry of the old house. I would
wrap and stamp the books and take them to the post
office. Often my brother Rick would take them in his
pony cart. We had time out to mow the lawn and run
errands."

Today the printing is no longer done by Unity School
of Christianity, but by commercial printers. In 1974 when
this change was made, twelve presses, all many times
larger than the original job press on McGee Street, and
rows of typesetting machines, folders, stitchers, and bind-
ers often ran night and day in the huge printing building
Unity School had erected at Unity Village. A force of a
hundred men and women was needed to operate this array of machinery.

Even with the printing being done commercially, in
order to get the millions of pieces of literature finished
and mailed, the publishing building is still crowded with
workers and complicated equipment, some of which has
had to be designed especially for Unity.

Only a large computer containing millions of names

and addresses makes it possible to fill the subscriptions and meet the orders that pour in. Before the computer was acquired, the files that contained these names and addresses had expanded till they filled whole rooms, and batteries of graphotype and addressograph machines were needed.

However the work has been done, the spirit of unity has always activated the work. It pervades the vast buildings at Unity headquarters where hundreds of people carry on the work, as it pervaded the small office in the Journal Building where there were only two people to do what had to be done.

In June 1891, after the name *Unity* had been selected by Charles Fillmore as the right name for the work, the first issue of *Unity* magazine appeared and the name of the company was changed to Unity Book Company. The magazine *Thought* also continued to be published, but *Unity* was started as a special organ for the Society of Silent Unity, which also began at that time. Most of the articles in it were reprinted from *Thought.*

With the first issue of *Unity* magazine, there appeared across the top of the first page the winged globe that through the years was Unity's emblem and often still appears on Unity letterheads and literature. Charles Fillmore wrote that the idea of having such an emblem came to him as a revelation:

> It is an ancient Egyptian symbol; and I remember that when I first saw it I felt that I had had something to do with it in a previous incarnation. I went to a local artist by the name of E. A. Fileau and described to him what I wanted, and he made it under my directions.

> The winged globe or sun disk, as a religious symbol, had its earliest use in Egypt, but it is found in various forms in the religions of other races. It represents the relation existing between Spirit, soul, and body. Soul gives wings to the body. Spirit is the enveloping principle, like the atmosphere in which both soul and body exist, and from which they draw their original inspiration.

The winged globe is also a symbol of the earth and its soul. The earth has soul, as have its products of every description. All exist in the ether, the *anima mundi,* the divine mother. When the people of the earth lift up their thoughts to God, the *Animus Dei* or directive Spirit, then the planet takes wings into a higher radiation of universal life—the mortal puts on immortality.

As man develops spiritual consciousness, he attains the realization of the soul as the wings of the body. Back of the soul is Spirit, which quickens and energizes the soul; that is, gives the soul wings. Artists paint their angels with wings, representing in this way their freedom from physical fetters. But the soul does not have wings like a bird. The life activity of the soul is quickened by Spirit until it rises above the thoughts of matter and floats free in the ether or fourth dimension, which Jesus called the kingdom of the heavens.

Although the Fillmores knew little about the publishing business when they first entered it, they did their best to make *Unity* a magazine that was attractive to the public. They were not afraid to make changes. At first *Unity* was an eight-page paper, the pages being slightly larger than they are now, with two columns of type on a page. After about a year, the number of pages was increased from eight to sixteen. This number has increased through the years. Also the size of the pages has changed. In the beginning most of the covers were white. Today color and illustration are used generously throughout the magazines published by Unity School, but when in the nineties the Fillmores tried dressing up the magazine with a colored cover, some of the subscribers wrote in to say that any color except white was inappropriate for a magazine devoted to such a serious subject. For several years the magazine was published twice a month, and the idea was advanced of making it a weekly. However, Charles Fillmore decided that there were not enough subscribers to warrant a weekly. In 1895 *Thought* and *Unity* were consolidated. By 1898 *Unity* had become a monthly periodical of approximately the size it is today.

One of the outstanding features of the early issues of *Unity* was the advertisements. Sometimes one-fourth of the space was given over to advertising. They were not commercial ads. Of these Charles Fillmore had written:

> Do not send us commercial advertisements. This is not a trade publication, and we do not desire to cultivate the cupidity of our readers beyond its present capacity. The world is now stark mad with the moneymaking thought—it is the most formidable disease we have to heal. Should we give up our pages to descriptions of schemes that will increase this crazy whirl, so potent in paralyzing brain and nerves? We had as well commend the advantages of live arc light and trolley wires as conducive to the health of those who will lay hold of them.

The advertisements were those of healers and other metaphysical publications. Although most of them were simple announcements, some of them made sensational claims.

The June 1894 issue of *Unity* printed this notice:

> To maintain the religious dignity of the doctrine we advocate, we must hold to the pivotal thought that it is a spiritual ministry, and not a new system of healing. . . . The tendency on the part of healers is to give curing too much prominence, and thus the world comes to regard the divine doctrine of Jesus Christ as merely a new departure in materia medica. This feature became so prominent in the advertising columns of *Thought* and *Unity,* and it was so rapidly increasing, that we were compelled to call a halt. We never object to printing the dignified announcements of those who trust to the Spirit of God to do that which is needful for the people whom the Father may draw to them; but we do have qualms of conscience when we give place to alluring bids for healing patronage that smack loudly of patent medicine methods.

Realizing that by so doing we can raise the standard of the doctrine we advocate, we have decided to discontinue display advertisements, and in their stead print regularly a "Teachers and Healers Directory." There will be no specific charge made for the carrying of names in this directory. We leave the compensation to the Spirit of justice working through each one. We want to co-operate with all true, honest, faithful Christian workers and will do any right thing to further the cause. We are one with you in advocating the doctrine of Jesus Christ, and the only title we need is "Christian Teachers and Healers." Let us be true to this modest yet dignified title, and impress upon our patients that it is their spiritual welfare that concerns us first, last, and always—that when this is made right the desirable things of the external shall be added.

Even after this announcement, ads crept into the magazines. The Fillmores had numerous friends in the metaphysical movement, friends with whom they had taken classes and attended conventions. These friends wanted to advertise, and it was hard to turn them down. The Fillmores were friendly, and as Truth students they had learned to respect individuality. No matter how much they disagreed with the methods of their friends, they continued to be friendly. It was several years before they were able to reduce the ads to a simple list of the names and addresses of Truth teachers, printed at the back of the magazine.

The Fillmores continually struggled against turning their organization into a commercial venture. For this reason, they changed the name of the Unity Book Company to the Unity Tract Society, by which name the organization was known until it was incorporated in 1914 together with the Society of Silent Unity as Unity School of Christianity. (This organization, which is now located at Unity Village, Missouri, is sometimes confused with the Unity Society of Practical Christianity, which was incorporated in 1903 and is now located in the Unity Temple on the Country Club Plaza in Kansas City.

Charles and Myrtle Fillmore were the leaders of both organizations, which were originally located alongside each other on Tracy Avenue; but the two have always had different functions. Unity Society is a Unity center, doing a local work; Charles Fillmore was its minister. Unity School of Christianity is the central organization of the Unity movement, doing a worldwide work. It conducts the Silent Unity ministry, publishes *Daily Word, Unity, Wee Wisdom, La Palabra Diaria,* and the Unity books and booklets; prepares radio and television programs; produces cassettes; is responsible for most of the Unity educational programs; and through Silent-70 distributes free literature throughout the world.)

When Charles Fillmore changed the name to the Unity Tract Society, he wrote:

> We have changed the name to relieve the Publication Department of the appearance of a commercial venture. The dollar tag has been so persistently hung onto this movement in its various departments that it has become known to the public at large as a new system of therapeutics, with the usual financial appendix, instead of a religion. That people may more fully understand that there is no element of financial gain in our Publication Department we purposely adopted the word "tract," which is a synonym of religious literature issued without the idea of gain. *This is not a business but a ministry.*

It was indeed a ministry that the Fillmores conducted. Despite the fact that they were having a constant struggle to find the finances to keep publishing *Unity* and take care of their family, Myrtle Fillmore felt that they could be of still further service than they were. At the very beginning of the Unity movement, she had had a vision. It had seemed to her that she was one of a vast congregation of people, many of whom were children. The children were completely undisciplined; in great confusion they were pushing and squirming through the crowd. As she watched them, the thought came to her that they needed someone to look after them. "Who will take care of the children?" she asked.

Even as she asked the question, it seemed to her as though a tremendous force took hold of her and impelled her to the front of the throng. As she was thus thrust forward, a voice spoke to her and said: "You are to take care of the children; this is your work."

Then she awoke; but the vision remained. As soon as she was able, she began a Sunday school that met before the regular Sunday meetings of the Unity Society, and commenced the magazine *Wee Wisdom.* In August 1893 the first number, a small, eight-page paper, was published.

The publication of *Wee Wisdom* brought new financial problems to the struggling couple. The subscription price was only fifty cents a year, far less than necessary to pay the cost of publication, and the subscribers were few. Mrs. Fillmore wote in 1895:

> The fact is that this little paper costs us more than we get for it, and during the past two years the cash outlay over and above the income has been about seven hundred dollars, not allowing anything for editorial services. It has been a debatable question whether to discontinue its publication, raise the subscription price, or cut its size. We are daily reminded by appreciative letters that it is doing a good work among the little ones, so we dismissed the idea of discontinuing its publication. It was not deemed wise to raise the price, so the one thing is to reduce its expense until it shall at least pay printing bills. The subscription list is steadily increasing, and just as soon as the income is sufficient, the former size will again be issued.

Most persons faced with getting out a magazine that cost more than it brought in would have discontinued publishing it; but Myrtle Fillmore was not in the business of publishing magazines, she was in the business of helping people and serving God.

Several times she had to reduce the size of the magazine. For a short time, it was combined with *Unity.*

Once it was sent automatically with a subscription for *Unity*, being treated as a sort of bonus. Nevertheless, the little magazine continued to be published. "You are to take care of the children; this is your work," she had been told.

Today *Wee Wisdom* is the oldest children's magazine in continuous publication in America, and it goes into many thousands of homes. It is published in braille for blind children and sent to them free of charge whenever Unity School is made aware of a need for it.

The statement, "This little paper costs us more than we get for it," has been true throughout its history, but this has never deterred Unity from publishing it.

Myrtle Fillmore was the editor of the magazine for almost thirty years and contributed many stories and poems to its pages. As a result of her vision as to the purpose of the magazine, *Wee Wisdom* has always presented the Unity idea and expressed a positive Christian philosophy of life, but it has kept its material so free from "preaching" that the majority of parents, teachers, and children do not even class it as a religious publication.

Only one book by Myrtle Fillmore was published during her lifetime. This was *Wee Wisdom's Way*, a story about children. This story originally appeared as a serial in *Wee Wisdom*, its initial installment appearing in the first number of the magazine in August 1893. Not only the children but grownups wrote in to comment on the simple language in which it presented metaphysical ideas. Brought forth as a book, it proved to be one of the most popular of the early day publications of Unity.

As Myrtle wrote the story, she would read it to her oldest son Lowell. When he would tell her, "Boys don't say it that way," she would rewrite it. Years later in a letter to a friend she wrote of the book:

> I'll send you the little book that I wrote when the boys were little. The healings were all true, the characters, of course, fictitious. Trixie really was my own little girl-self. I loved to keep a journal. Some people love this little story. Lowell, my eldest son, who was

my critic, almost cried when I told him I had finished the story, and said, "O Mama, please write more, nobody can tell it like Aunt Joy or write like Trixie."

Sometimes Myrtle Fillmore turned the publication of *Wee Wisdom* over to her sons Lowell, Rickert, and Royal. Usually the boys, who referred to themselves as "Wee editors," would edit the August birthday issue. When they were in charge, most of the material in the magazine was provided by *Wee Wisdom* readers.

Nowhere has Unity's wish to maintain a nonsectarian spirit been so clearly displayed as in *Wee Wisdom*. From the beginning, Unity School published the magazine with one purpose in view: to meet the needs of children. It has refused to use the magazine to advance Unity as a movement. The connection of Unity School with it has always been kept in the background. A worker at Unity School once told about a neighbor of hers who expressed antipathy toward Unity and all its works. Yet one day the worker discovered that this neighbor's children were readers of *Wee Wisdom*. Unity had so submerged its own connection with the magazine that the neighbor was not even aware that Unity was the publisher.

What may be the most popular single item ever published by Unity School first appeared in *Wee Wisdom*. This is "The Prayer of Faith" by Hannah More Kohaus:

> God is my help in every need;
> God does my every hunger feed;
> God walks beside me, guides my way
> Through every moment of the day.
>
> I now am wise, I now am true,
> Patient, kind, and loving, too.
> All things I am, can do, and be,
> Through Christ, the Truth that is in me.
>
> God is my health, I can't be sick;
> God is my strength, unfailing, quick;
> God is my all; I know no fear,
> Since God and love and Truth are here.

For years this prayer-poem has been circulated on

cards and in booklets and the Unity periodicals. Today millions of people are familiar with its message. Adults and children write to Unity School to tell how during some crisis of their lives they clung to one of the lines of this poem and found it a lifeline—their "help in every need."

Because of the faith of Myrtle Fillmore, thousands of children have learned to think of God as their help when they have things to meet in their life. They have learned to meet life courageously. They have learned to pray. They have learned to value honesty and kindness and cooperation. They are better, stronger, happier children; and they grow to be better, stronger, happier adults.

How much Myrtle Fillmore's insistence on taking care of the children has influenced the Unity movement was shown when work on Unity Temple (the present home of the Unity Society of practical Christianity on the Country Club Plaza in Kansas City) was begun in the 1940's. As construction proceeded, it became apparent that the entire building could not be completed at one time, as it was going to cost over a million dollars. This was an immense sum of money to raise for an organization that had no wealthy backers but depended for its income on small contributions. It was finally decided to build only part of the building and wait before finishing the rest. It was not the Sunday-school rooms but the sanctuary that was left unfinished.

The vision of the Fillmores found expression in many ways. It was not only through the things that they themselves wrote and said and did that they accomplished good. From the beginning of the movement, they showed a talent for calling forth the talent of others.

Among those whom they inspired to write about Truth was a doctor by the name of H. Emilie Cady. She had been a teacher in a little school in Dryden, New York, had left to study medicine, and had been a practicing physician in New York City for several years before the Fillmores heard of her. A little book that she had written fell into Myrtle Fillmore's hands. From that time,

Dr. Cady was to have a tremendous influence on the Unity movement although she never visited Unity School and the Fillmores did not meet her until 1926 when they visited her in New York.

The title of the booklet that Myrtle Fillmore found and was impressed by is *Finding the Christ in Ourselves*. Mrs. Fillmore passed it on to her husband to read, and he also was impressed by it, so they wrote to Dr. Cady and asked her permission to print and distribute the article in booklet form. They also asked her for contributions to their magazines. In the January 1892 number of *Unity*, the first article by H. Emilie Cady, "Neither Do I Condemn Thee," appeared. In ensuing numbers, there were a number of articles written by her, as well as some personal letters to the Fillmores. In August 1894 she wrote:

> My heart leaped within me when I read some time ago in your answer to a correspondent: "We do not need to battle for the right or for Truth. We do not need to resist evil. There is a higher way; just be still and know," and so forth.
>
> I was so glad to have that thought given to the hundreds of persons who maintain that they must resist evil in order to overcome it. "This is the victory that hath overcome the world, *even* our faith," and faith does not need to strive or battle.
>
> And then all my soul blessed you when you said, "We will no longer print ads or personal puffs." Will not Spirit do its own advertising if trusted? If Spirit desires to heal through me, does not the same Spirit live in those it would help through me, and will it not bring the supply and demand together if fully trusted? Surely.
>
> Oh, how the mortal needs this lesson of being willing to sink out of sight if only Spirit is manifest! How hard it is for this John the Baptist to say, "He must increase, but I must decrease." God does abundantly bless you for having taken the stand. Fear not. With great desire He has desired from the beginning to manifest Himself through you as your supply of

money, without intervention of human hands outside of yourself. "Faithful is he that calleth you, who will also do it."

To me the same call came four years ago, and well have I known ever since that that is my work in the world: to prove to the multitudes that the God within them is their supply, and that it must come forth from within to each one, independently, as his very own supply. I know that we are free today from the law of poverty and want, and further, from the law of work-and-get-pay-for-it. We are freely justified by His grace (or free gifts). Let us stand if all the world turns the other way, for thereunto has He called us. . . .

I am going to write again. May I send some little message through *Thought?*

At the same time, the Fillmores printed a letter from a subscriber suggesting a simple course of lessons:

There are some who are taking your paper for the first time and do not as yet even understand the principles of divine healing. Would you be so kind as to have one of your clearest writers, one who understands the principles, and the uninformed mind of a student, write an explanation of this grand Truth in very simple form and in simple, clear words. It would be a great help to some I know of. H. Emilie Cady or Mrs. Militz or Mrs. A. W. Mills, I am sure, would respond most gratefully if you would request them.

Following this suggestion, the Fillmores wrote to Dr. Cady and asked her if she would undertake such a task. At first, she was reluctant to do so. She explained to them that she was a practicing physician as well as a metaphysician and that because her practice kept her so busy she had little time for writing. Also she doubted her ability, but the Fillmores had no doubt. As a Unity booklet, *Finding the Christ in Ourselves* had been extremely popular with the readers, as it had been popular with the Fillmores. They felt that this woman had the ability to present simply and clearly the fundamentals of the Jesus Christ teachings that they were endeavoring to propound in their magazine. They recognized in her a deep spiritual insight and they called forth from her, as they were to call from many others, the inspiration and talent that were innately hers. They persisted in asking her to attempt this work, for they knew how much it was needed by their readers. There was at that time no simple set of lessons that presented the principles that they were teaching.

In September 1894, this letter by Dr. Cady appeared in *Unity* as an announcement of the forthcoming series of lessons:

> *Dear Mr. Fillmore:* Yours, asking me to write a consecutive course of lessons for *Unity,* received. These are the words given to me in reply: "Now therefore go, and I will be with thy mouth, and teach thee what thou shalt speak."
>
> So there is nothing left for me to say but yes. I will send you the first one in time for the October *Unity* if you will let me know when it has to be in for that.
>
> I shall not give any stilted or set form of lessons, but just the utter simplicity of the gospel in words that the wayfarer, "though a fool," may understand; for I believe that to be the need of the hour. Will this be satisfactory to you?

The first lesson appeared the following month. It was titled "Statement of Being"; it is now the second chapter of *Lessons in Truth.* In subsequent months, eleven other lessons were published. There had been other attempts to present some of the fundamental teachings in *Unity,* but they had never before caught on. These lessons caught the readers' interest as nothing else that had been published in the magazine. The response to them was immediate and great. The people who read them felt that here was a simple expression of the ideas they were endeavoring to assimilate. Here was something they could pass on to friends and neighbors that would explain their belief for them.

Mr. Fillmore decided to print the lessons in booklet form. Shortly after the last one appeared in the magazine, he issued three booklets, each containing four of the lessons. These booklets sold for twenty-five cents apiece, or all three for seventy-five cents.

It was several years before the lessons were printed in book form and appeared as *Lessons in Truth,* as we know it today, the most popular book ever published by Unity. It has been translated into ten languages, and about a million and a half copies of it have been distributed. Back in 1894, when the aspiring editors of the humble magazine *Unity* asked the homeopathic physician in New York to prepare a series of simple lessons presenting the fundamentals of Truth, they did not foresee the multitudes who were to be led by *Lessons in Truth* to a source of healing for their bodies and a light for their minds; neither did they foresee how the little magazine that after five years of publication still had a circulation of only five thousand subscribers would some day be expanded into the battery of publications that today flow into millions of homes.

But diligently, faithfully, they wrote about Truth as they saw it and inspired others, like H. Emilie Cady, to do likewise; and month in, month out, with little thought of personal remuneration but with the divine urge to serve, they sent their words out to all who would read them. Today because of their steadfastness these words echo around the globe.

Chapter VI

Silent Unity

"Pray One for Another"

IN THE APRIL 1890 number of the magazine *Thought,*
Myrtle Fillmore announced the opening of a new depart-
ment that she called at first the Society of Silent Help.
She wrote:

> All over the land are persons yearning for Truth,
> yet so dominated by the surrounding error that they
> find it almost impossible, without a helping hand, to
> come into harmony with the divine Spirit. To open a
> way for those and to help them overcome their sins,
> ills, and troubles is the object of the Society of Silent
> Help. The wonderful success of absent healing dem-
> onstrates that bodily presence is not necessary to
> those in spiritual harmony. Jesus said: "If two of you
> shall agree on earth as touching anything that they
> shall ask, it shall be done for them of my Father who
> is in heaven." Those who have had experience in
> asking understandingly know that this is absolutely
> true.
>
> Hence a little band in this city have agreed to meet
> in silent soul communion every night at 10 o'clock
> all those who are in trouble, sickness, or poverty, and
> who sincerely desire the help of the Good Father.
>
> Whoever will may join this society, the only re-
> quirement being that members shall sit in a quiet,
> retired place, if possible, at the hour of 10 o'clock
> every night, and hold in silent thought, for not less
> than fifteen minutes, the words that shall be given

each month by the editor of this department. The difference in the solar time between widely separated places will not materially interfere with the result, for to Spirit there is neither time nor space, hence each member should sit at 10 p.m. local time.

The words that were given to be held in silent thought every night at 10 o'clock from April 15 to May 15, 1890, were these:

> God is all goodness and everywhere present. He is the loving Father, and I am His child and have all His attributes of life, love, truth, and intelligence. In Him is all health, strength, wisdom, and harmony, and as His child all these become mine by a recognition of the truth that *God is all.*

The little band that met in silent soul communion at first consisted only of Mr. and Mrs. Fillmore and a few friends and neighbors who had become interested. They met every night at 10 o'clock in the Fillmore home to pray together and to give a blessing to all who tuned in to them in thought. Sometimes to open the meeting they sang a hymn or two to get themselves into a spirit of worship, then Charles or Myrtle led the others in affirmative prayer.

"Take with you words and return to the Lord," said the prophet Hosea. This is exactly what the first members of the Society of Silent Help did. They became quiet and meditated on the idea of God until the idea became a living reality in their minds and hearts and they felt God as a living presence in themselves. When they had gained a sense of oneness with God, they affirmed that God's goodness was being brought forth in their minds, bodies, and affairs. They made these affirmations for one another; they made them for others who had asked them for special prayers. If someone during the day had asked one of this little band to pray for him, they all spoke his name and declared Truth for him; that is, they affirmed his oneness with the goodness of God, with health and love and wisdom and harmony and any other blessing they felt he needed. All that they asked of the one for whom they prayed was that he join in silent prayer with them wherever he might be.

From the time that the Fillmores had started Unity, they had been praying each evening for those who came to them personally and asked for prayer. At this time, they enlarged the field of their service.

The Society of Silent Help is open to everyone. If you are sick, troubled, or unhappy from any cause whatever, sit in the silence with us every night and for a short time forget all your external thoughts. Give yourself up to the Spirit within for but a little while, and we assure you your heart will be lighter at the end of thirty days, if not in less time.

In establishing the Society of Silent Help, the Fillmores took a great step forward. From the beginning, they had been teaching that God is omnipresent, and suddenly they realized that if it were true that God is everywhere, that His power is everywhere and can be called into activity anywhere, it was not necessary for people to come to them for personal interviews in order to receive help. God's presence was not confined to the little room of their home where they prayed, or to their office; God was not something that acted only in their presence or when they spoke a word of Truth into the ear of someone sitting near them. God was omnipresence, God was everywhere, God was principle. The principle of God was not limited by space or time. The only limitation that there could possibly be was the limitation that existed in those who were attempting to work with the principle. "Whatever you ask in prayer, you will receive, if you have faith," Jesus had said; and so they asked in faith. Like the Master at the tomb of Lazarus, they declared with perfect faith: "Father, I thank thee that thou hast heard me. I knew that thou hearest me always."

Because they felt that God's will is always good, they had come to the conclusion that all that keeps our blessings from us are our own thoughts, our own lack of faith. They realized that if people can get their thoughts right, change their attitudes, their consciousness—as they called it—into one of receptivity, God's good flows into their lives.

They felt that there is power in united prayer, that when several persons with a high degree of faith in God's goodness join together in affirming Truth, a channel is cleared, as it were, through which His blessings may flow forth more freely and abundantly. Therefore, they felt that the location of those for whom they prayed did not matter. Though miles might separate the persons concerned, if they were together in thought, they were together in the true sense of the word. If one person prays in a spirit of love and faith and lifts himself into oneness with God, then all who are attuned in thought with him are lifted into that oneness, no matter whether they are sitting side by side or are on opposite sides of the earth.

This was a great discovery by Charles and Myrtle Fillmore: that people did not have to live in Kansas City in order to commune with them in prayer. Jesus said, "And I, when I am lifted up from the earth, will draw all men to myself." They could pray in the house on Elmwood Avenue in Kansas City or in their office downtown and if they could be lifted up in consciousness to an awareness of the Christ presence, all who prayed with them, no matter where they might be, would be lifted up into that same awareness. It was upon this idea that Silent Unity was founded and it is through this faith that Unity has grown.

At first, the department of Silent Help was supervised by Mrs. Fillmore, but in a short time, as this department grew rapidly, both she and Mr. Fillmore were thoroughly engrossed in it.

There was something about the idea of the little band meeting together in silent soul communion every night at 10 o'clock to help all those who were in trouble, sickness, or poverty, wherever they might be throughout the land, that appealed to the imagination. People began at once to write for prayers. Mrs. Fillmore wrote:

> This department is not intended for trained teach-
> ers, although many of them might be benefited by
> sitting in the silence each evening, but the object is
> to start into spiritual unfoldment those who are so
> situated that they cannot have personal teaching.

Charles and Myrtle Fillmore were in tune with their
time. They knew that people had come to the place
where they were seeking to find Truth within themselves. They knew that all over the earth there were people hungering for silent soul communion, people in need,
people sick and troubled, people looking for God. They
sensed that these people were not finding in the churches
the help in their trouble or the communion in their loneliness that they desired. It was for these people that the
Society of Silent Help was formed, and it was these people who stretched out their hands to the Fillmores for
help through prayer. From the beginning, no charge has
been made for this help. The Silent Unity ministry has
always been conducted on the freewill offering plan.

In the May 1890 number of the magazine, Mrs. Fillmore wrote:

> Although the Society of Silent Help [as an organi-
> zation] has been in existence but thirty days, it has in
> that short time demonstrated its efficacy as a factor in
> the new dispensation. Its potency in opening the way
> for the Spirit of truth will increase in proportion to its
> membership—purity and persistence of individual
> thought being always understood. At the end of one
> year, there ought to be at least five thousand people
> in this country alone who will give fifteen minutes
> each evening to the silent communion with the Spirit
> of God. With that number of earnest souls holding
> the thoughts of Truth, every member should be lifted
> above sickness, sorrow, and poverty.

From lonely farms and little villages, and from the
loneliness of big cities, the letters began to come almost
at once, from the people who were sick and the people
who were unhappy and the people who were seeking the
unfoldment of their own spiritual powers. In a short time,

all over the land, people were sitting down at 10 p.m. and joining in silent soul communion with the little band in Kansas City. From thousands of isolated rooms, isolated no longer, voices were declaring longingly and prayer-fully the silent thought provided by the Society.

Also in May 1890, the hour of prayer was changed from 10 to 9 at night. "This change," wrote Mrs. Fillmore, "is made to accommodate a number of persons living in the country districts who have written us that they should like to become members but were prevented by the late-ness of the hour of communion."

Each month in the magazine a new affirmation, or prayer, for the members of the Society to hold together in thought was printed. These were called "Class Thoughts." These were general statements like the first one, but in a few years two "Class Thoughts" were printed each month, one to cover healing and one to cover prosperity. Today when a person writes to Silent Unity for help he almost always receives a prayer state-ment printed on a leaf or card, but for many years this was not the case. If a person wanted Silent Unity's help he wrote a letter to the Society and at the same time began to use whichever one of the "Class Thoughts" best fitted his need. The "Class Thoughts" printed in *Unity* were the only prayers that the members of Silent Unity used.

At one time, the "Class Thoughts" were printed on a sheet that could be taken out of the magazine so that the subscriber could carry it with him wherever he went. For a few years in the early 1900's, this sheet was colored red and became known as the "red leaf." Some of Unity's subscribers began to apply this leaf literally to various parts of their bodies that needed healing, like a kind of charm. Charles Fillmore wrote that the "red leaf" was of value not because of any mysterious physical virtue it possessed but only because the diligent use of the affirm-ative prayer printed on it might quicken the one who used it into a realization of his oneness with the healing life of God. Many of his students, however, went on applying the red leaf to their bodies, and Unity received hundreds of letters telling of good results obtained by this method.

In time, the "Class Thoughts" came to be supplemented by other affirmations composed by Silent Unity to meet specific needs of correspondents. Today there are hundreds of different affirmations to fit every conceivable need.

In the beginning, the prayers of Silent Unity were almost exclusively concerned with the healing of physical ailments, and later with financial supply. It was only after several years that people began to feel free to write about other things. Today, of the more than a million and a half requests for prayer that are received every year, although many are still concerned with a need for physical healing and prosperity, the majority of requests deal with emotional problems, problems involving human relationships.

In the beginning, all requests for prayer came to Silent Unity in letters, but very soon people began to turn to the telephone and call for help. The Fillmores were always ready to answer the telephone, and since they stayed up every night to very late hours, they were usually available.

Before World War I they had begun a round-the-clock telephone service as part of the ministry of Silent Unity. In a room at the top of the building at Ninth and Tracy, they had someone stationed night and day to answer calls for help and to pray at any time with anyone who needed prayer.

The light shining at all times from the window of this room caught the imagination of Silent Unity workers. Walking by in the street outside late at night, they would look up and feel lifted in heart. This lighted window, they felt, was the symbol of all that they did in Silent Unity. They thought of Silent Unity as "the light that shines for you," and that is how people everywhere began to think of it.

Today the lighted window of the Silent Unity telephone prayer room at Unity Village has become famous throughout the world. People have traveled thousands of miles just to stand outside that window and look up at it. And a truly dedicated ministry is conducted in the room behind it.

While the majority of the requests for prayer still come to Silent Unity in letters, every year more and more people call on the telephone. By 1975 the telephone ministry had grown so much that Silent Unity installed toll-free lines. It was recognized that many people do not have the money to call and also that many people who need to call are doing so in a highly emotional state, perhaps at a moment of great emergency, from the scene of an accident or from a hospital, where they find it a nerve-racking task to have to carefully count out coins and drop them in a pay phone. The toll-free lines have helped many thousands of persons in difficult situations.

Today it takes a staff of more than forty dedicated workers to conduct the telephone ministry. People call from all over the world. Every day more than a thousand, some days more than two thousand, people call. On an average day, perhaps five thousand write. About two hundred people work in the Silent Unity building.

To everyone who calls, as to everyone who writes, Silent Unity answers with a letter, and usually an affirmation especially fitted to that person's need is sent. Also Silent Unity has prepared several hundred booklets that take up the various problems that people write about, and usually one of these is enclosed.

In the beginning, there were no special prayers sent out and letters that were received in connection with the Society were not always answered. Myrtle Fillmore wrote:

> In reply to the many letters to the editor of this department, we would say that our duties are such that we cannot personally answer each one, but that we do hold the writers in thought for what comes to us as their special needs. We are glad to hear from everyone who takes an interest in this society and

every letter will be filed in the archives and become
a part of our storehouse of good.

The new organization did not long have the name of
"Society of Silent Help." In the spring of 1891, less than a
year after the organization was formed, Charles Fillmore
had his revelation that the new movement should be
called "Unity," and the first *Unity* magazine was published in June of that year. It was published as an organ
of the new Society, the name of which was now changed
to "Society of Silent Unity," of which Charles and Myrtle
Fillmore were listed as the central secretaries. As the
Society of Silent Unity, it has been known ever since.
Through the years, the name of Silent Unity has come to
mean much to millions of persons (most of whom were
not yet born in the spring of 1891 when the Fillmores
gave it that name). It has come to be a symbol of love and
service and help in time of trouble.

Most of those who have written to Silent Unity for
help have never been in the Kansas City area. They have
never talked with a Silent Unity worker. Yet to them the
name Silent Unity stands for the "silent soul communion," of which the Fillmores spoke in the very first notice
that appeared in the magazine about the formation of this
new department. It stands for the outstretched hands of
prayer, outstretched in love and service, outstretched in
faith in God. It stands for help in every need, for healing
for the sick and supply for the needy, joy for the down-in-
spirit, freedom for those in bondage, and companionship
for those who are alone.

Relatively few who have turned to Silent Unity have
ever visited Unity headquarters; but even if they have
not, they know that there is today, as there has always
been, a band of faithful workers praying with them,
thinking of them, turning with them to God in prayer
each day. They know that if they should go to Unity
headquarters, whatever the hour of the night or day, they
would find someone in prayer, someone keeping the vigil
of faith that began almost a century ago. And they know

that they do not need to go in person, they only need to go in thought, only need to turn in heart and mind to Silent Unity to find the "silent soul communion" that is their need.

The infinite potentialities of the idea of Silent Unity revealed themselves almost at once. From many places, numerous people not only wrote for prayers for themselves, they wrote that they were having some of their friends who were interested in spiritual matters meet with them at 9 o'clock at night and form another Society of Silent Unity.

The Fillmores could see that Silent Unity, with little groups of persons in harmony of thought and purpose joining together all over the land to pray for themselves and for one another, might be developed into one of the most potent spiritual forces that had ever been created. They could see that in a short time thousands would be praying together, uniting their spiritual efforts in a common aim, and they could see that through this common effort a tremendous spiritual force was going to be unleashed. They could see how Silent Unity would grow into a great far-flung movement of mutual help.

"For where two or three are gathered in my name, there am I in the midst of them," said Jesus.

In Silent Unity, there would be, not two or three gathered together, but thousands. What immeasurable spiritual power must this united prayer release! In their magazine, the Fillmores published directions for forming Silent Unity Societies:

> Start a society at once if you have but two persons to begin with. Do not seek numbers, but harmony in those who meet with you. Meet regularly every Tuesday night, and the Spirit will eventually draw to you those desired. Two persons in perfect harmony will do the work of the Spirit more effectually than a hundred in discord.
>
> Begin with music and sing frequently during the entire time of the meeting. Immediately after each song, hold in the Silence for a moment some thought

of Truth. You cannot overdo this feature of the meeting. It is always uplifting and harmonizing to hold in unison some high spiritual thought. "Speech is silver, silence is golden."

The early part of the evening may be passed in a general discussion of matters spiritual. When the clock strikes nine, go into the silence and hold in consciousness a few moments: "Be still, and know that I am God."

Then after music hold the class thought for the month, in unison, for a few moments. It is sometimes advisable to repeat it audibly, then silently, until the mental vibrations become harmonious. In holding these universal thoughts, let your consciousness go out and take in all the minds of men. Feel that you are talking to every soul in the universe and that all are listening to your call. This mental drill will center your thoughts, and those of you who are spiritually alive will sense the vibrations of Spirit. Then is the time to do effective work. Take up those you desire to help and hold them in thought by name separately.

The only object and aim of this Society is to get people to listen to the "still small voice" and know that God will lead them into all wisdom, health, and happiness if they will spend but a few moments each day in His company—the silent realm of Divine Mind. Rules are but temporary leading strings and must eventually all be put aside. "Behold, the tabernacle of God is with men, and he will dwell with them, and they shall be his peoples, and God himself shall be with them, *and be* their God: and he shall wipe away every tear from their eyes; and death shall be no more; neither shall there be mourning, nor crying, nor pain any more: the first things are passed away."

All who desired to be identified with Silent Unity were invited to send in their names with a brief description of their troubles. No answer by letter was assured the writer, but they were assured that Silent Unity would respond in prayer. They could have a certificate of membership if they wanted one. If they wanted help for a friend, they could have that, but they had to promise to pray for the friend themselves.

In a short time, the Fillmores decided that the nine o'clock prayer period was not enough and members were asked to sit in the silence not only in the evening but also from 12:15 to 12:45 p.m. and join in prayer at that time. Today people join in prayer with Silent Unity at all times of the day and night.

The day begins in Silent Unity at 8 o'clock in the morning with a prayer service based on the prayer that is given in *Daily Word* for that day. (This is done also in all other departments at Unity School.) At 11 o'clock a recording of the Lord's prayer made by Charles Fillmore is broadcast from loudspeakers throughout the buildings. At this time, Silent Unity workers meet in the prayer room for a healing service based on the "Class Thoughts." Before a worker is permitted to take part in this healing meeting, he has been instructed in the principles of healing as taught by Unity School.

At noon there is another special period of prayer based mainly on the Prosperity Thought. Often at two-thirty in the afternoon the workers meet again. Most of the workers go home at 4 o'clock, but a smaller group comes in and remains all night long. It conducts the 9 o'clock prayer service, which is centered on the Healing Thought, answers telephone calls, and prays.

Workers who handle letters from correspondents, even if they are only filing them, give them a blessing. Night and day, day in, day out, every half hour, a worker goes into the prayer room alone to pray. Today prayer is truly continuous in Silent Unity.

The growth of the organization was rapid. In 1891, Mr. Fillmore asked for Societies of Silent Unity to be formed "in every town, city, and hamlet in the land. No formal organization of any kind is necessary—no creed, no leader, no authority but God." In a short time, there were hundreds of these groups. In five years, more than six thousand memberships were issued. By 1903 there were ten thousand members; by 1906, fifteen thousand; today Silent Unity receives many more than a million requests for prayers each year.

For several years, Charles and Myrtle Fillmore did all the work in Silent Unity. They called themselves "central secretaries" and they handled all the letters themselves, though often unable to answer them all. Occasionally, when there were many letters that had to go unanswered, Myrtle Fillmore printed in the magazine a general letter to all the Silent Unity correspondents who had not been answered personally:

> *Dear Friends:* Your loving words make us strong and glad. We never tire of them. The inspiration of them goes with us through all of our work. They shine out to us from shadows that sometimes seem. They refresh and bless us. God measure to you again increasingly.
>
> No less dear to us is your sacred confidence, dear hearts, who believe yourselves overshadowed by sorrow and disease. God loves you! We would rather be able to speak the word that hurls you from these mountains of belief than charm all earth with our eloquence.
>
> It is because so many ask for words of help and comfort that we have not been able to make our pens fly fast enough to get round to each. Our thoughts are not so slow. You have all, each and every one, been held in strong and loving Truth by us.

It was several years before the Fillmores were able to hire someone to help them with the Silent Unity correspondence. By the early 1900's they had a half dozen helpers working with them to answer the letters from Silent Unity correspondents. About one hundred letters a day were coming to the department, and Charles Fillmore was prophesying that the time would come when there would be twenty-four workers in Silent Unity.

To one looking back from the present when there are about 250 workers in the Silent Unity building at Unity Village, that may not seem like much of a proph-

ecy, but at the time it took courage and faith to make the
statement, and to those who were working with him it
seemed like a grand leap of the imagination.

At that time, the work was conducted on the third
floor of the new building that Unity had built at 913
Tracy. Here at the top of a narrow stairway, Silent Unity
had its prayer room into which no one was permitted to
enter except those who through years of silent meditation
and consecration to the Christ ideals had unfolded spiritually to the place where they maintained themselves in
a high consciousness of faith in God. Here the requests
for prayer were brought, and here the members of Silent
Unity met each day to take those requests to God in
prayer.

The workers of Silent Unity have always claimed
that they have no special power that is not also innate in
everyone else. "It is not I, but the Father who dwells
within me who does his works." When they meet in the
prayer room at Unity Village, this statement is always in
front of them. It is printed at the top of the lists of names
that they take into the room. But those who take part in
the healing meetings have consecrated themselves to the
service of God and their fellowmen by preparation in
prayer and obedience to the teachings of Jesus. To this
day, Silent Unity workers feel that their prayer room is a
sacred place, a place apart, a place that like the "secret
place of the Most High" within themselves is to be kept
inviolate and consecrated. Few persons outside of the
members of Silent Unity ever enter this room.

From the beginning, the prayers of Silent Unity produced results. In one of the first issues of *Unity* magazine, there were two letters from correspondents. The first
was from a woman in Dundee, Illinois, who wrote:

> My husband, a strong, healthy man of two hundred
> pounds, got out of bed perfectly well to all appear-
> ance, after a good night's sleep. All at once, he grew
> blind and fell forward. The fall awoke me, and I has-
> tened to him. He was trying to arise, and l helped
> him onto the bed.

Oh, the looks of him would have scared me a few months ago. The pulse was gone, and the heart's action was imperceptible. I said not a word but quietly lay down beside him, and burying my head in the pillow to shut out the terrible seeming, I mentally affirmed "Life, life, eternal life," over and over again. I said, "God is in that heart, and its action is perfect." I said it with all my might and soul.

Soon the heart resumed its action, the body became warm, and he slept, oh, so sweetly in those loving arms of healing mercy. I want to sing praises to God all the time.

I will just say that my husband was able to be about and do some work the same day.

And the other was from a Kansas City doctor, who said:

Last Tuesday night, I was watching at the bedside of an apparently dying woman. I had exhausted every resource. She was surely passing away, when I thought of Silent Unity. I prayed that I might have your help in saving my patient. It was about 9 o'clock, and I knew you were in session, so I shut my eyes and asked that the Spirit of truth might be poured out upon the dying woman.

Instantly the room seemed ablaze with a bright light, and I saw a stream of what seemed a luminous ether poured upon my patient. I saw it just as plainly as I could the sunlight coming through a window. Just how long it lasted, I do not know. When I opened my eyes, I found the woman sleeping. In about half an hour, she awoke greatly improved. Again she went to sleep. The next morning, I was satisfied she would live. Yesterday she started on a long journey.

It was to me the tangible evidence of an invisible healing principle of which our medical science is still quite ignorant. I can only say it must have been the power of God.

At first, the Fillmores were reluctant to print testimonials, but in succeeding issues under a column with the heading "Apples of Gold in Pictures of Silver" were

printed stories of the healing of many diseases. Through
the years that Silent Unity has prayed with those who
turned to God for help, the magazines published by Unity
have contained letters testifying to the healing of almost
every known physical ailment, including cancer, tuberculosis, blindness, deafness, insanity, arthritis, and many
others. There have been letters from those who found
through Silent Unity new faith in life after they had come
to the place where they had decided to make an end of it.
There have been letters testifying to the gaining of freedom from bondage to habits and false states of mind of
many years' standing. There have been letters that have
told how families have adjusted their lives and grown out
of chaos and bitterness into harmony and happiness.
There have been letters that have related seemingly mi-
raculous openings of employment and income where
before failure had appeared to be certain. There have
been letters proving over and over thousands of times
that *with God all things are possible.*

When they were the central secretaries of Silent
Unity, Myrtle and Charles Fillmore were close to those
who worked there. Every day, Mrs. Fillmore went from
desk to desk among the workers, bringing encouragement and words of cheer, perhaps leaving some small gift
that she wished to share with the worker. Mr. Fillmore
sat at his desk at the head of the department. When a
worker had some particularly difficult letter to answer
that he was not sure of, he took it to Charles Fillmore and
received advice and inspiration. Together the Fillmores
led the healing meetings and taught most of the classes
in Silent Unity that prepared the workers to conduct the
ministry aright. They were the mind and heart of Silent
Unity. Their prayers were at the core of it. Their ideas
were the inspiration for it.

Today the spirit of these two still moves through the
Silent Unity work. The same spirit of devotion to the
healing ministry of the Christ burns in the heart and
mind of those who serve there. Letters that go out declare
as reassuringly as ever the Truth discovered by Charles

and Myrtle Fillmore: that God is life, that God is love, and that His life and love are accessible through prayer to heal, to prosper, and to bless.

This year all over the earth, from city and village and farm, more than a million persons will call on Silent Unity for spiritual help, and they will find a faith that they would not have found had it not been that many years ago in Kansas City a man and a woman, Charles and Myrtle Fillmore, "agreed to meet in silent soul communion . . . all those who are in trouble, sickness, and poverty, and who sincerely desire the help of the good Father."

Chapter VII

First Years of the Ministry

"Pastors and Teachers"

ONE OF THE great needs of the Fillmores was a suitable place in which to conduct their ministry. The first office in the Journal Building, where Mr. Fillmore had conducted his mining and real estate business, proved almost at once to be unsatisfactory, and he moved to the Deardorff Building, where several other persons who were interested in the metaphysical movement had their offices. Here, with the help of some of these friends, he was able to establish a circulating library of books on metaphysics.

Visitors who were interested in any phase of the metaphysical movement were invited to drop into the offices regardless of what school of thought they might represent.

A few months later, the Fillmores moved their offices again, this time to the fifth floor of the Hall Building, on the corner of Ninth and Walnut Streets. The Fillmore boys loved these rooms because from the windows they could look "way down" to the street, and across the street was a fire station.

This move turned out to be a fortunate one, not only because of the more commodious quarters, but shortly after the move, the Deardorff Building burned to the ground. Several of Mr. Fillmore's friends who had remained there lost all the records of their work. One of them, Dr. J. S. Thacher, inserted a notice in *Thought* asking those who had been his patients to communicate with him again because he had lost even their names.

The offices in the Hall Building consisted of double rooms with a kind of archway connecting them. Meetings were held in the east half of this room. The Knights of Pythias hall in the same building was used for Sunday services.

Mr. Fillmore was not the only speaker at the meetings. Often some friend of the Fillmores who was active in the work was the speaker, or some lecturer on metaphysics who was passing through town was asked to conduct the meeting. At one time, on Sunday evenings, a course of lectures known as the "No Name Series" was given, the subject being announced ahead of time but the name of the speaker being kept secret. The Fillmores were not working to gain personal acclaim. They did not believe that they had sole title to Truth or sole access to it. They believed that each person had in him the potentialities of a son of God and they put their belief into practice by letting various persons who felt that they had something worth saying deliver addresses. Several persons who had taken classes under Emma Curtis Hopkins took charge of the "No Name" meetings.

Emma Curtis Hopkins came to Kansas City several times and taught a series of classes. Tall, slender, and good-looking, wearing a big picture hat while she spoke, she was a dynamic and eloquent teacher. Eighty-seven students attended one of her classes, the largest Truth class in Kansas City up to that time. When she came to Kansas City, arrangements were made so that students coming from a distance could find room and board in the same house with her. The times spent with Mrs. Hopkins were joyous times for the Fillmores, for they found with her and with the students that surrounded her the meeting of minds that as much as any other thing is conducive to happiness in human affairs.

In 1890, the Fillmores went to Chicago to attend a class review at Mrs. Hopkins' school. Both of them made speeches. There were over one hundred and twenty of

Mrs. Hopkins' students and graduates assembled at the seminary, and for ten days they threw themselves into classwork, prayer meetings, and joyous visits with others who spoke their language.

When they returned home to Kansas City, Mrs. Fillmore wrote a letter describing the visit to Chicago:

> There are so many things I wanted to tell you about our Chicago experiences. I got my black dress made up so that it is very stylish and becoming with velvet sleeves and collar and the front of the waist is velvet. The Rays fixed me up a velvet hat out of that velvet of your bonnet; they furnished a wing and trim. There were lots of beautiful dresses there but one didn't think much about such things.
>
> Of course we met all those whose names are so familiar in the literature: Ida Nichols, Nellie Anderson, Julia Twinchester, and so forth. A finer set of people I never met.
>
> We were fortunate enough to have a room under Mrs. Hopkins' roof. She is just lovely to be with. There were over a hundred at the Review and all ate at her tables. It was the happiest, most harmonious family meeting on earth—for that's what it seemed— everything seemed as free and natural as air.
>
> You can see from the program how we spent most of our time. Tuesday was a day off, for they were getting the seminary ready for ordination services. Charles and I wandered about the city, went to see "Jerusalem on the Day of the Crucifixion." It is a wonderful cyclorama.
>
> At night, we all went over to C. I. Thacher's—and such a time! Never was there such a jolly, happy set. He had cleared out the basement and decorated it and had an orchestra down there as a surprise to the party. You ought to have seen Doctor Gibbons and another old minister there trip the fantastic toe. Can you imagine John Thacher, Sullivan, and Barton dancing? I laughed till I could hardly stand up, it was so funny. As they closed about the fourth set, Charles rushed into the middle of the floor and shouted out: "I can't dance, but I can sing. Let's sing 'Praise God

from Whom All Blessings Flow.'" And before the orchestra could change its tune to fall in, the house trembled with the old hymn; it was powerfully done. Then followed a healing song, and next the dancing was resumed. The musicians looked funny. I suppose they thought they had struck a lot of lunatics. A nice supper was served about 11 o'clock.

Charles and I were invited out there the Sunday before to dinner. Doctor Gibbons, Miss Rix, Miss Austin, and several others were there. I tell you, they have an elegant home and things are served up in grand style. They keep three servants all the time, two girls and a man. And after our eight o'clock dinner, we sat in the silence, and such a wonderful power came over us. We gave it direction, and those we have heard from were wonderfully benefited. It was then our baby was named and blessed.

Up until this time, the youngest boy of the Fillmores had been known simply as "Baby," but at this party he was given the name "Royal."

The Fillmores knew many of the people who were interested in Truth, and whenever they could afford to, they went to gatherings of those friends. In the summer of 1893, they were back in Chicago, where a group of New Thoughters held a congress at the World's Columbian Exposition. In 1895, they were back once more for the meeting of the International Divine Science Association. There, much to their delight, it was voted that the 1896 congress should be held in Kansas City under the sponsorship of the Fillmores.

This congress opened on May 12, and the Fillmores were so busy seeing to the needs and the pleasures of their visiting friends that they did not even take time to publish the May 15 number of *Unity*, but omitted it and on June 1, put out an extra large one that gave an account of all the meetings.

The meetings were held in the Academy of Music, which was located on McGee Street, about four blocks from the Unity rooms, which were then in the Hall Building.

The first act of most of those who attended the congress, when they got off the train at the Union Station, was to take a cable car to Ninth and Walnut streets. The Fillmores had arranged for rooms and boarding places for most of them. Good room and board cost four dollars a week.

Most of the well-known metaphysical leaders and teachers in the United States were there. Many of those who did not attend sent papers that were read at the meetings.

This organization that met in Kansas City in 1896 later became the International New Thought Alliance, and during the next few years the Fillmores' association with this group was a close one, for they knew and liked many of the teachers personally. They attended several conventions, but in 1905 in an article in *Unity* Charles Fillmore wrote:

> So far as the Unity Society of Practical Christianity is concerned, we must candidly say that its teachings are widely different from those of the majority of New Thought doctrines, and we do not feel at home in the average gathering under that name, although we try to harmonize with all Truth seekers.

Charles Fillmore went to the convention of the International New Thought Federation, as it was then called, held in Chicago in 1906, but he was disappointed. The turnout was small, and the ideas that he heard expressed were a far cry from the ones that he had come to hold. He wrote:

> I asked several people to give me a definition of New Thought, and they differed greatly in their concepts. It dawned on me that the name "New Thought" had been appropriated by so many cults that had new theories to promulgate that it had ceased to express what I conceived to be absolute Truth. The New Thought Federation is attempting to carry this load of thought diversity, and I can see no success in it. There are too many lines of thought to harmonize. When I hear what to me is rank error set

forth by New Thought speakers, I protest, and say,
"If this is New Thought, I must find a new name for
my philosophy." In the face of these facts, I have
decided that I am no longer a New Thoughter. I have
a standard of faith which is true and logical, and I
must conform to it in my teaching without compro-
mise. We call it Practical Christianity, and under this
name we shall henceforth do our work.

From that time, Unity and the New Thought movement began to go their separate ways. The Fillmores continued to be personally friendly with many New Thought
leaders, and many of them who came to Kansas City were
invited to speak before the Unity Society, but there was
no official connection between the two movements until
1919 when Unity returned to the International New
Thought Alliance. At this time, Royal Fillmore and E. V.
Ingraham of the Unity staff were added to the executive
board of the Alliance.

Unity invited the I.N.T.A. to hold its congress in
Kansas City the next year. This invitation was accepted,
and the meeting was like a joyous reunion. But this
connection did not last long, for in 1922 Unity left the
I.N.T.A. once more.

Many times in his magazines, Charles Fillmore affirmed that he was not trying to establish another church
or sect; he was trying to establish an educational institution where people of all faiths could study the laws of life
as given by Jesus and learn how to apply them in order to
establish a more abundant life for themselves.

For several years after the founding of Unity, the
Sunday meetings were not held at 11 o'clock in the morning as they now are, but at 3 o'clock in the afternoon so
that they would not conflict with regular church hours.
Meetings were also held on Wednesday at 3 o'clock in
the afternoon. Before the Sunday meeting, Myrtle Fillmore conducted a Sunday school for children.

The meetings were as much like discussions as they
were like church services. There were singing and prayers much as in churches today. But for the main part of

the service, copies of *Unity* were distributed to the members of the group, and the Bible text for that Sunday was read aloud, the leader reading the first verse and the congregation the next. After that, each verse was taken up in a general discussion directed by a leader who had been chosen by the group.

Myrtle Fillmore was in charge of the Wednesday afternoon services, but she usually appointed someone else to lead the silence and give a short talk. This was followed by a discussion of the subject in which everyone present participated.

When the Unity Society of Practical Christianity was incorporated July 29, 1903, it was incorporated not as a church but as a "society for scientific and educational purposes, viz: the study and demonstration of universal law." Such it still is.

When Charles and Myrtle Fillmore later formed the Unity School of Christianity as the central organization to carry on their worldwide work, they called it a school rather than a church. The Unity movement is a religious movement and may be thought of as a church, since it does all the work that churches do, but it is a different kind of church from those of traditional Christianity. It is a new concept in religion that crosses all church lines. It does not ask anyone who takes its literature or calls for prayer whether he is a member of a Unity church or not; it does not ask whether he is a member of any church. It does not ask him to subscribe to a creed or to perform certain rites or practices. Unity leaves people free to practice their religion at whatever level they have come to, for it feels that there is good in all religions and that people need different approaches to self-unfoldment. It is not so much concerned with worship services as it is in helping people to apply spiritual principles to their daily problems. It is a week-long, rather than a Sunday-only religion.

Charles and Myrtle Fillmore never thought of themselves as preachers, but as teachers. They did not want a church, although from the beginning they envisioned suitable quarters from which they could carry on their work and to which people in need of healing and spiritual help could come.

In one of the first issues of *Modern Thought,* Charles Fillmore wrote that he thought Jackson County was intended to be a great spiritual center:

> That a peculiar psychic atmosphere prevails here is plain to everyone who has made any attainments whatever in the unfoldment of the spirit. Metaphysicians from all parts of the country have sensed it and observed its harmonious effect upon them. We have carefully noted their separate testimonies as to its quality, and they all agree that they have here a sense of freedom and peace which they do not feel elsewhere.

He quoted several spiritual leaders in corroboration of his intuition about Jackson County and Kansas City. He wrote that Emma Curtis Hopkins had intimated that the city might be the site of a great temple "which should heal of sin and sickness all who step over its threshold." From the beginning of their work, the Fillmores had a vision of such a temple, a great institution where Christian metaphysics would be taught.

Two rooms in an office building were unsatisfactory quarters for the spiritual work that Charles and Myrtle Fillmore were doing. As soon as they were able, they found a house that provided more room in which to do the things they had to do to carry on the expanding Unity work. In 1898 they moved into a house at 1315 McGee Street, which had belonged to a steamboat captain on the Missouri River. This house was situated a block from the cable car and was a homey place built of brick. It was set back from the street, with a steep terrace in the front, a large shady yard, and vine-covered porches on two sides. There were two large rooms with folding doors between them that could be used as offices during the week and for meetings on Sundays. Folding chairs were placed in these rooms to seat about one hundred. In two years, however, this room proved to be too small, and for the Sunday meetings a larger hall had to be rented.

On McGee Street, Unity entered a happy period. It was not rich in the world's goods, but the poverty of the first years had now been overcome and there was enough money coming in so that the Fillmores could live comfortably. The organization was not large but it was large enough to support the work and at the same time all the members could know one another. The Fillmores were gregarious people, they loved to have their friends around them; and on McGee Street there were wonderful social events. In the summertime, there was always the Fourth of July picnic in Budd Park, a small park in the northeast section of the city, to which the members could all go by cable car or horse and buggy. Usually about two hundred of them would turn out. Everyone brought lunch baskets, and they would all eat together on tables under the trees. The lemonade and ice cream were supplied by the Fillmores.

At Christmas, the Sunday School had a Christmas tree with toys for the children and food for the grownups. On Valentine's Day and Easter and Thanksgiving and at other times throughout the year, there were parties, and Charles Fillmore was always in the center of them, cracking jokes and making quips, enjoying himself and helping everybody else to have fun. There were songs and recitations and games at the parties. Charles Fillmore loved to recite and he could usually be prevailed upon to render a poem.

It was one of these entertainments that caused Mr. Fillmore to shave the beard that he wore in the early days of the movement. He had to deliver a dramatic monologue in which he dressed up as a washerwoman who takes her little boy to get a job. Because his beard spoiled the effect, he shaved it off.

There was a warmth about the Fillmores that drew friends to them. When people came for help, the Fillmores took them into their hearts. They were even likely to take them into their home. It was not unusual for them to take into their home someone who had no means and had come to them for help. The boys often had to double up for sleeping because one of their beds was occupied by someone who had come to the Fillmores for help and remained to live with them for a while.

There was a kind of family feeling about Unity. The group was growing but it still remained a family. Even the meetings that the Fillmores held were more like family gatherings than they were like church services. If someone felt like disagreeing with something that Mr. Fillmore said, he got up on the floor and did so. Charles Fillmore liked people who thought for themselves and he invited discussion. Sometimes he turned the meeting over to others, and when they said something he did not agree with he, too, felt free to express his disagreement.

Once Elizabeth Towne, the editor of "Nautilus," the most popular Truth magazine of that time, was in town and Charles invited her to speak at a Unity meeting. When she said something with which he disagreed, he shook his head as if to say "No."

"I see Charles Fillmore shaking his head," said the speaker, and forthwith challenged him to discuss the subject. He arose and refuted her point.

To the Fillmores for help, came not only the halt, the lame, and the blind, but also the peculiar, and as these were often the ones who demanded the floor, the meetings sometimes produced exciting surprises.

The joyous informality of his meetings delighted Charles Fillmore. He was a teacher and a thinker; he wanted people to think and to learn and to grow; and he found as he tirelessly and joyously presented his ideas of Truth that people were thinking about them and growing. The movement grew too, for in a short time it was too large for 1315 McGee Street.

By 1900 a hall had to be rented for the Sunday meetings. This arrangement was not satisfactory, however. The Fillmores wanted a place where they could house all the activities of their growing movement under one roof. In 1902, Charles Fillmore suggested at a meeting that some committees be appointed to supervise the activities, among them a building committee. During the first year of its existence, this building committee was considered to be a joke. One of the Board members started the building fund by giving a one-cent piece. But the one-cent piece was not a joke to Charles Fillmore. He took it, gave thanks to God for it, and blessed it. To him, the building was on its way. The fund grew very slowly; by the end of 1903, there was only twenty-five cents in it. Nevertheless, in February 1903 in *Unity* magazine, Mr. Fillmore gave his subscribers "the privilege and opportunity of contributing any sum from ten cents to one thousand dollars, or more," towards the purchase of a site and the erection of a building.

By 1905 only $601 had been raised. Some people might have lost faith and given up the project of a new building to house the work, but not Charles and Myrtle Fillmore. The financing of the Unity work had always been a matter that took a great deal of faith. As Charles Fillmore wrote: "The way has not always been strewn with roses...." Charles and Myrtle Fillmore had the required faith.

Chapter VIII

No Price on Their Prayers

"They Made a Covenant"

FROM THE BEGINNING, the Fillmores had traveled the road of faith. In 1888, when the bottom fell out of the real estate boom, Charles Fillmore was left not with assets, but with debts that he had to pay off. When he began the publication of his magazine, he had only a few hundred subscribers. After several years, this had grown to a few thousand, many of whom did not pay for their subscriptions promptly.

The Fillmores had set a nominal price of one dollar a year for a subscription to *Unity*. They had to set a fixed price on the magazine in order to conform to postal regulations.

In January 1891, an editorial in the magazine under the heading, "There Is Only God," explained the attitude of the Fillmores about charging for the magazine:

> This publication is turned over to and is now under the full and complete control of Principle. Personality has stepped aside in this, as it must in all matters connected with divine science.
>
> The nominal subscription price is $1 a year, but this is nominal only, as the value of Truth cannot be measured in dollars and cents, and no specific charge can be made for it. "With what measure ye mete, it shall be measured unto you," is the law which is affirmed for this paper. It will trust that law, and go far and wide freely and generously to all who are seeking Truth.

All matters of whatsoever nature pertaining to this publication are referred to Principle, and no personality is responsible for any action which is taken in its conduct.

In April 1891, when the Society of Silent Unity began, it was decided to make no fixed charge for its services, but to conduct the Society on the freewill offering plan. When Myrtle Fillmore had been healed, people immediately began to come to her for healing for themselves. She prayed for them and worked with them spiritually with no thought of charging for her services. She was on fire with the idea that had come to her; she wanted to help everyone who needed help. It never occurred to her to set a price on her services. Later when more and more people were coming to the Fillmores and rooms were rented downtown to carry on the healing work and publish the magazine, the Fillmores still did not charge for their prayers and time, although most of the metaphysical teachers and healers of the day did charge a fixed price—sometimes very high—for their services. The Fillmores were not led to follow such examples.

It is probable that at first they did not think of metaphysics as a way of earning a living, for Mr. Fillmore continued in the real estate business as his means of livelihood. They began to help people because they wanted to help them. As they continued in the work, however, they found that it was taking more and more of their time. Finally the demands people were making on them became so great and so continuous that they had no time for anything except the spiritual work they were doing; then the Fillmores realized that they had to be recompensed for their services. It would have been easy at this point to set a fixed charge for these services or, because the recompense was very small, to get out of the work. Charles Fillmore said:

Encouraged by my wife, I persevered when almost at the point of failure; and if there comes any universal success out of this continuous effort, she should

have the greater share of the credit. Had I been alone
I would more than once have thrown the whole thing
over and gone back to my real-estate business.

Little money came in. The Unity movement grew
very slowly at first, and many who came for help had
little to give. Mr. Fillmore has related that he was ready
to relinquish the love offering idea. Mrs. Fillmore, however, prevailed on him to continue it. "This is the right
way," she said, in effect, "and God will support us in it;
He will carry us through to success if we will follow as
He leads us." Jesus said: "He that followeth me shall not
walk in the darkness, but shall have the light of life."

Although they did charge a nominal price for their
magazine in order to conform to postal regulations, they
continued to set no price on the ministry of Silent Unity,
nor did they set a fixed charge for personal consultation;
they wrote:

> The Spirit moves members to contribute, and it is
> observed that those who manifest gratefulness either
> in money, in love, or in works, are helped more rap-
> idly than those who are neglectful.

The practice of making no fixed charge for classes or
prayers is still generally followed in the Unity movement,
though some of the churches now set a fee for special
classes, especially when they use teachers from other
groups. But Silent Unity has never charged for its prayers
and services, and Unity School still conducts all its many
classes at Unity Village on a love offering basis. Unity
firmly believes that if it trusts God and gives good service
its needs will be met and it will not constantly have to
ask for money or to charge high prices. This faith has
been justified. Today Unity School sends out at nominal
prices millions of attractive, well-printed magazines and
books; gives away thousands more; carries on a correspondence with millions of persons; prepares radio and
television programs for broadcast over hundreds of stations; and to do all this, trusts in God as the source of
supply!

In the first few years of the Unity work, the Fillmores must have needed money desperately. In 1889, they had written in their magazine that they could not even afford to hire a stenographer although they were so busy that they could not answer all the letters that came to them.

There were six in the family and little money to meet their needs. The first Christmas after they started the magazine, for instance, looked as if it might turn out to be a bare occasion. Mrs. Fillmore wrote in a letter:

> I had about decided that we must go without buying the children Christmas presents when a neighbor we have been praying for walked in and gave me a check for five dollars and insisted upon my keeping it. I got Lowell a two-dollar tool chest, and Rick had commanded me to get him a drum and a gun. I got the drum, a sword, and a military hat, so he is fixed for marching. A friend gave each a book, so all fared well; and your box came Christmas Eve, and the boys were perfectly wild with delight. Lowell was very anxious to help be Santa Claus, so I let him get candy and help fill some little bags I made.

Charles Fillmore's mother was a tremendous asset during these lean years. Her ability with needle and thread kept them all in clothing. Often in these early years, Mr. Fillmore wore the clothing that people who came to the meetings gave him. One time the boys wore suits that their grandmother had made for them out of old curtains.

Grandma Fillmore was a wonderful cook and could make the simplest foods taste delicious. Years later, when the Fillmores were more prosperous and entertained many friends who came to Unity headquarters, the letters from these visitors had as a recurring theme the excellence of Grandma's meals.

The Fillmores were not only hard pressed at home, but sometimes financial need visited the Unity rooms too. Once Charles Fillmore endorsed a note for a friend; the friend failed to meet the obligation, and Charles was asked to pay. The sheriff threatened to sell out the printing office, and for a time it looked as if the Unity work would come to a sudden end; but the Fillmores prayed and the threat was never carried out.

Another time, one of the men who had been associated with the Fillmores in the Unity work carried off most of the furniture from the rooms to start a work of his own. He claimed that this furniture was as much his as it was the Fillmores'. Instead of threatening him or suing to recover the possessions, the Fillmores went quietly on with their work, praying that they would have whatever they needed. They were able to carry on. In fact, when this man began a magazine of his own a few years later, the Fillmores had forgiven him—if they had ever had any anger against him—to such an extent that they ran a notice in *Thought,* praising him and telling about his new venture. Jesus said, "And if anyone forces you to go one mile, go with him two miles." They were His disciples and they followed His instructions as well as they were able.

> We shall make this [they wrote in January 1892, a time when they must have needed money badly] a grand co-operative brotherhood in which the severe chilling methods of the financial world will have no part. How glorious it will be when we can send our books and pamphlets to all freely and have just enough coming in without solicitation to meet the expense from day to day. This is to be a feature of the new—the old must surely pass out with its "pound of flesh."

When someone asked Charles Fillmore, "Will you send me a paper and wait until I can pay for it?" he replied:

> Certainly we will. We know that it will bring to you before the year is out that which will pay for it many times over. . . . It will pay its own way. If you do not feel before the end of the year that it has much more than paid its own way, you need not send us a cent, and you will never be dunned. No bills are ever sent out from this office. If you do not pay your

bill freely and gladly, it is evident that you have not
had value received, hence you owe us nothing.

And a little later he wrote:

Many think that we are doing work in which our
compensation in some way comes out of the air. To
dispossess this idea we find it necessary now and
then to make very definite statements of our position
on the compensation point, but we are striving to
relieve this work of commercial bondage. We send
no bills and hold no one in our debt. We only ask
that the just and equitable law be established.

The entire Unity work has always been based on
"the just and equitable law": "Give and it will be given
to you." In the beginning, the Fillmores set the standard
that Unity follows today; they decided that they and the
movement were to be dedicated to the Spirit of truth, that
the object of their existence was to be the service of God,
not personal reward.

In 1942, while looking through some old files, the
librarian at Unity uncovered among papers of Myrtle Fillmore's a document in Mr. Fillmore's handwriting that
had remained their secret for fifty years. The document
had remained a secret, but the spirit of this covenant—as
it has become known in Unity since its discovery—had
shown itself time and time again in the half-century that
had passed since the Fillmores had signed it on December 7, 1892, for it is the spirit that motivated their life and
work.

DEDICATION AND COVENANT

We, Charles Fillmore and Myrtle Fillmore, hus-
band and wife, hereby dedicate ourselves, our time,
our money, all we have and all we expect to have, to
the Spirit of Truth, and through it, to the Society of
Silent Unity.

It being understood and agreed that the said Spirit
of Truth shall render unto us an equivalent for this
dedication, in peace of mind, health of body, wis-
dom, understanding, love, life, and an abundant

*supply of all things necessary to meet every want
without our making any of these things the object of
our existence.*

*In the presence of the Conscious Mind of Christ
Jesus, this 7th day of December, A.D. 1892.*

Charles Fillmore
Myrtle Fillmore

The Fillmores held to their ideal. They were doing
God's work. They were not doing it to enrich themselves;
they were doing it because they believed in God and
wanted to help others to find Him and His blessings.
They wanted to do this work in a way that would enable
them to help the most people, to help people when they
were in need. They did not see how they could set a price
on their work, for that might result in the exclusion of
some of those who needed help most of all; and it was not
they, but God, who did the work. Then, how could they
put a price on God's work? Jesus helped those who came
to Him freely and with no thought of charge. They could
do no less. If they put a price on their work, it might be
that the very time someone needed help most would be
the time when he could not afford it. At the beginning of
their work, they established the principle of no fixed
charge for their prayers. They wrote of Silent Unity:

> The work of this Society is wholly voluntary, and
> no fees or dues of any kind are imposed upon mem-
> bers. Those who have been helped through its minis-
> trations, or those who feel that it is a worthy cause,
> contribute for its support as they are moved.

In the early days, the financing of the Unity work
was a continual struggle, but God could not have chosen
people more ideally suited than the Fillmores to make
that struggle. They believed what they taught. They believed that if they really sought the kingdom of God and
His righteousness, the things they needed would be
added to them. They did not doubt God's promises. When
they made a covenant with Him, it was in complete ex-
pectation that the covenant would be fulfilled. They in-

tended to do their part and they had perfect faith that God would do His.

The Fillmores taught that prosperity is governed by the same laws that govern physical health. They thought that if they could maintain themselves in a prosperity consciousness, an awareness of God as the Source of their supply, prosperity could not fail to be theirs. If the money did not come in, it was not because God had failed; it was only because they had not maintained a high enough consciousness of their supply in Him, and they redoubled their efforts in prayer. They felt that their supply depended on their maintaining the right consciousness. "Only be strong and very courageous, being careful to do according to all the law . . . that you may have good success."

The Unity work has always been conducted on this principle. For many years the workers in Silent Unity were compensated on a freewill offering basis. No fixed salaries were paid. It was up to each worker through prayer to maintain a consciousness of prosperity. Each one had his share in that responsibility. As the supply came in, it was divided among them.

The Fillmores were publishing a magazine for which they received only one dollar a year. Besides this, they were trying to issue a magazine for children that cost them much more to publish than they received from it. They were carrying on by means of letters a prayer service of silent communion that was being given to people all over this country and even in Europe. The only immediate source of their supply was voluntary contributions. Yet the Fillmores applied themselves to their ministry undaunted. They promised:

> We will send literature to anybody anywhere any time there is a possibility of benefit resulting to the recipient. [That promise has been kept.]

With nothing but the freewill offerings of friends to support their efforts, the Fillmores began to send their publications out to everyone who wrote and asked for them. By November 1894 they were writing:

> We hope our good friends and helpers will appre-
> ciate our position as regards the many appeals for
> free literature, and be sparing in their requests for
> free yearly subscriptions for their acquaintances. Our
> free list now costs us over ten dollars per week, and
> is growing very fast. We are not backed by a rich
> Bible society, and please remember that the dimes
> count fast into dollars where so many are looking for
> aid.

In 1910, The Silent-70 was organized, and through it
Unity literature was sent free of charge to everyone who
asked for it, some of whom at the moment were not in a
position to pay. Soon a stream of Unity literature was
going without charge to individuals and into libraries,
prisons, hospitals, and other public institutions.

Many times the Fillmores must have wondered
about the direction from which funds would come to
carry on the work, but they never wondered about
the Source—God. Always they prayed. Always prayer
worked. Always, however impossible it might appear to
be, the funds materialized. They moved out of the little
office in the Journal Building into a larger office in the
Deardorff Building and they moved from it into still more
commodious quarters in the Hall Building. From there
they were able to move into the house on McGee Street.
Still the work continued to grow. Still it needed more
space. In the early 1900's, the Fillmores decided that the
Unity movement was prosperous enough to justify their
thinking about buying property and erecting a building
in which to conduct the work.

This was the goal they set for the Unity Society. The
penny with which the building fund began had grown by
1905 only to $601. Nevertheless, the Fillmores did not
relinquish their goal. The building committee found a lot
and an eight-room house that were for sale at 913 Tracy
Avenue. This seemed an ideal place to buy. But the
money to buy was not forthcoming.

At a meeting of the Board of Directors of the Unity

Society of Practical Christianity several men pledged a hundred dollars apiece toward the purchase of the lot and the erection of a building. This was still far from enough. The Fillmores prayed and prayed, yet enough money did not appear. Then one evening, one of the members of the Board arose and announced quietly that he had decided to mortgage everything that he owned in order to provide Unity with the funds needed to buy the lot and begin the erection of a building.

He was not a rich man and he had a wife and four little children to provide for, but he had been attending the meetings for several years, and the Fillmores had inspired in him the same kind of faith that they had. He believed in their ideas and felt that it was important that those ideas be carried to as many people as possible.

His business associates tried to discourage him from taking the step. To them, Unity was not a good risk. But he was not to be dissuaded. Through him, Unity obtained the money needed. The house and lot at 913 Tracy Avenue were purchased. The plans for the new building were pushed ahead.

The man who had mortgaged his property did not lose one cent because he had been willing to stand behind Unity in its need, and in a short time he was the owner of a much more successful business than he had had before. "Give, and it will be given to you; good measure, pressed down, shaken together, running over. . . . For the measure you give will be the measure you get back."

In September 1905, the house was moved to the rear of the lot, and work was begun on a three-story brick building.

While Unity carried on its work from the house, the work on the building pressed forward. There were no funds on hand with which to complete it, but there was the faith of the Fillmores and of those who were associated with them.

By August 1906, over six thousand dollars had been received, and the rest of the money needed was contributed in the next few years.

On August 19, 1906, Unity students gathered from all over the country for a week of celebration, which was climaxed on Wednesday afternoon by the laying of the cornerstone of the new building. Several hundred persons, one of them from India, gathered to watch Mr. Fillmore lay the cornerstone, the inscription on which read: "Built upon the foundation of the apostles and prophets, Jesus Christ Himself being the chief cornerstone." There was a choir and several soloists. Charles Fillmore made a short talk. A copy of the first numbers of *Thought, Unity,* and *Wee Wisdom;* the August 1906 *Unity* and *Wee Wisdom;* a copy of the convention program; a copy of the Kansas City post containing a write-up of the new building; and a list of the names of contributors were placed in the cornerstone. Jennie Croft (one of the most faithful and versatile of the early Unity workers) tossed in a rose, and Charles Fillmore took a bouquet from his buttonhole and added it to the contents.

After the ceremony was finished, most of the group ate in Unity Inn, the vegetarian cafeteria that Unity had started for its workers. The Inn at that time was located in the house that had been moved to the rear of the lot. Inside were signs: "All the expenses of this house are met by the freewill offerings of its guests. 'Freely ye received, freely give.'" In keeping with Unity custom, the guests at that dedication ceremony paid for the dinner by freewill offerings.

On that August day in 1906, as Charles and Myrtle Fillmore stood in the new building, they must have felt that truly this was a reward of faith.

How ample the building must have looked to them then! It was forty by seventy feet, three stories high in front. The chapel would seat more than two hundred. The printing shop would handle the magazines. The reception room and offices were furnished in the latest style. There was a special healing room for the use of Silent Unity.

When the Fillmores had started the work seventeen

years before, there was no beautiful new building to move into. There was a real estate office in a downtown building—and their faith. They had started the work on faith; they had carried it on by faith. They had trusted in God as the source of their supply, and their trust had been justified. They had built this building and the work of which it was a physical representation, and except for the magazines, they had never made a fixed charge for the service they gave.

People had laughed at them; people had said it was impossible. Paying no attention, they had gone ahead—on faith. On this August day, they stood in the building faith had built, while around them milled a happy throng called together from all over the earth by the power of their faith.

They looked about them. They looked at the chapel, at their offices, at the printing shop, at the Silent Unity rooms, and they knew that all this had been brought about because of their trust in God. As they stood there on that August day in 1906, it must have seemed to them like the culmination of their fondest dreams. Yet it was not a culmination. It was only a beginning.

Chapter IX

Growth and Expansion

"He Shall Build the Temple"

ALMOST AT ONCE, the building at 913 Tracy Avenue was too small. In less than four years, an even larger building was going up on the lot next door, at 917 Tracy Avenue. The September 22, 1910, issue of *Weekly Unity* (a magazine no longer published) reported:

> The Unity printing plant has been moved to its new quarters at 917 Tracy. . . .
> A new Optimus press, thirty-nine by fifty-five, has been added to the pressroom equipment, making it quite complete. . . . This number of *Weekly Unity* is the first piece of printing done in the new building.

The first number of *Weekly Unity*, with Lowell Fillmore as editor, appeared May 15, 1909. Unity School had taken another step forward. Years before, Charles Fillmore had thought about making *Unity* a weekly, but the idea had not seemed practical then.

The new magazine had grown out of the weekly bulletin that described the activities of the Unity Society of Practical Christianity in Kansas City. People in other parts of the country had expressed an interest in these activities, and it was decided to publish a magazine that would tell about them. *Unity* announced:

> *Weekly Unity*, containing all items of interest to the Society, reports, readings, and so forth, will be mailed to any address fifty-two times a year for one dollar.

The popularity of the new magazine increased rapidly, and in the July 10, 1909, issue, the editor told his
readers:

> We have one subscriber as far east as New York
> and one as far west as California, with a sprinkling
> over the intervening States.

Weekly Unity grew until it had more than two
hundred thousand subscribers, but eventually Unity
School decided that it was not needed; *Unity* magazine
presented what was essentially the same message more
effectively at much less expense and without the escalat-
ing mailing problems involved in getting out a weekly,
so it was discontinued in July 1972.

The new building proved to be no more adequate to
contain the rapidly growing Unity work than the one at
913 Tracy had been. It had to be enlarged. The original
three-story section of the building had been placed far
back on the lot. Now a front section was added to this,
and a fourth floor placed over all. The dedication of this
enlarged structure took place at the stroke of midnight
December 31, 1914. Declared *Weekly Unity:*

> The opening of the Unity administration building
> was a great success. By 9 p.m., December 31, the
> Unity auditorium was full to overflowing. The Guild
> [a young people's group] had ready a multitude of
> talent with which to entertain the assembled guests.
> Near 10:30 the Unity Inn became a mecca for the
> hungry. Apples, sandwiches, cakes, cocoa, and ce-
> real coffee were served to nearly four hundred peo-
> ple. By the time everyone had finished his refresh-
> ments, the new year was almost ready to be born. At
> the stroke of twelve the darkened administration
> building suddenly flashed into light; the front door
> swung open and the chimes began to ring.

This building, which was later enlarged twice more,
was to house most of the activities of Unity School for the
next thirty-four years. Its front, which with its massive
white columns somewhat resembled a temple, became—

much as today the Tower and Silent Unity's lighted window have become—a kind of symbol of the Unity movement. It was pictured on the front of the prosperity banks for many years. Today the Tower and the Silent Unity Building with the lighted window are pictured on the banks.

The prosperity bank plan is one of Unity's most distinctive ideas. It was originated by the Fillmores in 1910.

Often those who wanted to buy Unity literature were persons of small means to whom a dollar, the price of a year's subscription, was a large sum of money. Also many of those who studied the literature liked to order subscriptions for the periodicals and buy books for their friends too. The prosperity bank plan was a convenient way of doing this.

Those who use the prosperity bank plan are provided with a small cardboard bank. The instructions are to drop a coin in the bank at a regular time each day for seven weeks and to concentrate on the statement printed on the bank. A typical statement reads:

> *The Spirit of the Lord goes before me and my health, happiness, prosperity, and success are assured.*

Bank users are expected to do their best at all times to feel that the statement expresses the Truth about them, whatever appearances may indicate. Repeating the bank statement daily reminds the user that God is the source of all financial supply.

From the first, the bank plan was popular as a means of saving for subscriptions. Also, users found it a convenient way to save for their offerings to the Unity work. The bank plan has been popular because through the years those who have used it have felt that they were truly helped and prospered by its use. There are many Unity students who are never without a prosperity bank.

It was fitting that a picture of the new Unity building should be printed on the bank, because it was prayers for prosperity that had built the Unity buildings and the whole Unity work.

Charles Fillmore felt that the main reason for the study of Truth is to develop spiritual faculties. He wrote that people were too prone to think of Unity simply as a system of healing. He taught that it is not primarily a system of prosperity either. He taught that spiritual development should bring in its wake both healing and prosperity.

"Some religious teachers," wrote Mr. Fillmore, "have tried to make us believe that it is our Christian duty to be poor. But this is not the doctrine of Jesus." It was not the doctrine of Charles Fillmore either.

Charles Fillmore believed in praying for prosperity. Although he and his wife discovered Truth because they needed healing, they were soon stressing to their students that all people have the infinite resources of Spirit within themselves and they can be successful in all their worthy undertakings. One of the first popular articles that Charles Fillmore wrote was entitled, "Overcoming the Poverty Idea," which was reprinted several times in *Unity* magazine and finally issued as a pamphlet. Silent Unity was not very old before a special time each day—noon—was devoted to praying for prosperity for all who asked for prayers.

Whenever Unity School had a need for money or there was an important decision to be made, the first thing that the Fillmores always did when they called Unity leaders together for a conference was to say, "Let's pray about this matter." Often the whole conference, as they conducted it, turned out to be a prayer meeting. The Fillmores would not only take the matter to God themselves, but they asked everyone else present to speak words of prayer aloud. They believed in the power of affirmative prayer, and they practiced what they believed.

When there is a financial need to be met, the management of Unity School calls on Silent Unity to pray with it, exactly as someone on the outside does, and Silent Unity takes up the needs of Unity School in prayer just as it does the needs of others.

Unity School does not have, as some institutions do, wealthy backers. Many persons have left legacies, but Unity has been supported mainly by the modest offerings of countless persons who have been helped through its ministry. For the most part, it has been the "widow's mite" that has sustained Unity. The workers at Unity feel grateful for every offering that is sent in. They know that it is not the size of the gift but the love in the heart from which it comes that counts.

Even as late as 1910, it was not unusual for the total offering at a Sunday morning service of Unity Society to be no more than ten dollars. One time early in the history of Unity, a subscriber sent in one hundred dollars for a hundred-year subscription to *Unity*. It is hard to imagine the gratitude to God that the one hundred dollars evoked in the Unity office.

The Fillmores did not seek money for themselves, although they felt that it was their right, as it is the right of all the children of God, to have enough to meet their needs. But they sought support for Unity, and they believed implicitly that God would supply the needs of this organization. If they had not believed this, they would never have had the courage to go ahead. Often as they pressed forward, expanding their services, enlarging their magazines, building buildings, there was no apparent worldly source of needed finances. Had they always waited until the funds materialized to do the things they needed to do, they would have been able to do little. They took a step—praying all the while in faith—and the supply came to meet the need. "And whatever you ask in prayer, you will receive, if you have faith."

It has been in this way, praying and working, trusting in God for supply, that the various Unity buildings, one after another, have been built. And the need for more buildings has been continuous.

The building at 917 Tracy, even though it was enlarged, still proved to be too small. Behind it another building was erected to house the radio studio, heating plant, repair shop, and other departments. It was in this building that Charles and Myrtle Fillmore lived in the apartment that she dubbed "Gasoline Alley." Later another building was constructed alongside this one. Also, on the corner of Ninth and Tracy, Unity Inn, erected in 1920, became one of the most popular eating places in Kansas City.

Finally Unity grew so large that it began to think of moving from Tracy Avenue. The center of population in Kansas City had shifted far to the south and the Unity Society of Practical Christianity needed a location that would be more convenient for those who attended its services. In 1928 it bought the lot on the Country Club Plaza where Unity Temple is now located. Unity School of Christianity, the sister organization, began to think about moving its activities to what was then called Unity Farm.

In 1953 Unity Farm was legally incorporated as Unity Village, Missouri, and it is now a full-fledged municipality with a mayor and several hundred residents, a waterworks, a fire department, and its own post office with its own ZIP Code, 64065.

Today it is there, in Unity Village, in some of the most beautiful office buildings in the country, in a setting so perfectly landscaped that it is becoming famous throughout the world, that Unity School is located. There more than five hundred workers carry on the work that Charles and Myrtle Fillmore began. There every year go thousands of students to study and to learn the teachings the Fillmores first propounded almost a century ago.

In the buildings on Tracy Avenue, there was not enough room nor were there the proper facilities for activities of a community nature. The Fillmores envisioned a place apart, a place where Unity workers and students could go out of the bustle of the world's affairs to pray, to work, to re-create themselves physically and spiritually. Unity workers have always been like a big family, liking to do things with and for one another. It was natural that the Fillmores should look for a place suitable for the activities of their "Unity family."

In 1919, shortly after Rickert Fillmore returned home from service in World War I, he and Lowell and their father began a search for such a place. One Sunday, they saw an ad in the paper that listed forty acres for sale a few miles southeast of Kansas City. They drove out to the place but when they arrived they found that it had been sold. The real estate agent was still there and he asked them what they had in mind. They told him that they wanted a small place that was removed from city noises and confusion and at the same time not too far out for easy travel back and forth.

The real estate agent replied: "I know just the place you want." He took them out to the location that is now Unity Village and showed them fifty-eight acres that were for sale. The Fillmores liked it and made a down payment. On March 1, 1920, Unity Village was born.

Slowly, more and more acres have been added to the original fifty-eight, until today Unity Village comprises more than fourteen hundred acres. When the first parcel was purchased, the nearest good road was several miles east of the property. Today U.S. Highway 50 goes by the main entrance to Unity Village; another concrete highway, Colbern Road, runs through the Village; and I-470, a major circumferential freeway, cuts across one corner.

The first buildings constructed were of the English Cotswold type. Among them was The Arches, which was built for Charles and Myrtle Fillmore about 1925. It stands near the farmhouse that was on the property when it was bought. After it was built, Mr. and Mrs. Fillmore would go out to The Arches on Thursday evening and stay overnight, going back to "Gasoline Alley" on Friday morning. Then on Sunday after the service was over, they would return to The Arches and stay until Monday morning.

Myrtle Fillmore called The Arches her dream house. Rickert Fillmore had built it for his mother exactly as she had dreamed of a house. Set in the middle of an apple orchard, with a high peaked roof of many gables and casement windows, the house was like one out of a fairy book. Myrtle Fillmore spent a great deal of time in it.

As a surprise for his mother, Rickert had built it without a kitchen, as she had said she wanted "a fairy home without kitchen or care." When the Fillmores were staying at The Arches they took their meals with Grandma Fillmore, who lived in the farmhouse just across the road. Myrtle wrote to a friend:

> Charles is doing his best to get some sort of im-promptu kitchen into our fairy home. But I say "Not while we have Grandmother's kitchen so close." We have entertained, doing our share, I think, in the past; and I do wish the fairy home to remain as it is, filled with food for thought and inspiration and blessings, but not the kind that makes stacks of dishes to wash.

Grandma Fillmore was the center of the life on Unity Farm. Resourceful, generous, energetic, she had been born for such a role. Although, when the Fillmores began to spend time on the Farm she was nearly ninety, she was still as capable of running a household as she had ever been. She was always happy and never seemed to run down. One of her friends once said of her: "She should have been sixteen years old all her life."

In her late nineties, she fell and broke her hip, but she refused to use a wheelchair. A wheelchair suggested "invalid" to her. That she never was. She had some roll-ers attached to a rocking chair and got about on that. Myrtle called this contraption "a roller skate motor."

"It is really a rocking chair with rollers," she de-scribed it to a friend, "like those on roller skates, and, my, how Grandmother does ride around on it. She 'mo-tors' all over the house, and she's the engine, the gas, the chauffeur, and the backseat driver all combined in one."

The first office building finished at Unity Village was the Silent Unity Building, which was designed in the Italian Renaissance style. It was completed in 1929.

In the summer of 1928, a great meeting of Unity leaders was held at Unity Village to bless the buildings and to make plans for the future. A tent city was erected.

Hundreds of Unity leaders, not only from the United States but from foreign countries, lived there for eight jubilant days through rain and fair weather.

It turned out to be mostly rain, and of creature comforts there were few. When it rained hard the water streamed through the tents between the cots; the only available shower baths were in the unfinished Silent Unity Building; the only place to eat was in the chapel in this building, which had been converted into a cafeteria serving fifteen hundred meals each day. But everyone sloshed through the rain to the meetings with sunshiny spirits that the weather could not dampen. There was no criticism, no complaint. There was little comfort, but a lot of consecration.

Meetings were scheduled from 8 o'clock each morning until 10 o'clock at night. Sometimes there were several at the same hour, so that it was impossible for one to attend all the events. One person was heard to say that he was kept as busy as if he were at a three-ring circus. And at the center of the celebration, greeting their friends, taking part in the meetings, sharing the meals, joining in the prayers, were Charles and Myrtle Fillmore.

At one meeting, more than four hundred workers from headquarters on Tracy Avenue formed a procession, passing in front of the assembled leaders, singing hymns while they marched. On the last Sunday, the whole conference came to its climax with the dedication of the Silent Unity Building, which more than two thousand people attended. The leaders returned to their homes rejoicing in the vision of the expanding Unity work and of the building rising to house it. The following spring, in 1929, Silent Unity moved from Tracy Avenue to its new building at Unity Village.

It was a triumphant moment for the Fillmores. It must have seemed to them then that one of their fondest hopes, the dream of a great spiritual center, was about to be realized. There were many years of prayer behind them, many years of trusting God for supply, many years of holding to their high purpose when there seemed little but their trust to hold to. But the lean years had changed into years of accelerating growth and prosperity. Not only had subscriptions to *Unity* and *Weekly Unity* and *Wee Wisdom* been soaring, but the last six years had seen three new magazines established: *The Christian Business Man* (later *Christian Business,* then *Good Business;* discontinued in 1966), *Unity Daily Word* (now *Daily Word),* and *Youth* (later *Progress;* discontinued in 1968). Subscriptions to these were pouring in. Silent Unity was growing. New centers were being opened in various cities. After almost half a century of strenuous spiritual effort, in that jubilant moment it may have looked as if Unity's prosperity was assured and Charles and Myrtle Fillmore could rest on their laurels.

But this was not to be. In the fall, the 1929 depression began. By 1930 Silent Unity was back on Tracy Avenue in Kansas City and its building at Unity Village was virtually empty.

In the 1930's the Fillmores' vision of a great spiritual center from which the Unity message would go out to all the world and to which students would come for spiritual instruction may have seemed to some almost a shattered dream. Unity School had never had a large reserve fund. Its income had always consisted largely of offerings sent in day by day. Since it had followed exactly the instruction of Jesus, "Do not be anxious about tomorrow," and had immediately employed in the expansion of the work whatever money it had received, it had not built up any surpluses.

In the 1930's, when great industrial empires with carefully hoarded reserves were going bankrupt, it might have seemed to an onlooker that an institution like Unity School, that had no source of income except the literature that was sold for a nominal price and the freely-sent offerings of people who were not even members of the organization and whose only connection was often only that of a letter and a prayer, could not possibly survive. But the casual onlooker could not have perceived the real source of Unity's strength, for this was invisible; it was

Myrtle Fillmore (*circa* 1863)   Charles Fillmore (*circa* 1876)

Unity Tract Society, 1315 McGee Street, Kansas City, Missouri (*circa* 1898)

Tracy Complex—913, 917, and the house that served as Unity Inn

Myrtle and Charles Fillmore seated on the platform
at a Silent Unity worker-prayer meeting in 1929

The Arches

The Fillmore Family (left to right): Lowell, Myrtle, Rick,
Charles, Mary (Grandmother), and Royal (*circa* 1917)

Full-page modern scene of Unity Village showing Tower, Silent Unity, and fountains

faith, the faith of the Unity workers, the faith of the Fillmores, the faith that had stood adamant in the beginning
when there was almost no income at all; the faith that
was steadfast when the first small building on Tracy
Avenue had to be built and there seemed to be no funds
with which to build it; the faith that had been tested over
and over throughout the years; the unalterable faith that
God is the supply of those who trust Him. "Put me to the
test, says the Lord of hosts, if I will not open the windows
of heaven for you and pour down for you an overflowing
blessing."

Now this faith triumphed as it has always
triumphed; Unity School not only weathered the depression but began to grow again. Although for ten years no
further buildings were erected, the Fillmores held steadfast to their vision of Unity Village as the center of the
work. In 1940 they began to build again.

Rickert Fillmore was in charge of this building program, and he quickly proved that he had in him the same
spirit as his parents, a spirit ready to use that which is at
hand, quick to see and utilize every natural advantage,
and willing to strike out on new paths and try the untried.

Beauty and utility have gone hand in hand in the
development of Unity Village. The Amphitheater, used
only rarely now, is as lovely a thing of its kind as can be
found in America. This is how it came into being, according to Rickert Fillmore:

> We needed a garage to take care of the cars of the
> workers at the Farm. There was a steep bluff at the
> most convenient location, so we built the garage up
> against this almost perpendicular bluff. When later
> we wanted a place for an open-air gathering, we
> found that we could use the flat roof of this garage as
> the floor of a platform or stage. The gentle rise of the
> ground eastward from this point made it possible to
> use it for outdoor meetings, and seats were set out.
> When we wanted to use it for larger gatherings, we
> graded it and built a regular stage, which rises about

four feet above the front level of the ground.

The land itself provided limestone for buildings, re-
taining walls, and roads. Oak and walnut trees, killed by
the drought that ravaged the Midwest in the thirties,
were turned into a blessing instead of a loss when the
lumber was salvaged for cabinet work in the new buildings. Even the Tower, which was completed in 1929 and
rises one hundred sixty-five feet above the ground, was
not constructed for decorative purposes alone. Rickert
Fillmore said:

> We needed water to operate the Farm, and every
> time we drilled for water we got oil and gas. So
> across the railroad tracks on our property we made
> an artificial lake. The lake covers about twenty-two
> acres, and has a drop of fifty feet at the dam. We did
> all the concrete work on the dam ourselves, and it is
> the only one of its kind in Jackson County. This was
> in 1927. Then we had the water, but we had to get
> the elevation and the pressure in order to distribute
> it where needed. So we built the Tower with its huge
> water tank at the top. It is a symbol and a delight to
> the eye, of course, but it also makes available a con-
> tinuous supply of one hundred thousand gallons of
> water without which the Farm could not be run and
> provides seven stories of rooms for office use.

An amphitheater stage roofing a garage, a tower that
masks a water tank, chimneys that look like bell towers,
mirror pools that are really part of the air conditioning
system—such things as these reveal the imagination that
has gone into the development of Unity Village.

In 1940, when it became possible for Unity School to
build again, it was well that there was such an imaginative spirit in charge of the building program. The short-
age of labor and material caused by the war made the
usual type of construction out of the question.

Rickert Fillmore turned to a new type of construction
—prefabrication. Tests proved that the idea was not only
practical, but economical. The result is that the new
buildings he built were cast in sections at the Village and

hauled to the place they were to stand, and there put together in a process that might better be called "assembling" than "building." Almost everything in the buildings was precast; even the "antique cut-stone trim" is only colored concrete made in molds. The result has been a tremendous saving with no sacrifice of beauty.

In 1947 the printing department moved into its new quarters. In the fall of 1949, work on the building that houses the administrative, publishing, and editorial departments reached the place where it was ready for occupancy. On a weekend in late October, a huge fleet of trucks backed up to the dock at 917 Tracy and moved all the departments of Unity School, except Silent Unity and the Editorial Department, out to the new quarters. On Monday morning, the work in the new building went on almost as if no move had been made. A week later, Silent Unity moved into the building that it had occupied for a brief time twenty years before.

For the first time since 1906, passersby on Tracy Avenue at night saw no light shining from the rooms where workers in Silent Unity had kept so long the constant vigil of prayer. The buildings on Tracy Avenue, however, were to continue to be identified with the work of Jesus Christ, for after several months they were sold to The Salvation Army.

The move to Unity Village involved Unity School in many new and greatly expanded activities and created a continued need for more facilities. Housing for workers, students, and visitors was needed; motels, cottages, a trailer court, apartment houses had to be built, some to be kept available for visitors, some reserved for workers and students. All the many services required of a municipality had to be provided. Roads, sewers, and lakes had to be constructed. New property had to be acquired, and existing buildings had to be modified and enlarged.

In increasing numbers, people had to be fed and had to have places to meet. A small tea room in an apartment building and a small auditorium in the Silent Unity Building, constructed in the twenties quickly became

inadequate. Various wings of the Administration Building, modified for use as meeting places and by Unity Inn,
became inadequate, too.

Charles Rickert Fillmore, grandson of the founders,
became President of Unity School of Christianity in 1972,
and embarked on a new building program. A spacious
new building for Unity Inn was completed in 1975, with
dining space for 500 persons and three private banquet
rooms. At the same time a beautiful 1100-seat Unity
World Headquarters Activities Center was constructed,
with movable soundproof partitions making it possible to
hold three meetings simultaneously. Unity Village
Chapel holds its services there every Sunday, but conso-
nant with the original policy of Unity that the main thrust
of the movement would not be the building of churches,
the building was conceived as an activities center rather
than a church, and has many uses other than for Sunday
services.

When Unity School, with its vast facilities and
hundreds of workers moved out and occupied its new
home, it was still called a farm. But this was obviously
not an appropriate name for it. The name was changed to
Unity Village, but no name describes exactly what it is. It
is the center of a big publishing business. It is a place of
prayer, a shrine to which hundreds of thousands of people all over the earth turn in their thoughts when they are
in need of spiritual help. It is a garden community where
Unity leaders and workers live. It is a recreational center
to which persons go for physical activities that build and
refresh the body and mind: to swim, to play golf and
tennis, to picnic, to hike, to dance, and to get together
with one another. It is a school and a retreat center to
which thousands of people come every year from all over
the world to study and meditate and pray. It is a farm
with orchards, vineyards, and crops in cultivation. It is all
these, and yet it is more than all these, for it is a place of
God—it is Unity.

To Unity School of Christianity, Unity Village, Missouri, go increasing streams of letters and telephone

calls, and from Unity, increasing streams of magazines, books, booklets, television, and radio programs pour out. From the Silent Unity Building shines more brightly than ever the light that shows that Silent Unity workers are always praying, a light that was lit almost a century ago in Kansas City, where two sincere people began to pray for those in need.

Many years ago, Charles Fillmore prophesied that Jackson County was to be the center of a great spiritual work. Today, like faith in concrete, the expression of the enduring faith of Charles and Myrtle Fillmore, stand the buildings of Unity School. The newest is the Silent Unity building, whose construction is planned to coincide with Unity's centennial celebration in 1989.* And still the dream is not complete. The plan for developing Unity School is being pushed ahead, the work of Jesus Christ grows and grows. "And of his kingdom there will be no end."

*At the time of this revision, construction has just begun. The present Silent Unity building will eventually house the Library and Unity School for Religious Studies.

Chapter X

The Spirit of the Fillmores

"Whosoever Would Become Great"

A UNITY CENTER LEADER once asked Charles Fillmore for an affirmation to use as a blessing for herself and for those who worked with her in her center. He was probably not aware that it was a description of himself that he gave her: *"I am dignified and definite, yet meek and lowly in all that I say and do."*

Other people recognized the greatness of Charles and Myrtle Fillmore and sought to honor them, but neither Charles nor Myrtle sought honor. "We have never cared to interest folks in our individual lives," Mrs. Fillmore wrote. "It makes no real difference to others what we have done, who we are." Their dream had been, not of personal advancement, but of the growth of Unity.

Once a group of students arranged a program, the purpose of which was to honor the Fillmores, who had not been told the reason for the meeting. Many flattering words were directed toward them before they understood the purpose of the meeting. Then Charles Fillmore arose and said: "'Why callest thou me good? None *is* good, save one, *that is* God,'" and he forthwith turned the meeting into a song service of praise to God.

When visitors came to Unity School, it was not unusual for Myrtle Fillmore herself to show them through the buildings. The first time a person wrote to Silent Unity, she answered the letter personally, until the work grew to the place where she could no longer do this.

After that, she did answer personally as many letters as she could.

Once a picture of Charles Fillmore was wanted for use on a Unity letterhead at Christmastime. It took two years to get it. "I don't believe in glorifying personality," he said. It was only after many friends had pleaded with him that he reluctantly agreed to let his picture be taken. However, once he had consented, he let the photographers turn him this way and that and sat patiently while the various props were arranged. He said:

> I remember the first photograph I ever had taken for *Unity*. It was back in the '90's. There were about six workers in Unity at the time, as I recall. The photographer was fiddling around the way you are now, so I went into the silence. I was sitting there with my eyes half-closed; suddenly the photographer said that he was ready to take the picture; then he added, "I wonder if the gentleman on the left (he was referring to me) could look just a little more intelligent."
>
> A short time before having the picture taken, I had shaved off my beard, and in commenting on the picture in the magazine, I mentioned the fact that this was the first picture I had had taken without a beard. One subscriber wrote in: "If cutting off your beard makes you look like that picture, I hope you will let it grow again."

Charles and Myrtle Fillmore did a serious work, and other people took them seriously. This was right, for often their words meant life itself to those who came to them for help. But Charles and Myrtle Fillmore had a sense of humor that ran through all they said and did, as a little melody sometimes runs through a great symphony and gives it life and light. Charles Fillmore was a born storyteller and he loved to inject humor into his sermons. He had the gift of all natural speakers to sense the mood of an audience; he could tell when the people were getting restless and he knew when to inject a story. "I do not mind your looking at your watches," he told his audience, "but when you look at them, then put them to your ear to see if they are running, that is too much."

It was this sense of humor that enabled Charles Fillmore to be undisturbed by criticism. Sometimes secular publications ran articles that were unfriendly to Unity, but he refused to let this disturb him. If he felt that they were amusing enough, occasionally he even reprinted them in *Unity* with comments of his own. Once the New York Times ran an article ridiculing Unity, entitled "Christian Science Outdone." "This is a good piece, with very good testimonials," wrote Mr. Fillmore, and he proceeded to reprint the entire article. He thanked the author for writing it, commenting that he had received numerous letters from people asking help who had never heard of Unity until they read the article in the New York Times.

Over and over the history of Unity has shown this to be the case: the main effect of critical articles has been to interest people in Unity.

Charles Fillmore was always ready to laugh and if the laugh was on himself he did not mind. There were many typographical errors in the first issue of *Modern Thought,* so in the second issue he wrote:

> We may not be able, outside a printing office, to convince our Christian Science brothers and sisters that matter really exists, but shall have no trouble in backing our position when once its portals are passed. What outside was a dream, a shimmering illusion, the "Maya" of the Buddhist, becomes cold, metallic facts within, endowed with a creative power that coins words and phrases, and plays such fantastic tricks before high heaven as make the angels weep. In the face of such facts it [is] useless to beg our readers' pardon for the many typographical errors in our last issue.

In the early days of Unity, someone brought some hot dogs to a Sunday-school picnic. This would not have been important if one of them had not been put on Mr. Fillmore's plate. He was a strict vegetarian. Instead of acting displeased, he took the weiner and with a great show and much laughter nailed it to a tree.

While on a lecture trip in Texas, he had a cold and could hardly talk. He started his speech with the words, "It ain't my father and it ain't my mother, it ain't my sister and it ain't my brother, it's me, O Lord, that's standin' in the need of prayer," and he had the whole audience joyously join him in prayer for himself.

Myrtle Fillmore had the same love of gaiety as her husband and at Sunday-school parties would dance with the children. Sometimes she would get off a witticism that would have pleased Charles Fillmore to make. Once, during a Unity conference, all the center leaders were present at the Wednesday evening healing meeting, which Charles and Myrtle Fillmore were leading. Although the chapel was packed with people, Mr. Fillmore announced toward the end of the meeting, "When this program is over you are all invited to come over to our place for a bite to eat." As he stepped back, Mrs. Fillmore rose and declared quietly, "If you do, there had better be another expression of the miracle of the loaves and fishes."

In the early days, the family did not have much money, but their hearts and their house were large and they found room in both for those who needed help. Grandma Fillmore could always be counted on to conjure up enough of her delicious food to fill an extra plate. They all prayed about their needs—and they had a wonderful time.

One time, when they were children, Lowell and Rickert played with a little boy who said that he was lost. When they went home that evening they told their parents about him. Mrs. Fillmore sent Charles out to find him.

Soon Mr. Fillmore returned with him. He was a little black boy. He was very dirty, and his clothes were in rags, so Mrs. Fillmore took them off and replaced them with some of Rick and Lowell's. She heated some water on the kitchen stove and gave him a bath in the tin tub that served the family.

While she was bathing him, she talked to him and tried to give him some Unity ideas about God. "God is everywhere," she told him. "God is in this very room." At that moment, Mr. Fillmore came through the room and went upstairs. The little boy's mouth fell open. "Is that God?" he asked.

The Fillmore family lived in the northeast section of Kansas City. They moved often, but finally settled in a house on Elmwood Avenue where they lived for several years. This was then far out in the suburbs. The barn on the lot was moved forward and joined to the rear of the house, and in this back part, which they called "the den," Lowell, Rickert, and Royal lived. Rickert painted the walls of "the den" with pictures of the Katzenjammer kids. Lowell was the gardener and filled the yard with flowers. There was a huge elm in the backyard, and in this tree Rickert built a series of platforms and ladders that enabled one to climb up high. Often his mother and he would climb up together, and he would play his guitar while she sat and meditated.

The Fillmores were a neighborly family and soon were good friends with most of their neighbors, many of whom became staunch followers of Unity.

To Charles and Myrtle Fillmore, life was a joyous and wonderful experience, and they were not content merely to make their own life wonderful; they tried to live so that some of the wonder spilled over into the lives that touched their own. To them, people were not merely followers, but lovable human beings in whose personal adventures, as well as spiritual welfare, they were interested.

A woman who worked at Unity told how, when her mother had given birth to her children, Mrs. Fillmore stayed up each time until she was informed by telephone that all was well. One time, the mother was unusually worried about some physical symptoms that had appeared. Before she went to the hospital, Myrtle Fillmore insisted that she be called as soon as the baby was born. No matter what time it came, she would be waiting up for the call. It was not until 3 o'clock in the morning that the baby was born, and when the Fillmore house was called Mr. Fillmore answered the telephone. He and Mrs. Fillmore had stayed up praying for the mother and child.

Myrtle, especially, had a way of making people feel that she loved them. She was always putting her arms around the people she knew; her conversation overflowed with compliments. She had a gentle smile that made her callers feel that she had been looking forward to seeing them especially. And on terminating an interview, she had a way of half-rising, sometimes going to the door, as if to say, "Oh, I wish you wouldn't go." Usually when she had visitors she gave them some gift. She herself received many gifts from everywhere; as she could not use all of them, she passed many of them on to other persons. She was not afraid either in her conversation or her letters to say, "I love you."

"How I wish I could write this letter to you right from my heart without waiting for this typewriter to form the words," she began one letter. It was right from her heart that she wrote—and felt.

Although she carried on a voluminous correspondence, and many of the letters were answered by secretaries, she was able to remember intimate details in the lives of the persons to whom she wrote. She always read the letters her secretaries wrote for her. Usually she added to them in her own hand a postscript or a word in the margin, perhaps inquiring after a father or a daughter whom the correspondent had not even mentioned in the letter that was being answered.

Charles Fillmore, too, had this faculty for remembering people. One woman wrote to Unity School that two years after she and her husband had met Charles and Myrtle Fillmore at a Unity conference, the couple paid another visit to Unity and on entering the building on Tracy Avenue happened to encounter Mr. Fillmore. When he greeted them personally, the woman said, "I believe you are mistaking me for someone else."

Mr. Fillmore replied, "No, a good shepherd knows

his sheep," and told her how shepherds have their sheep named. "The shepherd doesn't forget the names of the sheep," he said. "You were here two years ago with your husband; you are from Peoria, Illinois," and he called them by name.

To the Fillmores, people were important, all people, whether important in the world's eye or not. All people were important because they were God's children. The Fillmores loved them, great and small. A young girl who once sat next to Charles Fillmore at a banquet later said, "He made me feel as if what I had to say was of great importance."

One time a woman came to study at the Unity Training School and ran out of funds before the term was over. She heard that the Fillmores wanted to hire someone to pick berries on their farm, so she applied for the job. She was instructed to go out and bring in a large bowlful of the berries for Mr. Fillmore's dinner. Then instead of hiring her to work, Charles asked her to eat with him.

Years later, the woman described the incident: "When dinner was served, Mr. Fillmore, like any father serving his little girl who was hungry, took a spoon and served half his dish of berries to me. Then, when I was about to leave, without my asking, he let me have twenty dollars to help me with my expenses and carried me back to Kansas City in his pretty new red car. I loved the twinkle in his eyes. He did his good like a bad boy slipping things over on one."

The Fillmores did not believe in amassing wealth for themselves; they believed in passing it on. "Sometimes I have a very definite place for all my allowance, before I even begin on my own individual needs," wrote Myrtle. They carried no life insurance, made no financial provision for the future. Although Unity School now copyrights its publications for the protection of its authors, the Fillmores never copyrighted any of their writings; they wanted people to be free to reprint anything they wrote. People sent them many gifts of money, most of which they turned over to Unity. Myrtle wrote:

My husband and I have put ourselves into this
thing which God has given us to do, year after year,
without personal returns beyond our "daily bread"
and clothing. I work here in the Unity buildings every day, and receive a salary just as several hundred
other workers do. I think a ... businessman or
woman would not consider working for my salary.

Charles and Myrtle Fillmore thought of themselves
as Unity workers. They were "Papa Charley" and "Mama
Myrtle." They felt that every person who worked at Unity
School, everyone connected with the movement, everyone who wrote to Unity, everyone who even visited the
buildings, was a member of the Unity family. They felt a
oneness with them all, a kinship with all people everywhere. When Unity workers were having financial trouble, they sometimes found money left on their typewrit-
ers. It was from Myrtle.

The offerings in classes taught at Unity School in the
early days were likely to be very small. Myrtle Fillmore
knew this and she would often have her secretary slip
into a class that some worker was teaching and put something for the teacher into the collection plate.

Charles and Myrtle Fillmore often went with the
other workers for picnics on Cliff Drive, a scenic spot in
the neighborhood. They would build a fire and cook their
meal and after they had eaten they would repeat Truth
statements together or sing some of the Truth songs they
loved.

Mr. Fillmore loved to conduct what he called "joy
times" for the workers. He would tell funny stories, and
so would some of the others. Long before most places of
business were having recreational periods during working hours, the Unity Workers were given time to tell
funny stories, to sing songs they liked, and to meditate
and pray.

The Fillmores wanted their workers to enjoy themselves and to improve themselves. Interesting speakers
who came to Kansas City were often invited to speak to
the Unity workers. Once an adult educational program in

downtown Kansas City sponsored a series of lectures called "University Extension Lectures." Although these lectures were held during working hours, the Unity workers were given the privilege of attending.

The Fillmores believed in joy and wanted others to be joyful. They had a large tent erected on top of the building at 913 Tracy where Unity workers and students who lived in the neighborhood could sleep out of doors on hot nights. For several years on this roof, Charles Fillmore on his birthday, August 22, had a watermelon party for the workers.

Sometimes, on holidays or at other times when there were only a few workers in the office, he would invite the whole group into his office to have lunch. There he had a little hot plate. Sometimes all he had was soup and crackers. The workers would sit in his office and sip soup from cups or glasses, or any other kind of small container they could get.

A room on the roof of 917 Tracy Avenue was called "The Tower Room" and was used for night work. Often Charles and Myrtle Fillmore would come up to this room to have the nine o'clock healing meeting with the workers who were on duty there. In the winter there would be a coal fire in the fireplace. Sometimes Mr. Fillmore would come up alone and sit in the rocking chair in front of the fireplace. Sometimes he would not say anything, merely sit in the silence; sometimes, when the workers were not busy, he would sing. He loved to sing, especially songs that had amusing words, and he always smiled as he sang. One of his favorite songs was from "The Mikado," and his voice would ring out on the final words of the refrain.

> "Let the punishment fit the crime—
> The punishment fit the crime."

Mr. Fillmore did not believe in punishment. At one time, a number of workers at Unity School were won over by another teacher. This alone would not have disturbed

him, for in the early days of his ministry, when some
visiting lecturer would come to town with a lot of public-
ity and most of his congregation would go to hear the
visitor, Mr. Fillmore would just proceed as always, blessing the lecturer and blessing the people and saying to
any friend who was concerned: "Leave them alone,
they'll be back." And they came back.

But this time, the other teacher not only tried to win
away the workers, he tried to get them to procure for him
a copy of the mailing list of Silent Unity's correspondents.
These names, of course, are considered inviolate. (The
names and needs of all those who write to Silent Unity
have always been considered strictly confidential. All the
workers are impressed, when they come into the service,
with the fact that they are not even supposed to talk
among themselves about the correspondents; and some
months after the letters are answered, they are destroyed.) But even when Charles Fillmore learned of the
attempt to destroy the loyalty of his workers, he did not
become angry. He did not even dismiss the workers. He
merely told them that they were free to stay, or go, as
they felt led. If they wanted to follow the other man, they
were free to do so, only he felt that they should serve in
the other man's organization. On the other hand, if they
wanted to stay at Unity School and be loyal to Unity, he
was happy to have them stay; they were his friends.

The Fillmores had faith in people. They had faith in
them because they saw them as God's children; they did
not see the defects and shortcomings, they saw the spiritual potentialities, they saw the Christ Spirit. Most persons lack faith in themselves. The Fillmores knew this.
They had the gift of instilling in people faith in their own
abilities. Few persons have love's eyes to see and love's
heart to feel the unspoken need and the hidden talents of
another. The Fillmores were such persons.

Myrtle Fillmore, especially, was sensitive to others'
undeveloped possibilities. No small part of her influence
on the Unity movement was the work that she did with
the Unity workers. She was always among them, stop-

ping at their desks, praising them, encouraging them, drawing out of them some good quality that they themselves perhaps did not know they had. For example, for years Myrtle Fillmore went every day to the bindery to conduct the blessing of the mail.

The woman who was in charge of the bindery was a timid person; she felt that she could never lead the workers in prayer. But one day, Mrs. Fillmore turned to her and said, "You know, today I would like you to give the blessing. I'd like to hear what it sounds like." The worker was hesitant as to how to begin, but heartened by Mrs. Fillmore's smile, she started out. Before she knew it she had led the workers in a prayer service that she had had no idea she was capable of. After she had finished, Mrs. Fillmore lifted her hands over the mail and said, "There is nothing more to be said. God bless you." From then on the workers in the bindery gave their own blessing to the Unity mail.

Blessing the mail is still a Unity custom: every morning when the mail from the post office reaches the mail-opening room it is blessed. Every day when mail is ready to leave Unity School the workers in the mailing room gather around and place a blessing upon it.

Many who became successful Unity leaders felt that the encouragement given them by Myrtle Fillmore was in large measure responsible for their success. Some of them might not have stayed in the Unity work had it not been for her appreciation and understanding. She helped them to find exactly the right place for themselves. One young man came to work at Unity School about the time of World War I. Brilliant and restless, at first it did not seem that he would be able to find a place in Unity where he could use his talents. Myrtle Fillmore, however, recognized that he was a gifted person and encouraged him to stay and to have faith that he would find in Unity the right avenue for the expression of his gifts. In 1924 this young man, Frank B. Whitney, encouraged by Myrtle and Charles Fillmore, brought forth *Unity Daily Word* (now known as *Daily Word*), which has since become the most popular of all the Unity publications. He became the first editor of this magazine and one of the best loved of Unity's writers.

Charles Fillmore, too, knew how to call forth the talents of others. Many workers in Silent Unity remember an experience they had when they first came to work in that department: a difficult letter came to them that they did not know how to answer; they took it to Mr. Fillmore and asked him how to answer it, and he told them. This happened perhaps three or four times; then they took a letter to him, and he told them: "The Spirit that is in me is in you. Go back to your desk and ask that Spirit how to answer this letter. You can answer it." At first, the letter-writer might doubt that he could do it; but always in the end he discovered that he had the ability.

Charles and Myrtle Fillmore were leaders. Because they had courage and faith in themselves as children of God, they inspired those around them to have courage and to dare to step out on their own resources.

Charles Fillmore was a man of action. Everything he had to meet he took to God in prayer. He prayed. He looked for guidance. Then he moved boldly ahead. He once told a co-worker, "Go ahead with an open mind and, if you are not on the right course, something will soon appear that you will see is better."

Knowing almost nothing about the publishing business, he dared to publish a magazine. To a materially-minded world, he dared to proclaim a new interpretation of the Jesus Christ teaching. Rejecting approved financial methods, he dared to rely on God and accepted free-will offerings as his income. Down through the years when there were changes to be made, buildings to be built, steps to be taken, people to be entrusted with important parts of the Unity work—whenever there was a vital decision to be made—Charles Fillmore was there with a David-brave heart, a Solomon-wise judgment, and an unshakable faith in God.

Charles Fillmore was the embodiment of prayer in action. He prayed about everything that he had to do, then he did it. His daring faith had much to do with making Unity what it now is. He always seemed to say, "Where He leads me I will follow, I'll go with Him all the way."

Chapter XI

Their Healing Work

"Heal the Sick"

UNITY BEGAN when Myrtle Fillmore received the idea, *"I am a child of God and therefore I do not inherit sickness,"* and was healed by the power of God in her. The first fruit of Unity was the healing of the friends and neighbors who came to her with their physical ills and saw these dissolved through prayer. Unity has always emphasized healing through the Christ within.

When the sick heard, back in the 1880s, that a woman named Myrtle Fillmore had been healed of tuberculosis through her prayers and was having success in bringing healing to others, it was natural that they should start beating a path to her door. They have been coming down that path in increasing numbers ever since.

It was through searching for health that the Fillmores themselves discovered Truth. Although Myrtle Fillmore quickly found her wholeness, Charles Fillmore spent untold hours of the day and night, during the last sixty years of his life, working in prayer for healing for himself and others.

He never accepted the withered leg as a handicap that he would have to put up with all the days of his life; he believed that his leg could be made whole and strong and perfect, and he worked in prayer to make it so. Those who knew him over a long period of time attest that as the years went by Charles' leg responded to the faith of the man, for they saw it grow in strength and vigor; they saw him discard cane and braces; they saw the leg become more nearly like the other. Charles Fillmore practiced the prayer that he taught.

The Fillmores never insisted that those who came to them for help give up medicine or other medical aid. They left their students free, and today Unity is glad to pray with those who are taking medical treatment. Unity believes in people getting help in every way they can, and praises everyone who is helping people to find health. Unity cooperates in all possible ways with doctors. The Unity School for Religious Studies sends its students to hospitals for special training, and Unity School has prepared special pamphlets for people to take with them when they have to go to hospitals for treatment. H. Emilie Cady, author of the basic Unity textbook, *Lessons in Truth,* was a homeopathic physician and continued for many years to practice medicine. Other doctors have written for Unity. Many have subscribed for the magazines and have not only put them in their waiting rooms for their patients to read but have advised their patients to subscribe for them and study them at home. The Fillmores knew that people were at all stages of spiritual development and that everyone had to live according to his own faith. They were glad to add their prayers to the ministrations of the doctors. For themselves, however, they felt that prayer alone was enough to keep them whole.

At one time, Charles Fillmore was in an automobile accident. A doctor was called who treated the other persons involved in the accident.

Charles Fillmore was in a great deal of pain, but when the doctor came to treat him, Charles said to him, "Just leave me alone, please, I'll do this my own way," and he motioned the doctor aside.

"There," said the doctor, "is a man." Charles recovered very quickly.

This atmosphere of faith in God as the source of healing pervaded the Fillmore household from the early days of Unity. Once Lowell had the mumps, and Rick caught them in one jaw. That day his mother found him playing barefoot in the rain. When she reprimanded him, he asked, "Don't you believe what you say?"

The Fillmore boys did not worry much about getting sick. Their mother wrote: "Yesterday, there were about four inches of snow on the ground, and from my study window I saw Royal with bare feet and with legs bared to the knees taking a run in the front yard. 'Just to see how snow feels,' he said."

When people came to the Fillmores for help, they caught the simple faith of this believing family, and soon a constant stream of the sick were coming to the Unity offices. By the time the Fillmores moved their offices to the house on McGee Street, a crowd was coming every day to see if some of the healing faith of these two praying people might touch and restore their bodies. By the time Charles arrived at 10 or 11 in the morning, there were always at least a dozen persons waiting for him in the reception room, which was used for the meetings on Sundays. He had his office in the front parlor. There he took these persons one by one and listened to them and prayed with them. He knew that he of himself could do nothing, but his whole prayer and his whole life were consecrated to gaining a spirit of oneness with the God of life, whose power can bring perfection to mind and body.

All day long, into that little office went aching, often despairing, men and women. Perhaps they had suffered pain for years, perhaps they had been told that they had no chance to live. They went into the office fear-racked and suffering, and they found there a little, quiet, kindly man who invited them to sit down beside him and tell him what was wrong.

Charles Fillmore said that it often seemed to him that he said very little. Sometimes the patient spent the whole time telling him what was wrong. But this, Charles Fillmore always silently denied; and he always prayed. Usually he managed to get the one who was asking for help to pray also. They would sit still together and in that creative silence they would speak the powerful words of

Truth that, as Charles Fillmore had come to know, carried healing.

When those people rose to go, fifteen minutes or a half-hour later, often they were not the same persons who had come slumped and desperate through the door. Almost always, they went forth renewed in spirit and often they went forth renewed in body too; for in this small office in Kansas City the miracles of which the Bible speaks were coming to pass again: the lame were being made to walk, the dumb to speak, and the blind to see.

At first, the Fillmores did not publish many testimonials of healing in their magazines because, as they said, they wanted to place the emphasis on the teaching and on the spiritual results rather than on physical ones. Finally, in response to many requests for testimonials, Mr. Fillmore began to publish a column of them regularly every month under the title, "The Signs That Follow." At one time, he published a magazine by this name for the sole purpose of printing the testimonials. He wrote:

> It has not been our custom to sound our own praises, nor even to print the tons of good words of help received by those who have co-operated with us. Recently there has been a real demand for a sight of the unsolicited testimonial letters we are so freely receiving. People say it helps them to believe when they see how many are being benefited; so it is for your encouragement that we print a few of the hundreds of letters we are constantly getting.

From that time on, thousands of letters describing the healing of almost every known physical condition have appeared in the pages of Unity's magazines. Since the Silent Unity work is strictly confidential, no names are ever mentioned in the letters and permission to reprint them is requested before they are used.

The number of persons to whom the Fillmores have pointed out the way to health is impossible to estimate. To this day, people are still writing to Unity, or sometimes visiting headquarters, who say that many years ago they were ill and they came to Charles or Myrtle Fillmore, or they wrote to them, and were healed through prayer.

A few years ago a visitor came to Unity School in a taxi from Kansas City. When Lowell Fillmore accompanied this visitor out to his waiting taxi, the driver said: "You probably don't know me, Mr. Fillmore, but my brother came to your mother years ago and was healed through her. He is well and working now." And he gave Lowell his name. It was a name that Lowell remembered well. It was one of the first cases of healing that his mother had had, and Lowell had often wondered what had become of the man.

There were many healings in those early days. One woman had a tumor. The doctors wanted to operate on her, but she kept putting them off as she was afraid that an operation would be fatal. Finally she set a time for the operation—Saturday morning. Friday night, weeping, she called on Mr. Fillmore. "For God's sake help me if you can," she cried. She had not slept for many nights, but that night when she went home she fell asleep and slept until morning. When the doctors examined her the next day, they found no tumor.

A woman who had been told that she would not live until fall came to the Fillmores with tuberculosis of the lungs. A few months later she was able to tell Mr. Fillmore, "I am a strong, healthy woman, doing all my own housework." Her husband was one day brought home with a strangulated hernia and rushed to the hospital where the head surgeon told her that he would probably die within three days from blood poisoning. She wired for help to Charles Fillmore. As the man went under the surgeon's knife, he was repeating, *"I am, I am one with God."* On the third day, there was no fever, and on the fourth day, the wound was completely healed.

One woman who had had one operation after another came to Myrtle Fillmore. After four sessions of prayer, she was completely well.

Another woman with tuberculosis came to Mrs. Fillmore; while they were praying, the woman had a coughing spell. They prayed together about that. The coughing stopped. Then the woman said in a surprised voice, "What did you do to my ankle?" Several years before, she had dislocated one of the small bones in her ankle and had not been able to put her foot flat on the ground since then. While Myrtle Fillmore and she had been praying about the coughing, she had felt a strange sensation in this foot, and when she rose from her chair she found that she could walk on this foot as well as on the other. In less than a year, her tuberculosis was gone.

There was a state legislator who, on applying for an insurance policy, had been told that he had an advanced case of diabetes. He attended one of the classes in Truth principles taught by Charles Fillmore. During the fourth lesson, he said that he suddenly received the assurance that he was healed. From ninety-two pounds, he went up in one month to one hundred and thirty-two pounds in weight. He was able to discard the diet he had been following, and tests showed that the diabetes had disappeared. His right arm, withered and over one inch shorter than the left, had been useless for seventeen years. One day, he found to his astonishment that the right arm had become the same length as the left and was almost as well-developed.

By the early 1900's, the Fillmores had become so busy that they could not continue spending most of each day taking up the healing needs of individuals who came to them for help. However, they never entirely ceased this practice, and there were probably few days when they were not praying with someone about healing needs.

Years later, they were still having experiences such as the following one described in a letter to Unity:

> I was very ill in Kansas City, Missouri, where I had been living and doing office work for several years. I had been doctoring for about six weeks but steadily getting worse.
>
> One morning, when I was very low, my doctor brought a specialist with him, and after consulting

together for some time, they told me I had to be removed at once to a hospital and operated on, or I would not be alive twelve hours from that time.

I made up my mind that I was not going to be operated on and I told the doctors to go away. My sister, who had come from the West Coast to be with me, asked me what I wanted to do. I had myself carried downstairs to the telephone, and they left me alone.

I called up Silent Unity, and the young lady at the telephone could not understand me, as I could not speak above a whisper.

In a minute she said, "Oh, hold on a minute, here comes Charles Fillmore. You are very blessed that you can get him to help you." I had been to several Sunday meetings at Unity and had heard Mr. Fillmore speak and had faith that he could help me.

As soon as he spoke, I told him the doctors had told me I was going to die if I was not operated on at once. He asked me what the doctor said was the matter with me. I told him.

He was very firm, and said: "You are not going to die." He had me repeat after him the words of the last verse of "The Prayer of Faith," although that was the first time I had ever heard it. Many times since then, through the years, that prayer has helped me over a hard place.

"Now," he said, "you go to sleep and rest."

I said, "Oh, Mr. Fillmore, I haven't slept except by fits and starts for over three weeks."

"Well," he said, "you will now. Just repeat those words I told you, and go to sleep."

I went right to sleep and dreamed that I was in heaven and a beautiful angel was bending over me and smiling. I opened my eyes, and it was night. Standing there was a lovely girl smoothing my forehead. I said, "Who are you, an angel?"

She said, "No, I'm not an angel. I'm Myrtle Fillmore's secretary, and we thought you might like to see me."

She stayed a little while and left, and I slept fine the rest of the night. In three weeks from that time, I

was back to work at my desk in the office and four
years later, in another city, I was married. Later, I
brought my husband and year-old baby daughter to
Unity in Kansas City, and Mr. Fillmore held my baby
in his arms and blessed her.

Although they themselves no longer had the time to
spend each day handling the healing needs of individuals, the Fillmores had gathered about them a group of
devoted persons who they believed had a high spiritual
consciousness, and these persons took over this phase of
the work. Finally there were twelve of these counselors,
or healers, as they called themselves. Myrtle Fillmore
herself remained in charge of their activities, and every
morning at 10 o'clock, she led this group in a healing
meeting.

Mr. and Mrs. Fillmore together often conducted the
healing meeting that Silent Unity held each morning at
11 o'clock. Together, too, they conducted every Wednesday evening at 8 o'clock a healing meeting that was open
to the public. They always stopped this meeting exactly
at 9, when they asked everyone to join them for fifteen
minutes in silent healing prayer. This 9 o'clock healing
service was the one they had asked people to participate
in when they first formed Silent Unity. They were faithful
to it always.

Myrtle and Charles Fillmore had learned to pray at
all times, in all places, and under all circumstances, and
they never let what was going on around them keep them
from praying. Sometimes on Sunday morning after the
service, Charles Fillmore would come down from the
platform and see someone who was in need of prayer.
Right there in the front row of the chapel, with people
talking and laughing and milling about them, he would
have the one who needed help sit down beside him, and
it would be as if the two of them were completely alone.
In the midst of the confusion, he would sit quietly, close
his eyes, and speak words of prayer with the one in need.

Usually the Fillmores opened a healing meeting
with a song. After the opening song, Mrs. Fillmore led a

silence, which is what Unity calls a period of meditation. She would take up the theme of the meeting, discuss the affirmation that she was having the group use in prayer, lead them in declaring it and meditating silently on the Truth of it. Then Mr. Fillmore would rise and give a talk based on the healing prayer, after which he would lead the group in further meditation, using the prayer as a basis for it. Usually he gave the benediction at the close of the meeting.

It was not what was done at the meeting, it was not the words that were spoken or the prayers that were used that mattered; it was the spirit of the two who conducted the meeting. As they took turns speaking and as they sat together in the silence, a compelling spirit radiated from the platform that was felt by all who were attuned to it. As the sick and the lonely and the troubled of heart sat in that small chapel and listened to the quiet words and looked into the gentle faces of the two before them, it was as if the healing Spirit of the Christ passed among them.

Here were two who had dedicated their lives to the living God. With adamant faith, they spoke from the silence of their hearts the words that they believed to be the truest words that could be spoken of a human being, words that proclaimed divinity, words that affirmed wholeness in Christ. Earnestly, faithfully, thankfully they prayed and prayed again until the words they spoke were no longer words; they were living symbols of God's healing life, and all who heard them and joined in speaking them in prayer felt the power of them too, felt it not only with their minds but in their bodies.

When, at the end of the meeting, Charles and Myrtle Fillmore passed from the room something of them remained—the consciousness of life that they had kindled in the minds and bodies of those who had been praying with them. "For where two or three are gathered in my name, there am I in the midst of them."

Chapter XII

The Fillmores as Teachers

"Thou Shalt Teach Them"

IN *UNITY* MAGAZINE of February 1897, there appeared an announcement by Charles Fillmore which read as follows:

> Monday evening, March 15, 1897, at 8 p.m., I will begin another class of instruction in practical Christianity at Rooms 510 and 511 Hall Building, Kansas City, Missouri. These lessons are in a large measure the outgrowth of my experience in the regeneration through which I have been passing for several years, and are therefore very practical. I do not follow any teaching, but give the Truth as I have gotten it from spiritual experiences, which I find corroborated in a wonderful way in the Hebrew Scriptures. Theory has been replaced by absolute knowledge, and I am enabled to give many things that have never before been taught. . . .
>
> These lessons are twelve in number and will be given one each night, taking two weeks to complete the course. All are welcome, but no new students will be admitted after the first lesson.
>
> No charge is made for the lessons or treatments that accompany, when needed. All expenses are met by freewill offerings.

Charles Fillmore had been teaching such classes in practical Christianity for several years. At first, there were only a handful of students in the classes. They

would all sit around in a circle. Mr. Fillmore would ask
one or another of them questions; then the whole group
would discuss the answers that were given. He loved to
teach in this way, freely and informally, with a group of
students as sincerely interested in Truth as himself gathered around him.

As the Fillmores said over and over, they were not
trying to set up a church, they were establishing a school.
When the Unity Society of Practical Christianity was incorporated in 1903, it was incorporated as a scientific and
educational institution, not as a church. Later Charles
Fillmore even tried to conduct the Sunday services along
the lines of the informal discussions that he had had in
his early classes. At one time, after the Unity Correspondence Course was begun, he assigned members of his
congregation questions from this course, which they
answered. Then there was an open discussion of the
answers. However, his congregation preferred to listen to
him talk, so he abandoned this plan; but his talks always
had more of the feel and flavor of a lecture by a scientist
or philosopher—and one with a keen sense of humor—
than they did of a sermon, although they were based on
the Bible and the teachings of Jesus.

Charles and Myrtle Fillmore did not teach an ab-
stract theory; they lived what they taught; they put it into
practice. They worked for long hours in prayer and meditation to discover Truth and then they applied to their
own bodies and their own affairs the Truth that was unfolded to them. Charles Fillmore once wrote:

> I spend from four to six hours daily in prayer,
> blessing the various parts of my body, the centers. At
> first it was difficult to get started, and I had many
> backsets, but now it is quite interesting and I often
> stay up all night intent upon improving my control of
> these subjective functions of the body.

Long before newspapers and magazines began to
write about meditation as if it were a brand new discovery brought to this country by Eastern swamis, the Fill-

mores, making no charge, were quietly teaching their students to relax, to become still, to turn within, and to call forth the divine potentiality that they knew each individual has within him. Almost a century ago they were directing students how to go beyond the ordinary limits of consciousness and call forth powers beyond their usual ones. And ever since, thousands of Unity students have improved and expanded their lives by following their teachings.

The Fillmores believed that a man has in him divine potentialities far beyond any that he usually expresses, the potentialities of the Christ. They believed that throughout the body there are spiritual centers and that by concentrating on these in prayer one can release spiritual forces centered in them. This they worked to do. Later Charles Fillmore wrote a book about this idea called *The Twelve Powers of Man,* in which he names and describes these centers.

In an article he described his experience in unfolding his own spiritual powers:

> The most important phase of my experience however was the opening of my spiritual nature. I gradually acquired the ability to go into the silence, and from that source I received unexpected revelations and physical sensations. At first, the revelations were nearly all through dreams. I developed a dream code through which I could get information and answers of marvelous accuracy to my questions. I do not remember that I asked who the author of my guidance was; I took for granted that it was Spirit.
>
> Then the mental and spiritual developed into sensations at the nerve extremities. I was informed by the Presence that I was beginning body regeneration as taught by Jesus Christ. Neither physiology nor psychology offers a nomenclature describing it. The first sensation was in my forehead, a crawly feeling when I was affirming life. Then I found that I could produce this same feeling in the bottom of my feet and other nerve extremities by concentrating my attention at the place and silently affirming life.

I spent several hours every day in this process and I found that I was releasing electronic forces sealed up in the nerves. This I have done for nearly fifty years until now I have what may be termed an electric body that is gradually replacing the physical. It is even more than electric, and when certain spiritual emotions are imparted to it, it fairly glows and blends with an omnipresent etheric atmosphere that is highly charged with life energy. My physical organism is being transformed cell by cell, and the ultimate will be an entirely new body having all the perfections of youth in addition to ethereal life.

This, Spirit tells me, is the transformation of mind and body promised by Jesus. Paul called attention to it—"Be ye transformed by the renewing of your mind"—but he did not attain it. Now at the end of this age, the spiritual and mental conditions of the race are ripe for the entering into this new life of all followers of Jesus in the regeneration. It is through this transformation and rearrangement of the atoms of the organism that the Christ body is formed in man's consciousness. When the light of Spirit is allowed to enter the conscious and the subconscious minds, a great revelation takes place, and it is found to be literal fact that "your body is a temple of the Holy Spirit which is in you, which ye have from God."

The Fillmores were slow in putting down in book form the conclusions they reached. The only book that Myrtle Fillmore ever wrote is the book for children, *Wee Wisdom's Way*, no longer in print; and Charles Fillmore studied and thought for twenty years before he felt that his ideas were ready to be published in book form.

When the Fillmores first felt that a book on Truth principles was needed, instead of writing it themselves, they compiled H. Emilie Cady's *Lessons in Truth*, which had originally appeared as a magazine series. Meanwhile, they were praying and organizing their thoughts.

The subscribers for their magazines wrote in continually asking them to write a book, but they were not to be hurried. In 1902 Charles wrote in reply to some of these letters, "I wish to attain such command of my organism that I can demonstrate what I write." To him, any spiritual law worth writing about had to be demonstrable. He called his work and he labeled his classes practical Christianity. Part of the reason why he did not, for such a long time, put the lessons into print, but insisted that those who wished to study with him come to him in person, was that much of the course consisted of actually working with the ideas, putting them into practice through prayer and meditation. He wrote:

"My class lessons are not in print, and there is no immediate prospect of printing them, as they consist in part of the practical application of the Word and drills that vary according to the need of the class."

He would have felt that his classes had not been a success if, in the course of them, some of the students had not proved the laws that he was teaching them by attaining more health or prosperity.

Finally in 1905, he began the publication in *Unity* of some metaphysical lessons that he intended to publish in book form when they were completed. The twelve lessons were not completed until 1909. In that year his first book, *Christian Healing,* was published. The material in it was the summation of what he had been teaching in the classes in practical Christianity that he had been giving since the inception of Unity. For twenty years, Charles Fillmore had tested in his own body and life the ideas he presented in this book, and because of the results that he had personally secured, he was sure that the ideas would be of practical value to others.

The book was run through scores of printings, and although editing later changed it somewhat, the ideas remain the same. They had been tried, they had been tested, they had been found workable and true. They were clear, high expressions of Truth, and Charles Fillmore held to these ideas all his life.

Yet he never stopped looking for new ideas. In his nineties, he was still saying, "I reserve the right to change my mind." He did not believe in the closed mind.

Life to him meant new beginnings. He was a pioneer of spirit, an adventurer in faith. He wrote:

> Beware of the circumscribed idea of God! Always provide for an increase in your concept. Don't write down any laws governing your conduct or your religious ideas. Be free to grow and expand. What you think today may not be the measure for your thought tomorrow.

Unity existed for more than thirty years before he wrote, and then only in response to a prolonged and persistent demand from readers for a precise statement of his beliefs, the "Unity Statement of Faith," and to this he added:

> We have considered the restrictions that will follow a formulated platform, and are hereby giving warning that we shall not be bound by this tentative statement of what Unity believes. We may change our mind tomorrow on some of the points, and if we do, we shall feel free to make a new statement of faith in harmony with the new viewpoint. However, we are assured that there will be no change in fundamentals; the form of words may be clarified and the inner and outer meaning of the Truth may be more clearly set forth.

Often in his classes, a student would be answering a question and Mr. Fillmore would ask, "Where did you get that idea?"

The student would reply, "I read that in such-and-such a Unity book, Mr. Fillmore."

"Are you sure?"

"Certainly, Mr. Fillmore, that is right out of page so and so."

"You know," he would say, "that is not exactly right," and then he would go on to explain the point in a way that clarified it.

Often in his classes, he would interrupt his students, when they were quoting him, with the question, "But what do *you* think about it?"

The main aim of his teaching was to get his students to think Truth through for themselves. By Socratic questioning, he would draw out his students' minds. He felt that Truth meant little as long as it was only words in a book. He was constantly making a distinction between spiritual understanding and intellectual understanding. Although he recognized the importance of words, he was not content with them. He worked in prayer until he had made Truth part of his very flesh and life.

When a student in one of his classes answered a question, he would ask, "Any comments?"

Perhaps one or two would speak up and say, "Good!" Usually that was all.

Then he would say, "Any questions?" Silence.

"Any criticism?" Silence.

"Any 'blowholes'?"

Usually there would be a laugh at this. Then the class would begin to discuss the question freely, which was what he wanted. He knew that only out of free discussion would his students arrive at an understanding of Truth that was in their own language. This was his aim, for he knew that nothing means much to a person until he has made it part of his own experience.

It was because Charles Fillmore himself was so certain of Truth that he was able to let his students arrive at Truth for themselves. He had the courage of his convictions; he had faith in their validity. There were certain divine ideas that Charles Fillmore knew, and he knew that he knew them. He had tested them by the logic of his mind and by application to his life. Nothing could have shaken his belief in them. He wrote:

> I can remember with what satisfaction I used to imbibe the assumed wisdom of freshmen teachers. I knew nothing about God because I had never made an effort to get acquainted with Him and in my egotism, I said, "All these people that think they are in communion with God are deluded; I have never seen God. I believe in things you can see and I will take the testimony of Bob Ingersoll, who says you cannot

know God, rather than that of Henry Ward Beecher, who says you can."

But a time came when I decided to solve this question independent of any man's opinion. I set about to search for Him with my mind. And right here, I want to add my testimony good and strong with those who have said, *"I know God."* I talk and think to God, and He flashes His ideas into my mind. I am not deluded. I know His thoughts from the thoughts of men as they pass through the mental atmosphere. He also talks to me in certain dreams. I can distinguish these dreams from the other dreams. Repeated thinking about the presence of God makes Him increasingly plainer to my inner vision. I have thought about Him as the life of my body until every cell is athrill with an energy that I can feel as you feel the shock of an electric battery, and He tells me how to communicate this life to others who have not recognized it as I have. Don't let the fool say in your heart, "There is no God." I let that kind of fool talk in my heart and it set up a current of thought that kept me for years speechless in the presence of God.

Charles Fillmore knew God and he knew where he stood in relation to Him, and this was a knowledge not open to argument. He was a man of strong conviction, yet he had no trace of the fanatic. Sometimes people came to his classes to denounce his ideas. When this happened, he quietly turned the discussion to other matters. Although he loved to lead his students in metaphysical discussion, he knew that arguing about religion is fruitless. He refrained from criticizing other religious teachings; he did not feel that it was necessary to defend his own. When people needed Unity, they would turn to it, he felt.

The Fillmore spirit of tolerance permeates Unity today. When people write to Unity School denouncing its beliefs, the Unity letterwriters agree with the correspondent in all possible points, and in regard to points of disagreement, merely say that Unity leaves every man free to find Truth for himself and that there is some Truth in all teachings.

Unity is not a proselyting religion. People of all religions and no religion write and call Silent Unity for help and subscribe to the magazines, and no one is ever asked, "What is your religion?" Many persons get so interested in the Unity attitude that they decide to attend classes and services held in Unity churches; but if they are members of a denomination and prefer to remain in it, Unity hopes that it can make their religion of greater value to them.

The Fillmores believed in each person seeking Truth within self. They always began and ended every class they taught with a silence, where each student's mind would be free to contact God in a personal way. Usually it was Myrtle Fillmore who conducted the silence. She loved this part of the meetings. When she led a meditation, she had a way of speaking as if the words tasted good to her. She usually began her prayers by explaining what prayer is. "Prayer is communion with God," she would say. "God is in you, and you can come in contact with Him there; you can feel His presence in you. Turn within now and let His presence come forth as wisdom so that your words and your thoughts may be filled with His wisdom."

The classes that the Fillmores taught were joyous classes. One of the distinguishing points of their teaching is the emphasis it puts on joy. When Unity began, many churches were teaching that life is a vale of tears, a mere temporary halting place where trials and tribulation prepare the soul for the hereafter. However, the Fillmores taught that it is not at all necessary to be sorrowful in order to be spiritual.

They taught that God's will is joy. They emphasized the importance of living a full life here and now. "Live in the present. 'Now is the acceptable time,'" they declared.

The Fillmores emphasized not Jesus crucified but Jesus Christ resurrected. They chose for the symbol of Unity not the cross, which to so many persons represents the suffering of Jesus, but the winged globe of Spirit.

Charles Fillmore did not want his teaching to be

connected with symbols associated with suffering. He did not believe that true religion is sorrowful. Although he taught that conduct should be governed by the highest ethical standards, he did not teach that there is any virtue in suffering.

The determination of the Fillmores to keep their teaching joyful is shown by Unity's manner of observing Lent. Unity provides those who would like one a study guide that they can follow for each of the forty days preceding Easter. Through the years many thousands have joined in this Lenten program, observing the time not as a period of physical denial but of consecration and joyous release from old thoughts and limitations.

The denial that the Fillmores taught is the denial of sorrow, the denial of limitations, the denial of sin, sickness, poverty, and death. They made of their teaching a joyous affirmation of life.

There was never anything gloomy or dull about Charles and Myrtle Fillmore. A new center leader was asked to conduct a funeral service. Never having conducted one, he came to Myrtle Fillmore for advice. She told him, "Just because it is a funeral, you don't have to talk about death, do you?"

"What shall I talk about?" he asked.

"Talk about life!" she exclaimed.

In all their classes, the Fillmores talked about life, abundant life, joyous life. Both Myrtle and Charles Fillmore loved to sing. If he could find a bit of song that applied to some question, he would sing it out. Myrtle Fillmore wrote a number of hymns. Usually she wrote Truth words to be sung to a familiar melody. One such hymn that was often sung in early Unity meetings to the melody of "Rock of Ages," is the following:

> Burst with praise, O gate of song;
> Flow, O voice from sorrow free;
> Let thy currents, pure and strong,
> Roll in healing melody,
> Till in one harmonious voice,
> Pain redeemed, shall earth rejoice.

Break thy bonds, O child of might;
Claim the freedom of thy birth;
Joy and wisdom shall unite,
Health and power claim the earth;
Love and peace, one circling sea,
Compass man in unity.

Also Myrtle Fillmore wrote the following words to the melody of "The Rosary":

The hours I've spent with Thee, dear Lord,
Are pearls of priceless worth to me.
My soul, my being merge in sweet accord,
In love for Thee; in love for Thee.
Each hour a pearl, each pearl a prayer,
Binding Thy presence close to me;
I only know that Thou art there, and I
Am lost in Thee.
Oh, glorious joys, that thrill and bless!
Oh, visions sweet of love divine!
My soul its rapturous bliss can ill express
That Thou art mine, O Lord! That Thou art mine!

Charles Fillmore tried his hand at writing brief verses such as this:

Behold, what God hath wrought!
An ideal man, a mighty man—
A man supreme, who thought by thought
Must demonstrate what God hath wrought.

One song printed in the *Unity Song Selections* was written by him:

Healed, healed by His power divine!
One, one with His love sublime!
My life now is sweet and my joy is complete,
For I'm healed, healed, healed!

Both he and Mrs. Fillmore loved to write affirmations that rhymed, such as:

I am praying and blessing my basket and store;
The Christ mind increases my good evermore.

In an early issue of *Unity*, Charles Fillmore jok-
ingly asked his writers to get Satan behind them when
they felt tempted to put their thoughts in rhyme. One
subscriber wrote in and said that Satan was behind Mr.
Fillmore when he chose the poems that he printed in
Unity. Charles Fillmore replied that he wished he had a
poetry editor who knew something about the "stuff."
Actually he was fond of poetry and reprinted quantities of
verse in his magazine. From his earliest days, he had
read the works of the great poets; they had been a major
source of his self-education.

Myrtle Fillmore, too, liked poetry; she liked to write
it as well as read it. In her correspondence with her
brother David Page, she sometimes enclosed bits of verse
that she had composed, and he in turn sent her many
pieces that he had written.

The Fillmores believed in everything that was joyous and beautiful. "When joy is put back into religion,
there will be more religion in the world," Charles Fillmore wrote.

One time when he was in a restaurant, Charles Fillmore told his wife that he thought the waitress was a
Unity student.

"Why do you think so?" she asked.

"She looks like a Unity student," he replied, "she
has such a happy look."

When the waitress came to the table again, Mrs. Fillmore asked her if she was a Unity student.

"Why yes," she said in astonishment, "I am."

When she found out that she was waiting on the
Fillmores, she introduced them to several other wait-
resses in the restaurant who were also Unity students. In
a few minutes, the cook came smiling from the kitchen
with a big cake with "U N I T Y" written on it in sugar.
He was a Unity student too.

It was one of Charles Fillmore's greatest satisfactions
to feel that he had made people happy. He believed that
happiness is the divine right of human beings, and that
anything less than happiness is due only to our failure to

perceive the full Truth for ourselves. This he taught in all his classes and this he expressed in all his life. "Let the old world wag as it will," he loved to say, "I will be gay and happy still."

Chapter XIII

A School of Practical Christianity

"Teaching and Fellowship"

EXCEPT FOR a few classes taught in Colorado in the early 1900's, Charles and Myrtle Fillmore did little of their teaching away from Kansas City. Yet, all through the land, there were people praying with Silent Unity and reading the Unity publications. These people were hungry for Truth. They were grateful for the opportunity to unite in prayer with Silent Unity and grateful for the publications. But in many cases there was a demand for more; they wanted to probe deeper into the principles that Charles and Myrtle Fillmore were teaching. Many of them were unable to make the trip to Kansas City to study or take the class work.

The Fillmores did not feel that they had time to teach in other cities, but they wanted to help these persons. They knew how avidly they had sought for inspiration when they had first discovered Truth. There was one teacher whom they especially wanted to come to Kansas City. This was Ursula Gestefeld, of Chicago, whose books on Truth were among the clearest and simplest written in the last century. She did not come to Kansas City, but finally she had mimeographed copies of her lessons sent to the Fillmores for them and their students to study.

In 1909 the Fillmores decided that they, too, could teach students in other cities in this way. They wrote about their new service:

For years, requests for lessons in the science of Being have been coming to the Society of Silent Unity, but the way never seemed open to take up the work until recently.

Early in April of this year [1909] we received a letter from a correspondent who asked that we send her immediately the first lesson in our correspondence course. It was one of those faith demands that cannot go unrewarded. She took it for granted that we had the lessons to give, and it was no doubt her unquestioning faith that brought our Correspondence School into manifestation. We had often considered the matter of opening such a school, but there seemed to be so much to do that was more pressing that the school remained merely an ideal to be fulfilled sometime in the indefinite future.

The faith shown in the friend's letter quickened our faith, and we felt moved to undertake the work at once. So an agreement was formulated and sent to this friend to sign, and in the few days' time required for the return of the agreement, the first lesson was written and was ready to be mailed to her when the signed agreement came back to us.

And so our first pupil was enrolled, and the Unity Correspondence School, so long a dream, was at last established in the manifest.

When the April number of *Unity* went out, April 15, it carried the first announcement of the school, and in a few days applications for membership began to come in. At this writing, June 4, the enrollment is 268.

The original lessons were written by Charles Fillmore. They were sent out on the freewill offering plan.

In a few months, not only were students enrolled in this new school from all parts of the United States, but also from Canada, Cuba, Hawaii, England, and India. By 1911, over two thousand students had been enrolled. For years the Unity Correspondence School was a principal source of instruction in the Unity teachings and it became one of the bases of study for those who desired to become

Unity teachers and ministers. Its courses are still available for home study to those who have a deeper interest in the teachings of Unity than they can satisfy by reading the books and magazines.

But today most of those who become deeply interested in Unity's teachings want personal instruction. Many of these persons seek out one of the centers and attend classes there. Those who can, come to Unity Village for instruction. Here they may attend Unity Retreats or the Unity Institute for Continuing Education, or they may apply for admittance to the School for Ministerial and Religious Studies—all of which offer a variety of courses and are developments of the Fillmores' early classes.

For several years in the early 1900's, Charles and Myrtle Fillmore taught summer classes in Pueblo and Denver, and in August 1901, they conducted a school in Manitou called "The Colorado Summer School of Metaphysics." Most of the classes of this school were held in a large tent, which seated about 150 persons on its wooden benches. At night, the tent was lighted by coal oil lamps. In the daytime, some of the meetings were held in the open, where the people gathered to hear Mr. Fillmore and the other teachers make their talks.

The Fillmores and some of the students lived in tents set up on the grounds. Grandma Fillmore was along and did her cooking in the Fillmore tent. The three Fillmore boys hiked and played in the mountains. Rick had just become interested in photography. By day he took pictures of the meetings and the teachers and by night he developed his films in the waters of a stream that ran through the grounds. They last taught classes in Colorado in 1902.

The Fillmores had not named their organization Unity School of Christianity idly. Few weeks went by when they were not teaching classes. They taught classes in Truth principles, in prayer, in healing, in prosperity, in numerous allied subjects.

Most of their students came from Kansas City, but always there were a few from other places. Each summer, they conducted what was known as the "Intensive Training School," which drew students from all over the country. This course lasted two weeks and was the origin of the Unity Training School, which for many years was conducted in the Silent Unity Building. In 1930 when Silent Unity moved back to Tracy Avenue, the large building that it had occupied at Unity Village was left empty. So the Fillmores decided to use it to educate Unity teachers and ministers, and they set up the program they called the Training School in it. For years all Unity leaders received their training there, living in the building, a large portion of which was remodeled for use as a dormitory.

Today the building is once more occupied by Silent Unity until completion of the new building in 1989. Then it will once again house the educational facilities. But Unity Village is the center of a number of different educational programs. The Training School has become the Unity School for Religious Studies/Continuing Education Program (CEP). To it go those who wish to experience more understanding of Unity teachings, and those who want to become teachers and counselors in Unity centers. Students go from all over the world. A single class at this school often has many times more students than sat in an earnest circle around Charles and Myrtle Fillmore in the early days of Unity and discussed with them the principles of Truth. Yet it is out of those first small classes in practical Christianity that the larger school has grown.

Each session at USRS-CEP consists of two weeks. Several sessions are held each year, and many students come for more than one session. The curriculum includes classes in public speaking, world religions, New Thought ideas, Bible history and interpretation, Unity principles, counseling, prayer, and other subjects of interest. The students live at Unity Village as if in another world—and such it is, a world apart. As once Jesus went up into the mountain to pray, so today students withdraw into the spiritual environment of Unity Village. At the end of the two weeks when they return to their homes to give to others the ideas they have learned, most of them go fortified in spirit and renewed in mind and body.

Besides USRS-CEP, there are many retreats, each lasting a week, held at Unity Village. The retreats offer a varied program intended to help persons unfold spiritually. They include meditations, lectures, workshops, music, singing, and, of course, much time for relaxation and quiet contemplation.

Also, a part of USRS is the Ministerial Education Program (MEP). This is a school for the preparation of Unity ministers. The school is conducted on a quarterly basis with no summer vacations, and a full two years of class work are required for completion.

The Unity Library, open to all who visit Unity School, contains one of the largest collections of metaphysical and New Thought books in the world.

Many students as well as workers live at Unity Village where there are houses, apartment houses, motels, cottages, dormitories, and trailer courts. Hundreds of visitors eat every day at Unity Inn, a cafeteria famous for its food—especially the vegetarian dishes—throughout Jackson County. Today meat is served, but for years the Inn was strictly a vegetarian cafeteria.

Charles and Myrtle Fillmore did not eat meat. Soon after the founding of Unity, they decided that a meatless diet was conducive to spiritual thinking, and from time to time in their magazines they advocated vegetarianism. They felt that it is more humane and more healthful.

In the early days, when Unity was located on McGee Street and there were only four or five workers, these ate together. There was a stove in the house, and one of the workers was appointed to prepare something hot for everyone. The workers discussed food and its relation to the spiritual life and decided that it would be better for them not to eat meat.

Later when Unity moved to Tracy Avenue, the workers still chose to have their lunch together, so lunch was prepared in the house at the rear of the lot. At first, only workers ate there, but other persons who were interested in vegetarianism expressed a wish to eat there too, so Unity bought a larger house on the corner of Tenth and Tracy and opened a restaurant.

For several years, no set price was charged for the food served there. Those who ate were left free to pay what they wished for their food.

At first, meals were prepared by Unity workers, as had been done on McGee Street. Some of the women from the office would go over and lend a hand at the noon hour, serving at the steam table, clearing tables, and doing whatever was needed. Myrtle Fillmore acted as hostess, going from table to table, talking to her friends, making everyone feel at home.

In a few years, the house on the corner of Tenth and Tracy became too small to accommodate all who wished to eat there, and in 1920 a large restaurant building, decorated by Rickert Fillmore, was erected on the corner of Ninth and Tracy, to which Unity Inn was moved. Here, for thirty years the public and Unity workers were served meatless meals in cafeteria style at nominal prices.

In regard to vegetarianism—as with most of the things they taught—the Fillmores left their students free to accept the teaching or not, as each felt led. The Fillmores were not trying to put forth a creed that their followers had to accept; they were not trying to convert people to a new religion. Those who studied Unity were of all religions (such they still are); they were Methodists and Catholics and Presbyterians; many were not even Christians. To all these, the Fillmores said in effect: "Here are some ideas that we believe to be true. Examine them; study them; accept those that you can use in your life. For the rest, do not let what you cannot accept keep you from accepting what will help you now. The time may come when you can accept these other ideas too. However that may be, if some of our ideas are of practical value to you now, we are happy to be of service." They wrote:

> The first step is to grant all people entire freedom to follow their own understanding no matter how wrong they may appear to us. If they will listen we may express our ideas, but further than that we should not go. They should be free to accept or to reject, as seems good to them.

It was with a great reluctance that Charles and Myrtle Fillmore set up a fixed procedure for becoming a teacher of Unity. "The doors of Unity," they said, "swing in for all who want to come and study, and they swing out just as readily for those who want to go forth and teach."

Charles and Myrtle Fillmore had their own ideas that they believed in passionately. They had even withdrawn from the I.N.T.A. because they felt that their teaching had little in common with that of most of the members of that organization. They felt, however, that everyone should be free to interpret Truth according to his own light. In an early issue of the magazine, Charles Fillmore wrote that the Unity rooms were open to everyone "interested in progressive thought. Teachers, healers, or lecturers passing through the city are invited to make any announcement they wish in connection with their work."

If other teachers wished to sell Unity literature, the Fillmores were happy to have them do so and did not ask what they taught. Their names were listed as Truth teachers in the back of *Unity* magazine at their request. When New Thought lecturers came to Kansas City, many of the regular Unity audience went to hear them. Sometimes the Fillmores themselves went.

When a lecturer who had been a fellow student with the Fillmores at the school of Emma Curtis Hopkins came to Kansas City, Mr. Fillmore heard that a number of Unity students were going to hear him. "There's nothing wrong with him," he said. "He's fine, only he doesn't put Truth in as simple language as we do, and he charges a good stiff fee for it."

Nevertheless, the Fillmores found at last that they had to place limitations on what could be taught in the name of Unity. All over the country, little groups of students who were studying Unity literature began to meet together and to start classes in the Unity teachings. Often those who led these groups knew very little of the teaching of the Fillmores. They held séances, cast horoscopes, told fortunes, read palms, and practiced numerology. The Fillmores themselves did not believe in any of these things and spoke out against them in their magazines. Still they were reluctant to tell other teachers what to teach—even when the teachings were put out under the name of Unity.

In the summer of 1925, at a conference of Unity teachers, a group that did not approve of some of the things that were being taught in the name of Unity but were unlike the teachings of the Fillmores, met together in the Pergola Room at Unity Inn one afternoon and formed what they named "The Unity Annual Conference." They adopted a set of rules to govern the teaching and conduct of leaders of Unity centers and classes.

Although Charles Fillmore told them at first, "I can't see why you want to bind yourselves with a lot of rules and regulations; leave yourselves free," he could see presently that the step they had taken was a necessary one.

This step was taken to assure those who might attend a Unity center that they would receive the same simple, practical teaching of the Fillmores that they were receiving through the Unity literature. The organization changed its name in 1946 to the "Unity Ministers Association." By this time scores of groups had sprung up, not only in the United States but also in many other countries, to study the Unity teachings. Because the Fillmores felt strongly that their movement should not become another denomination, none of these groups at first referred to themselves as churches. Most of them called themselves centers or societies. But today most of them call themselves churches.

Although the Unity centers had their own organization, the Unity Ministers Association, they depended upon Unity School for guidance, leadership, and often financial help. Also, Unity School took full charge of the education of Unity teachers and ministers, and Unity School ordained the ministers when their preparation was completed.

In 1965 Unity School decided that the centers were mature enough to stand on their own feet. It decided that it should no longer be responsible for centers and their leaders; the centers were churches now, and the School's thrust was nondenominational; its literature and prayer ministry served not only those who attended Unity centers, but people in all churches and many who had no church at all. So Unity School asked the centers to form an organization that would take responsibility for all their affairs. The School would continue to help in any way it could, but if problems arose within the churches or among them, they themselves would have to make the decisions concerning them rather than look to Unity School.

In 1966 the centers formed the Association of Unity Churches. They rented space from Unity School and established headquarters at Unity Village, but they became a separate organization, responsible for their own affairs including the licensing and ordination of Unity ministers when their education is completed. The Association of Unity Churches has organized a number of conferences, conventions, and lecture series for those who attend Unity churches. The hundreds of Unity churches throughout the United States and other countries look to the Association for guidance, for help with internal problems, for materials useful in conducting Sunday schools, youth groups, and the like, and for a new minister when one is needed.

Each Unity center or church, however, is an independent organization, financially self-supporting and governed by its own members. Unity remains a very free and loose-knit movement, drawn together more by mutual interest and common spiritual principles than by rules and organization.

The great majority of those who are attracted by the Unity ideas remain in their own churches.

Charles and Myrtle Fillmore did not believe in applying restrictions to the teaching of Truth because they knew that Truth is largely an individual matter: the Spirit of truth is in every person, and it is only through the awakening of this inner Spirit that anyone can come to know Truth. Books and teachers may be of value along the way, but in the final analysis each individual has to find Truth for himself, within himself. It is this belief that is the basis of Charles Fillmore's teaching about the Bible.

Several of Charles Fillmore's books consist of interpretations of the Bible. As early as 1889, he was printing such interpretations in *Unity* magazine.

> Scripture as mere history is not profitable to the overcoming metaphysician; what he looks for is practical instruction in mind operation. . . . When we look deeper than the mere historical recital, we find that there is a veiled meaning, which may be understood by one who is familiar with the operations of his own mind.

Few men have thought more about the meaning of the Bible than Charles Fillmore. To him, it shed light on every phase of human existence, and one of the great tasks that he set for himself was the exposition of the Bible's inner light to men. To him, the Bible was valuable not because it is a history of people who lived thousands of years ago, but because when properly understood it sheds light on our own problems and shows us the way to more abundant health, prosperity, and happiness. To him, the Bible was valuable because of its practicality; he thought of it as a guidebook to daily living.

To Charles Fillmore, the Bible was more than the Word of God. The Word of God is the spirit in man, and the Bible is an attempt "to describe that invisible Word which cannot be described, but must be lived." He wrote:

> Practical metaphysicians do not study the letter of the law. . . . They study mind in its original purity as manifest in themselves and all men. Then they find that the Scriptures are written in cipher—that they veil the movements of ideas under the symbols of men and nations. Bible writers were dealing with ideas all the time. . . . These they represented by the things of sense because they were writing for the instruction of a people who, like children, had to be amused by pictures and catchy stories.

Charles Fillmore's study of the Bible culminated in 1931 with the publication of the *Metaphysical Bible Dictionary,* the most pretentious work published by Unity School. This work is an analysis of the hidden meaning of all the names that appear in the Old and the New Testaments. Although Charles Fillmore had assistance in preparing it, the original idea was his and most of the interpretations that appear were taken from his writings and lectures.

There was much of Daniel in Charles Fillmore, who spent countless hours in prayer. He delighted in hidden meanings. He loved to dream and to interpret dreams. He wrote that God spoke to him through his dreams. He loved to explore the mysteries of spirit. Yet always, he was interested in these matters with a practical end in view. He explored the hidden meaning because he felt that it might contain something that could be applied to the everyday world of fact, something that would help men to live more abundantly. He sought arcane truths, and he sought to apply them to everyday problems. On his winged imagination, he made far flights of mind, and always it was in the hope that he could bring back to the footweary world trudging through its workaday existence some idea that would prove to be of comfort, strength, and inspiration.

Charles Fillmore once said that Unity could be defined as pure "Christian mysticism practically applied to everyday living." He was a mystic, as was Myrtle Fillmore; but they were mystics with a mission, and that mission was to help people have healthier, happier, richer lives. This is what made his approach to religion such a scientific one. In him, the scientific and religious approach to life were a step toward the abundant life that he was preaching.

At the time when Unity was first founded, Darwinism and materialism had taken hold of the minds of people. The church was denouncing science as denying the truths of the Bible, and the exponents of science were claiming that the Bible is full of falsehoods. In the very first issue of *Modern Thought,* Charles Fillmore had an article to the effect that science and religion should resolve their conflict. He saw clearly that the only religion that can stand is one based on Truth and that the only science that will not destroy itself is one based on religious principles.

One of the goals of his writing was to show that science and religion are but two different approaches to the same Truth. He felt that modern physicists, with their theories about the ethers and energy, are approaching with a different set of terms the same truths that Jesus taught when He taught about the kingdom of the heavens and the power of faith and prayer.

In an address that he made at a meeting of the World Fellowship of Faiths held during the Century of Progress in Chicago in 1933, he declared:

> My aim is to prove that science, in developing the unseen forces of the ether is merely revealing the mechanical side of that realm which Jesus called the "kingdom of the heavens."
>
> The approach of religion to the "kingdom" is through Spirit; the approach of science to the same, under the name of the luminiferous ether, is through physics, chemistry, and kindred fields of research.

That science and religion have not worked in unity is borne out by history. Religion functions in the realm of ideas and science in the realm of facts. By facts we mean anything that may be proved by material tests. Christianity has been very jealous of its revelations and has assumed that they are far more valuable than the discoveries of science. When Saint Augustine proclaimed that "nothing is to be accepted save on the authority of the Scriptures," a wall of ecclesiastical authority inclosed Christianity, and the pages of church history testify to the entrenchment within that inclosure of millions of followers of Jesus. There could be no new revelations from God; the slogan of religious authorities was, "Where the Scriptures speak, we speak; where they are silent, we are silent." Then followed the persecution even to death of anyone who dared to discover anything that seemed to conflict with the accepted interpretations of the Bible. The horrors of the Inquisition are almost unspeakable.

But the proved facts of scientific research and discovery have bit by bit broken down the wall of narrow dogmatic assumptions reared by Christianity, and we are finding that we have, like the Pharisees of Jesus' time, been making the dead letter of Scripture revelation take the place of the living Christ. Jesus was a demonstration of the fact of God's existence and power in this world, and when charged by the ecclesiastical congress with breaking their law He thundered, "Ye search the scriptures, because ye think that in them ye have eternal life; and these are they which bear witness of me; and ye will not come to me, that ye may have life." . . . Jesus loved to talk about this kingdom of the heavens and He compared it or said it was "like unto" this and that in many parables and mind pictures. . . .

To perform its miracles, modern science draws upon the kingdom of the heavens. It tells us that out of this kingdom come light, heat, power, color, sound, electricity, magnetism, life, and substance; in fact, that everything that exists in this universe came out of this invisible, omnipresent kingdom of the heavens, the luminiferous ether. Scientists tell us that in their discoveries they have merely touched the hem of the garment of a kingdom that, by further discoveries along the same line, will revolutionize our whole civilization.

It is this scientific approach that especially distinguishes the Unity teachings. Charles Fillmore did not believe that God is an arbitrary and extraneous Being who answers or fails to answer prayer according to His changing whim. He taught that God is law. He taught that life is governed by law, every incident in life, and that as we gain an understanding of the divine law, we can use it to change our life.

"The world," said Charles Fillmore, "is governed by the law of mind action." It was through this belief that he came to Unity's unique concept of prayer—the use of affirmations and denials, spiritual decrees rather than petitions, in addressing God.

Affirmations and denials are statements that deny the reality of undesirable conditions and affirm the reality of God and His good, such as: *There is nothing in all the universe for me to fear, for greater is He that is in me than he that is in the world,* and *I am a radiant, all-wise, all-loving, all-conquering son of God.* Charles Fillmore wrote:

> Prayer is not the beseeching a reluctant God. It is intercommunion with God. "Ye ask, and receive not, because ye ask amiss." Not that we ask for what God is not willing to give, nor what we, as His children may not rightfully ask for and claim; but because we beseech and supplicate, as though God were not willing but possibly might be induced to change and grant our petition. This is a false notion.
>
> "For I, Jehovah, change not." "Jesus Christ is the same yesterday and today, yea and for ever." If God ever did answer prayer, He always does, being the same God. Therefore, if there seems to be any lack of principle, it is in the one who prays. Misunderstanding of the will and nature of our God prevents prayer from being answered.

Prayer does not change God, the unchangeable, but it changes mortals and makes them receptive to that good which is being given without limit. "God is Spirit: and they that worship him must worship in spirit and truth." Translate material desires into their spiritual correspondents and then declare that in Truth and in Spirit you receive that which you desire, and then you will have it materially as well as spiritually. "But seek ye first his kingdom, and his righteousness; and all these things shall be added unto you."

Fifty years before the inception of the science of psychosomatics, which treats of the relationship of the mind to bodily illness, Charles and Myrtle Fillmore were teaching that the ills of our body are the result of our wrong thinking, that disease has its origin in negative mental and emotional states. Over and over, in the early pages of *Unity*, they traced physical disturbances to mental causes. Many years ago, Myrtle was writing to a correspondent:

Perhaps it will help if I tell you that I suffered with a trouble similar to yours for years. And I prayed for healing, many times; and did all I knew to please the Lord; and still my healing did not come. I tried to look over all my faults, and to bring myself into harmony with Truth. After asking the Lord to show me just what was hindering, Spirit spoke to me very clearly, saying, "You have looked among your faults; now, suppose you look among your virtues." And I did; and there I found the cause of the deep-seated physical suffering and congestion!

I had considered it a virtue to control my feelings; to never give way to them, outwardly; to never let anyone know when I was hurt or angered. I kept a calm and pleasant exterior, but inside I sometimes grieved and resented and worried and rebelled. And, my secret thoughts and feelings were cutting and congesting and weakening my vital organs and the walls of my body. As I turned the light of Spirit upon these hidden things, and sought to have Divine Mind transform my very subconsciousness, so that I should

work from an entirely new basis, I was healed and
restored to harmony and strength. There were times,
after the first revelation, when I would forget and
give way to old ways of thinking, and there would
come a physical warning. I have found that whatever
thoughts I harbor do produce some sort of results in
me or my environment; that if I want perfect health, I
must let the law of God, the rules of harmony and
health, come first, regardless of what they do to old
habits and thoughts.

The Fillmores taught that the way for a person to
change a physical condition is to change his thinking.
"People come to me and they ask me for help," said
Charles Fillmore. " 'Ask me to do anything,' they say, 'but
don't ask me to change my thinking.' But they have to
change their thinking if they want to be well."

Over and over, the Fillmores echoed the words of
Paul, "Be transformed by the renewal of your mind."
Charles Fillmore wrote:

> What can a man do with the thoughts of his mind?
> He can do everything with them. They are under his
> absolute control. He can direct them. He can coerce
> them. He can hush them or crush them. He can dis-
> solve them and put others in their place. There is no
> other spot in the universe where man has mastery.
> The dominion that is his by divine right is over his
> own thoughts. When man apprehends this and com-
> mences to exercise that dominion, he has begun to
> open the way to God, the only door to God—through
> mind and thought.

"The purpose of prayer," the Fillmores taught, "is to
change your thinking. God does not change; His will is
always, only good. All that keeps you from your good is
your failure to unify yourself in thought with the Source
of all good, God."

Following this line of thought, the Fillmores worked
out a new technique of prayer, which they called the
silence, using affirmations and denials. They instructed
the student to relax in mind and body, to turn to God in

thought, to think not about the problem but about God, whose wisdom, love, and power are mighty to solve every problem. To enable him to keep his mind away from the problem and on God's presence and power, they taught the student to use affirmations and denials, repeating them over and over. The words themselves had no magic power, but continued concentration on them brought the student to realize the Truth in them. "You will know the truth, and the truth will make you free."

Jesus taught, "And whatever you ask in prayer, you will receive, if you have faith." The Fillmores' technique of prayer is based on this idea of Jesus', and those who apply this idea rediscover what many persons have forgotten, that faithful prayer gets results.

The Fillmores did not advance new teachings. All that they taught is based on the Bible, and especially on the teachings of Jesus. They saw Jesus as the Son of God, the Master, conscious of His oneness with our Father, demonstrating His Sonship in His life, the perfect channel of God's power and love. They felt that Unity is a return to His original teachings, a return needed for centuries. Before they decided to call it "practical Christianity," they had called their teaching "primitive Christianity."

The Fillmores went back to the original teachings of Jesus, and came forth with a modern, seven-day-a-week religious teaching, expressed in up-to-date, easy-to-understand language. They demonstrated that religion has practical value in helping people handle today's problems.

Jesus taught that God is loving and accessible. "The kingdom of God is within you," He said, and Paul told the Athenians, "In him we live and move and have our being." But through the centuries, people had come to believe in God as a stern judge, living in a far-off heaven to which people went after they died.

The Fillmores restated in modern language the great truths that they found in the Bible: "God is within you. You can find Him there. Heaven is a state of mind. You can enter into heaven now."

"God is your loving Father and you are His beloved children," they taught, and repeated as had Jesus the words of the Psalmist, "You are gods, sons of the Most High, all of you."

"Christ in you, the hope of glory!" they declared. "The Christ Spirit is in you, and the Christ power. Claim it now, use it now to remake your life."

The Fillmores lived by the Bible. They studied the misunderstood teachings of Jesus—about the immanence of God, the love of God, the power of believing prayer. Jubilantly in their magazines, in their books, in their talks, they proclaimed these teachings until thousands on thousands of people were putting the teachings into practice and proving with quickened bodies, with minds set free, with lives renewed, that the teachings are true.

Charles and Myrtle Fillmore were people of vision. Their vision is expressed in Mrs. Fillmore's first affirmation, *I am a child of God and therefore I do not inherit sickness.* It was the vision of a way of life better than that which people have so long felt that they are heir to.

The teaching of Charles and Myrtle Fillmore was an affirmation of life. "Live!" they proclaimed. "Live free! Live whole! Live eternally!"

Chapter XIV

The Later Years

"Unto Eternal Life"

CHARLES AND MYRTLE FILLMORE did not believe in
age. They believed that they had constant access to a
fountain of youth, the Spirit within themselves. "Whoever
drinks of the water that I shall give him shall never thirst;
the water that I shall give him will become in him a
spring of water welling up to eternal life."

When Charles Fillmore was nearing fifty, he wrote
in *Unity:*

> About three years ago, the belief in old age began
> to take hold of me. I was nearing the half-century
> mark. I began to get wrinkled and gray, my knees
> tottered, and a great weakness came over me. I did
> not discern the cause at once, but I found in my
> dreams I was associating with old people and it
> gradually dawned upon me that I was coming into
> this phase of race belief. . . .
>
> I spent hours and hours silently affirming my unity
> with the infinite energy of the one true God. I asso-
> ciated with the young, danced with the boys, sang
> songs with them, and for a time took on the frivolity
> of the thoughtless kid. In this way I switched the old
> age current of thought.
>
> Then I went deep down within my body and talked
> to the inner life centers. I told them with firmness
> and decision that I would never submit to the old age
> devil, that I was determined never to give in. Grad-
> ually I felt a new life current coming up from the life

199

center. It was a faint little stream at first, and months
went by before I got it to the surface. Now it is growing strong by leaps and bounds. My cheeks have
filled out, the wrinkles and crow's feet are gone, and
I actually feel like the boy that I am.

Early in his study of spiritual principle, Charles Fillmore came to the conclusion that ill health is unnecessary, that old age is unnecessary, that death is unnecessary. The Fillmores believed in reincarnation; they
thought that they had lived many times before. Charles
even thought that he knew who he had been in previous
incarnations. But the Fillmores did not believe that reincarnation is the final answer. They believed that the recurring process of birth and death over and over again is
not essential, that it is possible for a human being to
come into so great an awareness of his spirituality and of
his life in Spirit that he can transform the very flesh of his
body into spiritual substance, living energy, so that the
body becomes an immortal vehicle of the immortal Spirit
of which it is an expression.

"Science," wrote Charles Fillmore, "is proving by
experimentation that living cells have within them the
elements of continuous life, and scientists are at a loss to
know why man's body should ever die, if it were properly
fed and cleansed."

To the question "Do you expect to live forever?"
Charles answered:

This question is often asked by *Unity* readers.
Some of them seem to think that I am either a fanatic
or a joker if I take myself seriously in the hope that I
shall with Jesus attain eternal life in the body. But
the fact is that I am very serious about the matter. . . .

It seems to me that someone should have initiative
enough to make at least an attempt to raise his body
to the Jesus Christ consciousness. Because none of
the followers of Jesus has attained the victory over
this terror of humanity does not prove that it cannot
be done. . . .

I do not claim that Jesus has unconditionally promised me that I shall overcome death as He overcame

it. The promise is conditional. "He that overcometh, I will give to him to sit down with me in my throne, as I also overcame, and sat down with my Father in his throne," I am trying to come up to His standard. . . .

No man will ever attain anything unless he attempts attainment.

Charles Fillmore never swerved from this belief. In 1919 he went through an illness so serious that some of those who were close to him did not think that he would survive, even though they were affirming Truth for him. For months, he was unable to deliver the Sunday talks. Yet whenever he was able, he was at his office, doing what he could; and always, steadfastly, whatever appearances might indicate, he was affirming health for himself. He came out of the illness with renewed vigor. Through the 1920's, the growth of Unity made ever-increasing demands on his time and energy, but he was able to meet them all.

In 1923 the Fillmores' son Royal passed on. Charles and Myrtle Fillmore had had great expectations of the part that he was to play in the Unity work. Royal had been a big, good-natured, exuberant person with a host of friends, and active in a score of civic enterprises.

Charles and Myrtle Fillmore felt deeply the passing of their son, but even more deeply they felt the truth of the principles they were teaching and the need to cling to those principles with redoubled courage and faith. They had dedicated themselves to helping mankind find a way of life free from sickness, poverty, and death—and they held to their high purpose.

They knew that the way they were trying to go was not an easy one. Charles Fillmore often repeated the words of Napoleon, "There shall be no Alps!" He saw the Alps clearly enough; but he knew that great faith would overcome them.

The Fillmores had been pioneers all their lives. They were not dismayed by appearances. They kept on praying in faith. They kept on affirming the Truth they believed. They kept on affirming life. They knew that unless someone tried to make the overcoming, it would never be made. Someone had to make the start. Even if the first ones who tried did not succeed, nevertheless a first step would be made. They dared to try.

The next few years were years of joy and action for the Fillmores. Unity School was growing at an unprecedented rate: new magazines were being established; the old services were being augmented; new centers were opening; the headquarters at Unity Village was being developed.

At home, they had their family. The Fillmores were people with a warm sense of family ties. Both Lowell and Rickert entered the Unity work, and their parents were able to turn over to them many of the details of running the organization. Both of them married women whom they had met at Unity School. Rickert married Harriet Collins in 1919, and they had two children, Charles Rickert, born in 1921, and Rosemary, born in 1925. Lowell married Alice Lee in 1926. Frances, Royal's daughter, made her home with Lowell and Alice.

Today there are seven great-grandchildren in the family. Charles Rickert married Anne Jones in 1943. Their children are Harriet DeBauge, born in 1944, and Constance Fillmore, born in 1948. In 1976 Constance graduated from Unity School for Ministerial and Religious Studies and is an ordained Unity minister. Rosemary married Ralph Rhea, a Unity minister, in 1968. She has two children by a previous marriage, Stanley Rickert Grace, born in 1948, and Rosalind Grace Tanner, born in 1950. Frances married Robert Lakin in 1945. They have three children, Robert Fillmore Lakin, born in 1946, Charles Edward Lakin, born in 1948, and Frances Lakin Lenzo, born in 1952.

Lowell and Rickert had their homes on Unity Farm, and as their parents spent part of each week at The Arches, they were all often together. Charles and Myrtle Fillmore had many happy times with their family. Like most other grandparents they were sometimes called upon to play the role of babysitter.

"You'd smile," wrote Myrtle Fillmore to her sister, "to see me rushing around, trying to keep up with the many things I find myself 'in for.' First, I want to look after some little thing at home; then meetings; then the letters in the office; then another meeting or two; then a trip downtown; then a nap (if I can crowd one in); then an evening out; then a trip to the Farm, and sometimes the care of one of the little folks; then the trip back, to take up work where I left off! And I just keep getting stronger, and younger, and happier, and more interested in things than ever."

There was scarcely time for a vacation. There was much work to be done, not only their work with Unity School but the spiritual work they were doing with themselves. Mr. Fillmore received many requests to make talks in other cities; his wife wrote in answer to one such request:

"He just isn't much interested in traveling about, and being looked at, and talked to, or even entertained. If he had been the type who likes to travel about, it would have proved that he thought more of such things than he did the delving into the unseen realms of spiritual ideas —and this school, so far as we are concerned, would never have been successfully established."

March 29, 1931, was Charles and Myrtle Fillmore's golden wedding anniversary. It was a Sunday, and when they entered the chapel at 913 Tracy Avenue the congregation was waiting to honor them. They were ushered up to the platform and there, as a tribute to their golden wedding, Ernest C. Wilson performed the Unity marriage ceremony. Myrtle wrote to a friend, "We were quite satisfied to trust the half-century knot that had held us so well, but the new minister surprised us by making it time proof."

That afternoon in Rick's house on Unity Farm, the family had a party for them. Rick took motion pictures of them as they sat on the lawn outside his house. With their children and grandchildren gathered around them and the Unity buildings rising like a backdrop to their joy, this must have been a moment of fulfillment.

A few weeks later, they opened the Unity Training School. In the new school Charles and Myrtle Fillmore taught a class in "Fundamentals of Practical Christianity." That had been the title of the first Unity class that they had taught. Around them once more, a group of students gathered, as students had gathered for forty years, to hear them teach Truth and affirm their faith in life. But this was to be their last class together.

On October 6, 1931, Myrtle Fillmore passed to the invisible side of life.

Those who knew her closely felt that in some way beyond their own power to understand, Mrs. Fillmore had willed to make this change. For months, she had had her secretary put everything in order as if she knew that she was going.

Several times, in earlier years, she had told friends that she personally felt that she had accomplished all that she was able to in this lifetime and wanted to pass on, but that it had been revealed to her that it was not yet time. This time, she had felt strongly that she was going to make the transition.

A short time before her passing, she had been visiting with one of the Unity workers. It was the kind of visit that she liked to make with all the workers, stopping by a desk to pass a few words and to give a benediction and a smile. In the course of the conversation, she mentioned that she wanted to make a change.

"That's fine," the worker answered. "What kind of change?"

"I believe that it would be easier to do the work that is ahead of me from the invisible plane," she said.

"Oh, you mustn't do that," he replied. "We need your help and inspiration, your spiritual guidance here."

"You know that you will have that anyway," she said smiling.

On the Wednesday before her passing, she helped Charles Fillmore lead the evening healing service and the next day she was around the office all day in a gay mood, talking with the workers, writing letters, receiving callers.

That evening, as was customary with her, she left the office in Kansas City and went to The Arches where she usually spent Friday and Saturday. She spent the evening picking apples from the trees around her home. Some friends who came to visit her found her up on a ladder in the orchard. The next morning, she was ill, and on the following Tuesday, she passed away.

Two Sundays later, Charles Fillmore was in his regular place, conducting the service at 913 Tracy Avenue. For forty years every Sunday, Myrtle Fillmore had led the meditation at this meeting. Now Mr. Fillmore took over this part of the service and said:

> Dear friends and co-workers in Christ: It is not our custom here at Unity even to mention the visits of the "last enemy," whom we have resolved finally to overcome, as taught by Jesus.
>
> But there are certain conditions under which we should exchange sympathy and give thanks for that universal unity which these days of stress and strain have brought. I feel your sympathy and I thank you from the bottom of my heart for your many expressions of comfort in thought and word. This occasion is so pregnant with the absence and the presence of the one who has for years stood in my place at this point in our Sunday morning lesson that I am constrained to speak a few words of consolation and comfort, not only for you but for myself.
>
> Personality sorrows and grieves when the bodily presence is withdrawn, but the sense of absence can be overcome when we realize that there is a spiritual bond that cannot be broken. We do not look at life as a "night between two eternities," as do those who, Paul says, "have no hope," because they live and have been educated in a foolish fashion, looking at life as a transitory, material thing; but we who are following Jesus Christ in the resurrection know life as a spiritual thing, and that we live spiritually, if we understand the law of life, and that we shall continue to live in Spirit, "whether in the body or out of the

body." And we know that this spiritual bond is the
only bond that will really endure.

Now where there had been two to think together, to
plan together, to work together in the cause of Unity and
in the service of the Truth that they had discovered and
believed in, Charles Fillmore was alone. Yet he was not
alone. He was a man with friends in every part of the
world. And the Father abiding in him was a real and
living presence in his life.

For thirty years, except for two brief visits to Chicago
and one to New York, Charles Fillmore had stayed at
work in Kansas City. During all that time, he had never
taken a real vacation. Everywhere there were thousands
of people who wanted to make his acquaintance, who
wanted to see and hear this man whose teachings had
meant so much to their lives.

Charles Fillmore began to turn over more and more
of the details of running Unity School to the people
around him, especially to his sons, Lowell and Rick.
Lowell became President of Unity School and Rickert
became Secretary. Yet Charles did not retire as active
head of Unity. He was like the captain of a ship who
turns the helm over to the mate. He was there in the
cabin if he was needed, and occasionally he came out on
the bridge to keep a weather eye on what was going on.
Few steps were taken without his approval.

In December 1933, Charles Fillmore, after more than
forty years of continuous service, retired from the pulpit
of the Unity Society of Practical Christianity in Kansas
City.

On December 31, 1933, he married Cora G. Dedrick,
who had for many years served him and Myrtle Fillmore
as private secretary and at one time had been the director
of Silent Unity. They were married at Lowell Fillmore's
home in Unity Village.

The next day, the two left for California; and Charles
Fillmore, who had always been trying the untried, was
off on yet another new venture. He went on a lecture

tour, the first of many that were to fill the remainder of his life and take him to every part of the nation.

The tour got off to an exciting start. The first lecture was in Los Angeles. Into the Shrine Auditorium, seven thousand two hundred persons jammed to hear him speak, while more than one thousand others were turned away for lack of room.

Charles Fillmore looked the crowd over (many times larger than any he had ever addressed) from behind the red plush curtain. When at last he went out to face the audience, "I feel like a little boy away from home," he began. When the speech ended the crowd rose from its seats and in a wave of applause swept onto the stage to tell this "little boy away from home" how much they loved him and how much his teachings had meant in their lives. He had to be hurried out of the press of his well-wishers.

From Los Angeles, Mr. Fillmore went to San Jose, where the Unity center was in need of funds. He gave a series of talks and turned over the offerings to the center. Then it was on to San Francisco where thousands more thronged to listen to him and to give him an ovation. It was late in the spring of 1934 before he was back in Kansas City, in time to teach at the Training School.

The next winter, Mr. Fillmore was off on another lecture tour, this time through the northeast section of the country. This tour, like most of those that were to follow, was made by automobile. Although at home he was a late riser, when he was traveling he was up early, ready for the day's drive to the next town. He usually stayed in tourist cabins and stopped to eat his lunch by the side of the road from an icebox carried in the car. Often, if he did not have a speech to make, in the evening he would go to the motion picture show, which he loved to attend. Charles Fillmore was a good traveler. Once when his companions thought to fix some pillows in the back seat so that he could lie down, he had them taken out, saying he wanted to sit up and see what was going on.

All his life, Charles Fillmore had unusual stores of

energy. He once wrote in *Unity:*

> Complaints are coming in that *Unity* is not being
> issued on time. I am the one responsible for this. The
> Publishing Department waits on my matter and is
> delayed when I am not prompt. I have undertaken
> more writing than I can well accomplish with my
> other duties. Yet I work twenty-one hours out of
> twenty-four and have kept it up at this pace for sev-
> eral years. It is daylight every morning before I catch
> the few hours' sleep that "knits up the raveled
> sleeve." This three hours' waste will eventually be
> overcome, and I shall work right through without a
> wink.

Later when the Fillmores became interested in radio,
Charles Fillmore would often stay up most of the night in
order to broadcast a talk in the early morning hours.

The Fillmores were among the first to see the possibilities in radio; Unity was probably the first organization
to give religious broadcasts. In 1924 Unity School purchased radio station WOQ, the oldest licensed broadcasting station in the Midwest. Unity speakers had been giving talks over the station for two years before that time.

The first Unity talks were broadcast by Francis J.
Gable from the window of a downtown store, where a
crowd could gather outside to watch the newfangled contraption in operation. When Unity bought WOQ, the studio was moved to the building at 917 Tracy.

Charles Fillmore loved to speak on the radio and
would make two or three talks a week. The studio had to
be completely closed during broadcasts, even in hot
summer weather; use of electric fans was prohibited because it would interfere with the broadcasting. Nevertheless it was not unusual for Mr. Fillmore, with the perspi-
ration streaming from him, to deliver an hour's speech
over the radio.

Every week or two, he would stay up until 3 or 4
o'clock in the morning and make an hour's talk at that
time. He would prepare a long time ahead for these
speeches. In those years, there were few stations and

none that gave all-night programs, so in the early morning WOQ had the air waves virtually to itself. It was on a good frequency and its programs were picked up all over the country. Charles Fillmore had announcements of many of these early-morning broadcasts in the magazines, and Unity students everywhere were able to tune in and receive the program. People wrote from the farthest corners of the country to Mr. Fillmore that they had set their alarm clock and gotten up to listen to him.

Those were the years when owners of radio sets tried to see what distant stations they could receive, and many people had their first introduction to the Unity teaching on these early-morning broadcasts. Letters came from night watchmen and fire stations and garages all over the United States.

Charles Fillmore never ceased to be a man of action, a man of decision. On one of their lecture trips to Florida, Charles and Cora Fillmore stopped at a tourist court. Their cottage had a large porch in front of it that caught Mr. Fillmore's fancy. Cora Fillmore owned a piece of land with a small cabin on it near Unity Farm, and they had talked about building a home on it.

"You know, Cora," Charles Fillmore told her, "it would be nice if we had a place with a porch like this." Right then he measured the porch. Late into that night, he was planning exactly the kind of home he wanted. Before he fell asleep, he had sent a night letter to a builder in Lee's Summit describing the house that he had planned and ordering its construction. He wanted it ready, he wrote, when he returned home from the trip.

It was in this house that Charles Fillmore spent most of his last twelve years. It was located in some wooded hills about one quarter of a mile southwest of Unity Village. Because Mr. Fillmore always loved to have people around him, this house, like his others, was often filled with guests and visitors. Sometimes friends would come and stay for weeks at a time.

He had some apartments built over his garage to provide a place for some of the young people employed at Unity to live. Often late into the night, his young tenants sat around the Fillmore hearth talking and laughing with their host—and also praying.

A few years later on one of his lecture trips to California, Charles Fillmore bought a house in the San Fernando Valley outside Los Angeles. Thereafter, he divided the year between his two homes, writing and lecturing in California in the winter and teaching at the Training School at Unity Farm in the summer.

To those around him, Charles Fillmore never seemed to grow old. Those who were close to him said that throughout the last years of his life his crippled leg was constantly improving, filling out, growing stronger. One of the features that strangers noticed first about him was his radiantly pink skin. "The skin on his face shone," perhaps as that of Moses had shone as he returned to the valley from Mount Sinai after having received from God the Ten Commandments.

He discovered on his lecture tours that many in the audience expected a large, aggressive man and were astounded at the slight, gentle, twinkling person who came out upon the platform. He liked to tell the story of how on one of his first tours, as he walked onto the platform one evening, he saw two little old ladies sitting down in front peering eagerly up at him. As he seated himself and closed his eyes to enter into the silence—as was his custom when he had a speech to make—he overheard one of the ladies remark to the other: "So that's him, is it?—all washed and pink and powdered like a baby."

Charles Fillmore had a fountain of youth within him, and the waters were forever joyously bubbling up. Life to him was a journey in jubilance. In his eighties, he started taking singing lessons. As his crippled leg improved, he told his friends he was considering taking dancing lessons.

He loved to make up affirmations and would write them on large sheets of paper in heavy black characters. Charles Fillmore had an unusual handwriting. The powerful lines of his signature almost always brought comment from persons who saw it for the first time. At ninety-four, his handwriting was as vigorous as a young man's. He used special writing crayons, and with these he wrote out by hand all his works, books, lectures, affirmations. He left a trail of affirmations wherever he went, like sparks struck from the anvil of faith. A few months before he passed on, he wrote this one:

> *I fairly sizzle with zeal and enthusiasm and spring forth with a mighty faith to do the things that ought to be done by me.*

A short time before his passing, he was approached with the suggestion that he get together some biographical material about himself. "Wait another hundred years," was his reply.

Charles Fillmore never gave up his hope of eternal life in the body, in his body. When he was ninety-two he wrote in *Unity* magazine:

> In my article in the August 1946 *Unity*, I stated that I had such a vital realization of Jesus' promise "If a man keep my word, he shall never see death" that I should never pass out of this body. Subscribers are now asking if I mean that I shall live forever in the flesh body. I answered that point in the article as definitely as it can be answered in words. I expect to associate with those in the flesh and be known as the same person that I have been for ninety-two years, but my body will be changed in appearance from that of an old man to a young man with a perfectly healthy body.
>
> I do not claim that I have yet attained that perfection but I am on the way. My leg is still out of joint but it is improving as I continue to work under the direction and guidance of Spirit.
>
> Some of my friends think that it is unwise for me to make this public statement of my conviction that I shall overcome death, that if I fail it will be detrimental to the Unity cause. I am not going to admit any such possibility; I am like Napoleon's drummer boy. I do not know how to beat a retreat and am not going to learn.

Charles Fillmore worked on as long as his undefeatable spirit could move his body. In February of 1948, he was still making speeches at Unity centers in Los Angeles. There he became ill. It was the same ailment that he had had some thirty years before when some of those around him had felt that he would not survive.

In April he came back to his home near Unity Village. From then on, he began slowly to slip away. Occasionally he was able to sit up, but for the most part he lay in bed.

He showed no fear of death. "I am facing it, but I am not afraid of it," he said.

He never lost his sense of humor. When someone made a witticism or said something pleasant to him, he never failed to smile.

Often Cora Fillmore would read him things that he himself had written. Sometimes he did not recognize them, as they were the manuscripts of talks that he had delivered and forgotten years before, but he always liked them. "That's logical," he would say of some passage as she read. "I can see that."

Once he asked of a friend who came into his room, "Do you know what the most important words in the world are?"

The friend shook her head. "No, Mr. Fillmore, I don't," she replied.

"'Christ in you, the hope of glory'—those are the most important words in the world." He lay silent for a moment, then he repeated, "'Christ in you, the hope of glory.'"

Several days before his passing, he slipped into a coma from which he emerged only for brief intervals. He knew that death was not far away. He said, "I am going to have a new body, anyway, and this time it's going to be a perfect body."

Still he did not accept the necessity of death. All his life he had affirmed life, believed in life, lived to the full. "The last enemy to be destroyed is death," Paul had said. To Charles Fillmore, this was the goal. He had believed in the divine possibility of its attainment all his life and, though it did not look as though he himself was to attain it, he was not going to relinquish it. He held steadfast to his faith. Even at the end he expressed it.

He would have kept his body, however unsuited it may have been as a vehicle for such a vital spirit. Charles Fillmore could not have willed otherwise. "I do not know how to beat a retreat," he had written. He did not know how to affirm anything else than life.

Shortly before his passing, he began to have a vision. It recurred several times, always the same one, a vision that he had held to all his life, that he had done his utmost to make a reality upon the earth. "Do you see it? Do you see it?" he would ask, staring intently upward. "The new Jerusalem, coming down from God, the new heaven and the new earth—don't you see it?"

His son Lowell spent the last night at his bedside. Charles was asleep throughout the night. At 10 o'clock on Monday morning, July 5, 1948, he woke, smiled as if at someone that he saw and recognized, and was gone.

Across the way at Unity Village, the activity had come to a halt because of the Fourth of July holiday. The shells of the buildings that were in process of construction stood empty. The printing presses were idle. The workers were gone from their desks in the building at 917 Tracy Avenue. Only a little group in Silent Unity was keeping the constant vigil of prayer.

The next morning, Unity Village rang with the sound of men and machinery at work, rushing the buildings toward completion. The presses were thundering out the magazines that bore witness to the faith of the Fillmores. The Unity workers were back at their desks in Kansas City, sending out books and magazines, answering the cry for prayer. From fifty radio stations scattered in many parts of the globe, the Unity Viewpoint was being broadcast. The work of Unity was going right on. It was as Charles Fillmore would have wanted it to be.

Chapter XV

A Worldwide Influence

"That They May Have Life"

THE WORK OF UNITY is going right on. Many years have gone by since the passing of Charles and Myrtle Fillmore. Cora Fillmore passed in 1955. Rickert Fillmore passed in 1965. Lowell Fillmore made his transition in 1975. Under the direction of Charles Rickert Fillmore, the organization that Charles and Myrtle built grows on; the ideas that they taught have an everlasting, ever-expanding influence; their teaching plays a powerful part in the lives of more and more people.

Because Charles and Myrtle Fillmore built on the rock of principle instead of on the sands of personality, they are as much alive today as they ever were. They live in every prayer uttered at Unity School; they live in the words of this book and in all the words of all the magazines and books that go forth in the name of Unity; they live in the lives of all—perhaps you are one—who have changed their lives by using Truth.

How shall we measure the influence of Charles and Myrtle Fillmore? Can it be measured by the Unity literature?

Almost two-hundred million pieces of mail pour out from Unity School each year. There are three English language magazines: *Unity, Daily Word,* and *Wee Wisdom,* and there are almost two million subscribers to these magazines.

Besides the magazines, Unity publishes scores of

books and hundreds of pamphlets. The Unity Book Club
with selections every two months brings Unity's books to
tens of thousands of readers. These books and magazines
go to people of all faiths, Christian and non-Christian.

Daily Word is published in eight languages. One of
these, *La Palabra Diaria* in Spanish, printed at Unity Village, goes to fifty thousand subscribers. The other trans-
lations are all printed in other countries. The French
edition, *La Parole Quotidienne,* goes to thousands of subscribers in Quebec, Canada, as well as to those in France.
Unity literature has been published in Dutch, French,
Afrikaans, Tamil, Gujarati, Greek, German, Portuguese,
Spanish, Russian, Ibo, Japanese, Swedish, Italian, and
Korean. Once Unity printed a peace prayer in sixteen
languages, but these were not enough to meet the needs
of all its students. A letter came to Unity headquarters
from a small town in the interior of India. A copy of *Daily
Word* containing the prayer had reached there, and a
man who had read it wrote in to ask why the prayer had
not been printed in Hindustani. He sent a translation of it
in that tongue.

Through its literature Unity's influence spread
through many countries long before anyone from Unity
headquarters ever visited them. Many years ago, a Nige-
rian visiting the United States liked the Unity literature,
took it home with him, and it turned out to be popular
with his fellow countrymen. Later, a geologist making
notes in Nigeria wrote that there is even a drumbeat that
signifies Unity, and today there are many Unity churches
and thousands of Unity students scattered throughout
that country. The Unity influence is spreading rapidly
throughout all of Africa.

For years, the interest in Unity has grown throughout
the West Indies until today there are many thousands of
Unity students and readers in all those islands and in
Central and South America. In San Juan, Puerto Rico,
there is even a school, the *Instituto Unity de Christian-
ismo Practico,* that trains Unity teachers in Spanish.
Throughout this area, too, the work grew through the

literature, though today there are a number of Unity churches and study groups in the area.

Unity's literature has penetrated into the farthest corners of the earth. Sheep ranchers in the interior of Australia and Eskimos in Alaska subscribe to its magazines, and read its books and pamphlets. Some of it is carried behind the Iron Curtain and into China.

Through Silent-70 the literature goes free of charge to about eight thousand public institutions in the United States and other countries. *Lessons in Truth, Finding the Christ in Ourselves, Unity* magazine, *Daily Word,* and *Wee Wisdom* are printed in Braille and distributed free to the blind, and new Unity literature will continue to be printed in Braille. Into leper colonies, orphanages, prisons, and hospitals, the Unity message freely given goes to bless hundreds of thousands of "sick" and "unfortunate" persons in every part of the earth.

If we measured the influence of the Fillmores by the scope of the Unity literature, we should conclude that their influence goes far. But their influence goes beyond the printed word.

Their influence goes beyond the spoken word, too. Today in Unity centers and churches in hundreds of cities, classes in Unity are taught, Unity lectures are given, Unity services are conducted.

Every week at Unity School of Christianity and in Unity centers, lectures, lessons, meditations, programs of every description are recorded on tape and distributed to eager listeners; thousands of cassettes go out from Unity School each month.

In 1934 radio station WOQ was discontinued, but today Unity School produces radio and television programs that are broadcast from hundreds of stations. Its public service program, *The Word,* reaches uncounted millions, and celebrities from many fields have taken part in it. Besides the programs that originate at Unity School, Unity ministers in many cities have their own radio and television programs. It is impossible to estimate the number of people the Unity message is reaching through radio and television.

Yet the influence of the Fillmores is even wider than this. Countless numbers of writers and teachers and ministers have absorbed the Unity idea, and from pulpits and books that have no "direct" connection with the Unity movement, the Fillmores' idea goes forth.

Protestant ministers have used Unity materials to enhance their sermons; Catholic priests and nuns have used Unity ideas in their work. Perhaps the greatest and subtlest influence of the Fillmores has been this: the unavowed and silent impact their teachings have had on the religious life of our time.

Their emphasis on positive thinking, their philosophy that life is consciousness and we can change our life by changing our thinking, their doctrine of the divine potential, their insistence that the world is the good work of a perfect Intelligence, their refusal to believe that God's will for us can be less than ultimate perfection, their teaching that the purpose of prayer and meditation is not to change God but to change us—all this has affected the message of thousands of traditional ministers and popular writers, served to midwife the birth of new organizations, both religious and secular, and inspired material for countless newspaper and magazine articles and radio and television programs. The influence of Unity has not always been avowed; perhaps it has not even been recognized, but it has not been a small one.

How then shall we measure Charles and Myrtle Fillmore's contribution to humanity? The contribution of some people can be measured by the buildings they left behind them. Can we understand the Fillmores better by looking at the buildings they built to house the Unity work?

The Fillmores began their work in rented rooms in a downtown building in Kansas City. Today on the Country Club Plaza of Kansas City stands the Unity Temple, a magnificent edifice with a sanctuary seating fifteen hundred, a fellowship hall seating eight hundred, and two smaller chapels—the Charles Fillmore Chapel and the Myrtle Fillmore Chapel—and an array of Sunday-school rooms. This handsome building is only one of seven Unity centers that serve the Kansas City area.

And in many other cities, Unity centers have erected their church buildings, some large, some small, some elaborate, some plain—but all of them there because the Fillmores lived and taught. And the building has scarcely begun. Year by year, more and more Unity churches and centers and study groups open in more and more cities.

Yet the contribution of the Fillmores cannot be measured by all these buildings. It cannot be measured by the more than 1400 acres that are Unity headquarters at Unity Village. Walk here among the lanes and paths, across the lawns, through the gardens and the orchards, or pause beside a wayside bench where two students are discussing some point of Truth, and you may begin to catch something of what Charles and Myrtle Fillmore mean to humanity, for there is a tranquil air about this place that blesses everyone who visits it. Here are rock walls covered with rambling roses, and crude stone bridges arching over quiet streams. Flights of stone steps climb up and down green slopes. Lanes wind past slate-roofed cottages, lanes rimmed with poplars that reach up like spires. Fountains laugh in the sunlight, and calm pools reflect the stillness of the trees that edge them round and the peace in the hearts of those who come to discourse or to meditate by their still waters. The sun sparkles on the red-tiled roofs of the many-windowed, cloistered buildings where the spiritual work goes on night and day. Beside the highway rises the Tower, a waymark, a guidepost, a symbol of strength, an emblem of faith, a promise of prayer.

You may come even closer to understanding the contribution of Charles and Myrtle Fillmore if, some dark night, you will enter the grounds at Unity Village. From a window of one of the rooms in the Silent Unity Building a light will be shining. This is a window in the Silent Unity telephone prayer room. There workers remain on constant

duty, serving and praying, waiting for a call that may
come from a home nearby or from the farthest ends of the
earth, waiting not only for a call that may come over the
telephone but also for a silent call that may come from
the sick and lonely heart of someone somewhere who in
the moment of his need is silently, and from afar, turning
in his mind to God through Unity. This year, almost half a
million persons will call Silent Unity by telephone, and
more than a million others will write for prayers.

The contribution of the Fillmores is more than one of
words or buildings. It is one of hearts and minds and lives
rebuilt by the transforming touch of their ideas, centered
in Christ.

Human beings have always been burdened by the
belief that they were born to suffer and die, to be buf-
feted by evil chance. They have thought of God as far
removed from them, willing suffering and death.

The Fillmores dared to set us free. They knew that
God is near, as near as one's own thoughts, as near as
one's own heart, as near as one's own faith and love and
wisdom. They saw that we are bound not by the will of
God but by the limitations of our own minds and they
dared to strike off the shackles of the mind. They turned
people back to the teachings of Jesus—"Ask, and it will
be given you"; "According to your faith be it done to
you"; "Love one another." They showed that by the application of His simple teachings to daily living we can
transform our lives.

If you wish to catch the meaning of the Fillmores, do
not seek in printed page and spoken word. Look about
you. Seek for their meaning in the lives they have transformed. You may find it in the life of your own neighbor.

On a ranch in western Texas, a rider dismounts from
his horse. As he stands looking out across the plains, his
thought turns to his wife who is ill. As anxiety starts to
surge into his mind, he thinks of the words of the prayer
on the card that came from Unity, and for a moment he
repeats them silently.

In a room of a London hospital, a mother is waiting.

Her daughter has just been taken to the operating room. The doctors have given her little hope. But the mother is not thinking of her fears; instead she has taken from her handbag a little magazine. On the cover is the name *Daily Word*. She opens it and turns to the lesson for the day and she reads: *I am enfolded in the one great Heart that beats for all. My mind is at peace, and I am healed.*

On a ship in the Pacific, a sailor has been reading a magazine called *Unity*. He never heard of Unity before, but he found this magazine among those placed aboard ship for the men to read. He has read it through. Now he is reading it again. He does not know much about religion, but these ideas sound practical. He has a lot of time. He has decided he will see what prayer can do. He quiets his thoughts. *"God is my help in every need,"* he declares silently.

A woman sits alone in a small house in Florida. Her husband went to work disheartened despite her efforts to cheer him up. With the rising prices, they seem to be getting farther and farther behind with their bills. Now she takes out her prosperity bank. She drops a coin into it. She repeats the prayer printed on the back of the bank: *"The Spirit of the Lord goes before me, and my health, happiness, prosperity, and success are assured."* Silently she prays for God's wisdom and love to make their way clear.

In a Roman villa, a countess is preparing to go to sleep. From the drawer of the table beside her bed, she takes out a typewritten letter. It is creased and blurred from many readings; but she reads again, as she has read many times since she received it long ago: "Dear Friend: Silent Unity has received your letter and is praying with you."

In Lee's Summit, Missouri, a worker from Unity headquarters has just turned away from the telephone. When she arrived home after her day's work, she found her little girl ill. Now as she hangs up the receiver, the familiar words are ringing with reassurance in her mind: "Silent Unity will be praying with you; God is with your little girl."

A young man is sitting alone in a hotel room. Tomorrow he is going to see the head of a company about a new job, and he is anxious. He has turned on the television, but is paying no attention. Suddenly his thought is caught by the words a well-known television star is saying: "It may seem like a platitude to say that you can accomplish whatever you really want to accomplish. Platitude or not, it's obvious that the words 'I can't' are the most futile words we can use." He listens as the words go on and end, "Remember, the word is *can*." "Yes, I believe I can," the young man says to himself.

A prisoner in a penitentiary in New York has been studying a book that he received from an organization called Silent-70. The name of the book is *Lessons in Truth*. He began to read in doubt but as he read, something about this book caught hold of his imagination; this is a different kind of religion. He turns to the first lesson; "Bondage or Liberty, Which?" he reads.

If you would find the true message of Charles and Myrtle Fillmore, turn into your own heart and pray. Live for a time by the Unity idea: dare to believe that God is your health; dare to believe that He is your support; dare to believe that you have in you all the ideas that you will ever need for a happy and successful life; dare to be generous, loving, free. Then in your own liberated spirit, in your own liberated life, you will understand what Charles and Myrtle Fillmore came to teach.

"I came that they may have life, and may have it abundantly."

"According to your faith be it done unto you."

Appendix A

From the Writings of Myrtle Fillmore

Letters to God

Some of the letters I addressed to God and some to Christ Jesus. I wrote just as one would to a kind, loving, and generous parent . . . a parent whose delight it is to provide every rich and beautiful blessing for a much-loved child. Of course, I did not mail these letters, but put them in a drawer, and about once a week I would take them out and read them over, and bless God for His goodness and wondrous love.

To the Lord of my manifestation: I heartily desire to purge myself of personality—I would know no man after the flesh, only Jesus Christ, and Him crucified. I would stand, so conscious of my oneness with Thee, that personal affection would have no power to move me. I would be so immersed in Thy love I could not feel the neglect— nor the withdrawal of human affections. I would be so far-seeing and wise that nothing on the plane of personal affection could make me unhappy or divert me from the consciousness of the Love that never faileth.

I would not be swerved by personality.

I would be so unified with the knowledge of my wisdom and strength and ability in Thee that I could always speak the Word with power, clearness and conviction.

I would know no authority, lean on nobody's thought or opinion.

I would stand fast in the knowledge that I am Thy thought going forth into unhindered expression.

Dear blessed Lord, strengthen me, in this blessed purpose and deliver me always from the adverse and personal sense of existence—I in Thee, blessed One, and Thou in me made perfect in harmonious Mind. Hold me to the knowledge that by divine inheritance I am beyond the influence of personal and external conditions—and that I do always recognize my inherent powers and assert my divinity in Christ. Witness this Spirit of Truth.

To Him my soul adores:

Holy One, I would do Thy will—I will—I would give all that I am, all that I am capable of being into Thy keeping. I would think Thy thoughts after Thee. I would give my life in making manifest Thy will in all my words and works. I would be dependent on Thee alone for my inspiration and incentive. I would know or acknowledge no other source. Thou in me and I in Thee and they in us made perfect in one. Thou has sent me into the world. Thou only can direct and vitalize my effort. Help me realize this momently. There are none beside Thee.

Dear Lord of my Being, alone with Thee I am asking, What am I? Who am I? Where am I? In answer there comes from within, "I am not what I seem." Flesh and blood do not reveal me to myself. Back of personal estimate comes the consciousness that some way I am inseparably joined with Thee, and until my union is acknowledged and consummated through divine cooperation of Spirit, soul, and body, I am not content nor at-one with Thee in consciousness. "I am that I am." I am Thy all possibility. Where I am in reality is in Thy bosom. Where I am in the world of effects depends upon what I think I am.

Lord of my Being, I would be unentangled from the servitude and vicissitudes of the formed world. I would do all Thou wouldst have me to do. I would be "in the world but not of it." I would dwell in the gloriousness of Thy omnipresent companionship. I would always be still enough to hear Thy voice instead of the confusion and clamor of the senses. I would know and not assume. I would truly live and not exist. Give me, dear Lord, Thy conscious support and let me be filled with the love and zeal that give character and direction to the activities of mind and body. "I am in Thee and Thou in me and they in us, made perfect in One."

Jesus Christ

The Unity teaching is based on the Jesus Christ teaching, and naturally we advise all people to hold firmly and steadfastly to the principles taught and demonstrated by this first Christian metaphysician. We have found in Christianity rightly interpreted more Truth than in any of the other religions we have dipped into; consequently we advocate it.

We have found Jesus to be the Great Teacher, accessible to all who have faith in and understand the spiritual principles that He sets forth. Jesus as a superman is here in our midst and we can every one of us receive instruction direct from Him if we ask Him, and agree to carry out in our life what He teaches. So if we want all that is contained in Christianity, Mohammedanism, and every other religion or religious cult that came out of Christianity, we should ask Jesus about it and He will show us the Truth just as fast as we develop our own spiritual nature to the point where He can import it to us. Jesus cannot reach the minds that are immersed in materialism. By those immersed in materialism we mean not only those who deal with the most material elements in the world but also those who have materialized Christianity.

To insure success and to inspire faith and confidence in ourselves and our undertaking, we should always have Christ as the source of our inspiration and prosperity. Our success and satisfaction in business, in home, in our social life is always greater when we take Christ Jesus as our partner; it is "Christ in you, the hope of glory." Why not follow in the footsteps of One who has demonstrated and proved every step of the way?

God's love for us, for all His children, is so great that He sent Jesus Christ to be the Way-Shower to lead us to a greater realization of our heavenly Father's love and will for us. Jesus Christ is not merely a divine man who lived many centuries ago and whose life and works are to be considered past history. The Christ presence within our own soul is the Great Physician who has wisdom and power to heal and to adjust in divine order every function of our body temple.

There's a distinction between Jesus Christ, the man, and the perfect-man idea that God has created and implanted in each of us, His children. The Christ Mind is the crystal-clear mind that is not blurred by the "becoming" things of which the senses tell us, nor by the reports of the intellect which are records of man's experiments day by day. The Christ Mind gives us an idea in its entirety and then we work it out in our own consciousness and body and affairs.

For example, the Christ idea of love is given us, God love. Love unifies us with God, our source, and we know that we are good and true and fearless from within, because we let these God qualities well up from the center of our being. But love alone would not enable us to keep our balance; it would draw us here and there without regard to what we accomplished. And here is where we begin to see the difference between the man Jesus Christ as we know Him, and the men who have fallen so far short of what we term goodness and real power. Jesus exercised all the God qualities we have yet been able to discern in a masterly way. God love was expressed by Him; but it was supplemented and balanced by God wisdom, and power, and judgment, and will, and zeal, and life, and renunciation, and strength, and order, and imagination, and faith. Love drew Him to people; but good judgment held Him to a course of action that resulted in a success more far-reaching than any of us have yet realized.

Jesus is the individual who made the complete union of mind, soul, and body in Spirit. He brought forth into expression the Christ, the God-Mind within, and consciously identified Himself with the Father. God is not a person; "God is Spirit."

Jesus Christ has merged His wonderful consciousness with the race consciousness, that we may turn to Him and receive into our own mind the understanding of life and the activities of mind that result in freedom from the limitations of the race beliefs and the intellectual reasonings. We can each quicken our own Christ Mind, by dwelling upon the Truth that we are one with Jesus Christ and one with God, through the understanding that Jesus the Christ helps us to unfold.

Prayer

Sometimes we pray to a God outside of ourselves. It is the God in the midst of us that frees and heals.

With our eye of faith we must see God in our flesh, see that wholeness for which we are praying in every part of the body temple. "Know ye not that your body is a temple of the Holy Spirit which is in you . . . glorify God therefore in your body."

Prayers aren't *sent out* at all! Sometimes that is our trouble. Where would we be sending our prayers? As individuals we should direct them to our own mind and heart and affairs. We commune with God-Mind within our own consciousness. Prayer is an exercise to change our own thought habits and our living habits, that we may set up a new and better activity, in accord with the divine law rather than with the suggestions we have received from various sources.

We sometimes think that we pray when we read and declare certain statements of Truth. We have very little idea of the way in which the answers to those prayers are coming. And we do not prove that we expect them to be answered. For almost immediately after praying we go on doing the things we have been doing, which does not allow of any answers. And we think and say that which is not in accord with the prayers we have made. For example, we go into the silence and declare statements of prosperity. Then in writing a letter we speak of lack and failure and longing. Which proves that we have those thoughts and feelings of lack in our heart and that we are really dwelling on them more strongly than we do on the Truth that we have prayed.

Prayer, then, is to change mind and heart so that God's omnipresent good may fill our mind and heart and manifest in our life. If we do not keep on thinking in accord with the prayers we have made, we do not get good results. For all thought is formative; all thought has its effect in our life. When some of our thought energy is expended in negative beliefs and feelings, and we show that we have old mental habits in the subconscious mind, we get those old negative results—even when we are praying daily and when others are praying for us.

We have a very decided part; we are to cease worrying, and being anxious, and thinking and speaking of the past and of the apparent lack and idleness. We are to concentrate all our attention upon the Truth of God, and the truth of our own being, upon the very things we would see taking place in our life. We cannot do this so long as we have negative thoughts in our heart.

As we pray, the word of life is going down into us, breaking up old fixed beliefs and reorganizing our life. The word of life—life as God has planned it—is taking hold of our subconsciousness, and we know that we are free and will begin to use our freedom. Working in the consciousness of freedom, we will be happy and well and busy and prosperous. But our attention will be upon what we are doing rather than upon outer results. The results will take care of themselves once we have started our foundation in Truth.

"With God all things are possible." Those who receive spiritual help are the ones who place their undivided faith in God and who bring their thinking in line with His Truth. "Ye shall know the truth, and the truth shall make you free."

Prayer, as Jesus Christ understood and used it, is communion with God; the communion of the child with his Father; the splendid confidential talks of the son with the Father. This communion is an attitude of mind and heart that lifts the individual into a wonderful sense of oneness with God, who is Spirit, the source of every good and perfect thing, and the substance that supplies all the child's needs—whether they are spiritual needs, social needs, mental needs, physical needs, or needs of a financial nature. Positive declaration of the truth of one's unity with God sets up a new current of thought power, which delivers one from the old beliefs and their depression. And when the soul is lifted up and becomes positive, the body and the affairs are readily healed.

Sometimes I have written a letter to God when I have wanted to be sure that something would have divine consideration and love and attention. I have written the letter, and laid it away, in the assurance that the eyes of the loving and all-wise Father were seeing my letter and knowing my heart and working to find ways to bless me and help me to grow. So I suggest that *you* write a letter to God, telling, putting into words, that which your heart holds and hopes for. Have faith that God is seeing your letter and your heart, and that there is wisdom and power and freedom and love to accomplish that which will meet your needs. After you have placed your heart's desires with God, don't be anxious, or worried, or negative. Don't even be looking for signs that He has responded. Just busy yourself with the work He gives, and with study and prayer to develop yourself into a real companion and a real radiator of happiness and inspiration. As you do so you become the radiating center toward which those are drawn who will add to your happiness and cooperate with you in making of your life a beautiful success. Spirit intends you to be a radiating center that will draw to you whatsoever you need to be well and strong, successful and prosperous.

Quickened by the Spirit

You remember the spiritual inspiration that Paul had, an inspiration that is also ours as we claim the light and power and love that are God's expression through us:

"If the Spirit of him that raised up Jesus from the dead dwelleth in you, he that raised up Christ Jesus from the dead shall give life also to your mortal bodies through his Spirit that dwelleth in you."

It isn't individuals at Unity who quicken and heal. It isn't the human desire of the individual's own heart that makes the life to flow through his organism more freely. It isn't the thing that we usually think of as Christianity that brings one into the quickening, healing currents of Christ life. It is the stirring in us of the same Spirit of

Christ that was and is in Jesus Christ—the Spirit of God, standing forth in individual consciousness and expression—the stirring up in our mind of divine ideas from the mind of Being. It is the soul's willingness and effort actually to live in its daily thinking and acts in the Spirit of Christ—that same Spirit which made Jesus to forget Himself in doing the good and perfect will of His Father. It is not church-going and praying and the observance of moral laws, but vital, loving, powerful words and acts of helpfulness to others. Jesus' consecration was a living, constant thing. He adored the Father and sought constantly to glorify Him in making the things of His Spirit manifest in the lives of His children. Jesus was eagerly discovering the real purpose of life and fulfilling it not for Himself alone but for all of us. And Jesus says: "Follow me." "If ye love me, ye will keep my commandments." "He that believeth on me, the works that I do shall he do also." "Feed my sheep." "As ye go, . . . Heal the sick, raise the dead, cleanse the lepers, cast out demons."

To be truly healed and quickened by the life more abundant, one must forget the past, and the limitations of the past, and offer every thought, every ounce of energy to Spirit, to be used in bringing God's kingdom of light and love and order and beauty and health into the earth, into the lives of all people. This giving is not to be done in human consciousness and might; but in the realization that it is God working through one's soul and body to increase constantly one's life and strength and substance, to fulfill His perfect plan. One's body is to be thought of as the temple of the living God. One's arms and hands are to be thought of, and used, as God's arms and hands, the expression of God-Mind's ideas of power and loving service and splendid work. The executive power of the mind, in its relation to things that we think of as belonging in the three-dimensional world, is expressed through the arms and hands. One should think of whatever one is led to do as being God's work. One should know and rejoice in one's innate ability to accomplish that work.

One should realize that one is free to decide wisely, and to do whatever will benefit oneself and others. One should see others in this beautiful spiritual world of activity and bless them.

God is in us as the very life and substance that we use, and our use of His gifts increases our ability to use and to direct them. God is life; we make that life into living. God is love; we make divine love into loving. God is substance; we take the substantial reality and bring it through into the manifest world. God is wisdom; we claim oneness with divine wisdom and it expresses through us as wise thoughts and decisions and actions: the light of life that glows from heart and face, yes, every cell of the body.

Permanent Prosperity

The only way to become permanently prosperous and successful is through the quickening, awakening, and bringing into righteous use all the indwelling resources of Spirit. When we develop our soul and express its talents and capabilities in loving service to God and mankind, all of our temporal needs will be supplied in bountiful measure. We have access to the realm of rich ideas; we enrich our consciousness by incorporating these rich ideas into it. A rich consciousness always demonstrates manifest prosperity.

"The kingdom of God is within you." Jesus said, "Seek ye first his kingdom, and his righteousness; and all these things shall be added unto you." This means that we are to find the wealth of capabilities and spiritual resources within us, and bring them into expression. When we develop the power to accomplish things and the qualities that we need in order to accomplish them, our success is assured.

We must depend wholly on the *inner* kingdom of supply and the indwelling Christ, for this inner way is the only way to receive permanently. We are to cease depending on outer, material avenues for prosperity, because when we look to the outer we look away from the one resource that is within us.

Prosperity is the result of complying with definite laws that are revealed by the Spirit of truth within. Those who are prosperous and successful are the people who have a rich consciousness. They open their minds to rich ideas, and then cash in on these ideas in an outer way. The men who are famous and successful are the ones who have developed their innate abilities and used the success-producing ideas that have come to them.

Sometimes we begin at the wrong end of the prosperity line, and our methods need changing. Perhaps we try to accumulate money to meet our temporal needs without first laying hold of the equivalent of money on the inner planes of consciousness. This inner equivalent consists of our rich ideas, our innate capabilities and resources of Spirit.

One great help in realizing permanent prosperity is to come into the realization that we do not work to earn money to meet our expenses! This is a delusion of mortal mind. In reality, in earning money we are expressing the God-given faculties and powers to bless others, and to keep our part of the divine law of giving and receiving. The supply is a gift of God and is ours because it is a part of His plan. We are to accept it in faith as such. Expect it to come, and it will.

Prosperity is not an accumulation of money or other so-called wealth, as we have sometimes thought. Wouldn't it really be a terrible thing if we were obliged to be eternally surrounded with the material baubles that we in our childish fancies believe to be prosperity? Wouldn't you dread to think of spending eternity with chains of houses and lands, and storehouses of food, and wardrobes of clothing, and garages of cars, and chests of silver? Wouldn't you dread to think that men and women were always to be deluded with the belief that these formed things are the realities, the truly valuable things of life? Why, we'd always have to be employing guards and giving our thought to caring for our wealth! And we'd never get to the place where we could really get still and learn from the Father the deeper things, the soul-satisfying things—the lessons there are for us ere we arise into the majesty of sonship—the realization of oneness! Let us rejoice then that our resources are the God qualities, the spiritual sources and substances from which our consciousness, our body, our home, come forth in response to our need and our word of faith and wisdom and authority. Let us rejoice that our good is in the realm of Mind, where it is instantly available and responsive to our thought and word and need. Rejoice that it is all under law, that it holds us to the law, even though a negative attitude does fail to produce desirable results! The lessons of experience are helpful to us until we learn the unchangeableness of the law and determine in our own mind that prosperity is progress, accomplishment of that which one has an urge to do, gain in spiritual, mental, physical or financial matters, attainment of that which is good and needful. Supply in abundance for the so-called temporal needs is a part of prosperity. And surely, since God has given us this physical being, and the physical earth, and all its bounty, it is not wrong for us to get the understanding of the full free use of it all!

If we are ever to understand and use the higher spiritual laws, we must learn to use the laws governing our present state! As we do this, we shall see that they are really different phases of the same law.

"The Lord is more willing to give than we are to receive."

The bounty of God is within us, undeveloped, and all about us, unused and misunderstood. It is ours to use all that the Father has.

Did I hear you say that healing comes from the Spirit within but that prosperity comes from without, or is something outside? Well, now, are you sure? Let's see. Spirit within is the quickening, adjusting, harmonizing force, yes. We must agree to think health, and to bless the body, and to express that which causes all the functions of the organism to work perfectly. But there is the physical side of health, also. Spirit must have substance through which to manifest! You must provide the manifest substance and life elements in proper food, and drink, and sunshine, and air. Without these Spirit would have no vehicle—and these are drawn in from the outside! Do you see?

And so it is with prosperity. The Spirit of Christ in you reveals the plan of God in your life and quickens in you the urge and the desire for the activities and the appropriations that fulfill the divine law in your being. Your faculties must let Spirit work through them, and develop them to the point where they can express the Christ ideas. They must learn to draw upon the universal spiritual substance and life, and mold it, and make use of it either for health or for prosperity. We have accepted the suggestions of those whose judgments in other things we might not be willing to abide by, and have thought that some things are "food which perisheth." The consciousness determines whether it is food that perishes, or whether it is living substance that is building an eternal temple. The results we get from the full, free use of life and substance are determined by our beliefs and our habits.

When you develop your soul and express its talents and capabilities in loving service to God and mankind, all your temporal needs will be supplied in bountiful measure. You have access to the rich ideas of Divine Mind; enrich your consciousness by incorporating rich ideas into it. When you make righteous use of all your indwelling resources of Spirit, then you will become a magnet to attract success.

A splendid prosperity lesson is found in the 1st chapter of Joshua. "Only be strong and very courageous, to observe to do according to all the law . . . turn not from it to the right hand or to the left, that thou mayest have good success whithersoever thou goest. This book of the law shall not depart out of thy mouth, but thou shalt meditate thereon day and night, that thou mayest observe to do according to all that is written therein: for then thou shalt make thy way prosperous, and then thou shalt have good success . . . for Jehovah thy God is with thee."

When you "observe to do according to all that is written," the law will open all the ways and outer avenues of supply for you.

True prosperity is not making money, or putting out goods, or developing property. It is determining what our own individual soul requires in order to cause it to unfold more and more of God; and then how to harmonize its expression with the needs of our fellow men so that all are really benefited and inspired to unfold and express more of their inner spiritual resources. The exchange of merchandise and money is merely incidental to this spiritual association and growth. Money success comes as a result; but there are other results that should be sought and rejoiced over even more than the financial returns.

Radiant health and physical freedom and the greater awakening of all the faculties and their physical centers of activity is another more valuable gain than the increase in salary and the promotion to a greater chair in the management's office.

The feeling that one is doing something to help in the establishment of the kingdom of heaven in the earth is great compensation for the hours of prayer and the effort to swing clear of the old commercial bondage and ways. We are to have whatever we require, yes. But we are making progress toward the time when we shall work at something really constructive, something that reveals God in man and in His world, something that gives us the privilege of deciding for ourselves, under guidance of Spirit, when we are to go and when we are to come. As soon as we are capable of it, the Lord will place us in such a position among our fellows. But before we are given this place, we are to prove that we are ever considering the highest good of our neighbors, and that we have the ability really to discern what it is they need and bring them face to face with it. Spiritual growth, you see, as well as temporal ability and success!

Helping Others

Instead of thinking of the people whom you have believed to be evil and an undesirable influence, begin to think of the goodness of God in the life of all His children. Think of God as everywhere present light, and love, and peace, and power, and life. Think of all men, all women, all children as ever abiding in His presence and expressing His qualities. As you do this, you will touch the reality of individuals, and you will invite only the best from them. Spirit will respond as you expect it to, for the Spirit of God is in each and every person. Some persons have not yet wakened to this realization, but as you declare the Truth for them and expect to have it express through them toward you, you will receive only loving and considerate treatment from them. As you read these explanations of the way in which a soul may lay hold of its inheritance from God and exercise its God-given freedom in the endeavor to develop and use its powers, pray for more light to enable you to see just how precious these individuals are and how important it is that we all have freedom to correct our mistakes.

The best way to help your brother is to pray for him to be spiritually illumined. Then if he has come to a place in his soul development where he is ready ·to accept Truth, he will have the understanding and desire to seek the indwelling Christ.

It is never wise to try to force Truth upon anyone. Place your brother "lovingly in the hands of the Father," and know that his own indwelling Lord will take care of him until he is open and receptive to ideas of Truth.

You are good, yes. But it is a negative goodness. You haven't realized your powers and made positive and purposeful use of them. You have been made to feel that nonresistance, and righteousness, and Christianity, and loving service are all passive. You have allowed your personal ideas of love and good will to make you too sympathetic and inclined to give, without seeking and asking for wisdom and good judgment to direct you.

Now while it is a virtue to be always ready to help others, we must be sure that we are truly helping them, and not hindering them by allowing them to continue in the unwise habits that have brought them to lack.

The greatest help is to be able to show others how they may help themselves and become self-supporting and resourceful. Study and prayer, along the lines of the Unity literature, will give you the knowledge and power really to help others to understand and bring forth their prosperity.

You have a store. Have you taken God into partnership with you? Do you start every day with quiet, purposeful communion with God? Do you really ask God to show you just what to do in each and every transaction?

Do you bless your store—the room, the stock of goods, the accounts, the customers, the salespeople? Do you fill the atmosphere with thoughts and words of love and wisdom and prosperity?

Do you demand of others that which you demand of

yourself, that they use good judgment, and self-denial when necessary? Do you make them understand that God prospers those who do their part; and that you expect them to do their part to pay their bills, so that you can pay yours and go on with the store, the service you feel led to offer?

Or do you think of the sickness, and the poverty, and the inharmony about you? Do you let folks have merchandise because you think them in need, or because they are God's children, and you are in this way helping Him to prosper them and make them happy; and because your business is going to prosper all and result in greater blessings? Do you pray for their prosperity? Do you expect God in these people and God in you to prompt them in doing that which is right by you?

By studying this matter you will come into a better understanding of the law of prosperity and you will be led into a much happier and more successful handling of your everyday problems.

Don't feel that you must just open your hands and pass out everything that you have. Conservation is one of the rules of success. You must expect others to do their part. And everyone, no matter how many failures he has had, can do his part.

———————

You aren't really giving Spirit much credit for ability to work in your brother's consciousness and affairs, are you? You say in the same breath that he has been upheld by the Spirit these months and that you feel he cannot stand the strain much longer! Don't you see what a mixed state of consciousness that is, and how foolish it is to pray and to expect Spirit to express its harmony and order and light in yourself or another, and then to feel that you or the other may at any time collapse because of the lack of spiritual power or light or life or substance?

Suppose "his mind," this tense, mortal state of mind

that has been causing him the worry and anxiety and weariness, does give way! What then? Why, that's the very thing that must come! This old fixed state of mind must give way, or be given up, that the Christ ideas may flow freely through his consciousness and give him the new life and light and poise and power and substance that he needs! Encourage him to let go, to place himself in God's care and keeping. It is personal assumption of responsibility that makes him feel he must cling so tenaciously to some of his opinions and ways of working.This is the only thing that keeps him out of the kingdom of heaven and its blessings! The treatment he has had, if he were cooperating, would have raised him into the Christ consciousness of peace and order and success long ago.

We are asking you to place him confidently in the care and keeping of his own indwelling Lord and to take your mental hands off! Don't even treat him! So long as you are trying to force something into him, you keep his attention divided, and he doesn't really get within and quiet enough to let his own soul commune with God. Leave him in the secret place, with the Father. Jesus has promised, you know, that those who go to the Father in secret, shall be rewarded openly!

The spiritual light coming to him from within will show him the utter foolishness of struggling and worrying and striving. It will reveal to him the right relation of things spiritual and things manifest. And he will see clearly how the right mental attitude and physical poise and health will result in instant and constant progress and prosperity and satisfaction. You can't give him this. Nor can we. It is the free gift of the Father within him.

What are you believing about this Father, who Jesus Christ proved was willing always to hear and to answer every call in the name of His Son Jesus Christ?

You are looking for a call. Do you really know when

you are called? You are to go straight to God to talk over these things. Go into your closet of prayer, into your "secret place of the Most High," and *shut the door;* then really pray.

We are not promised the Father's attention when we merely moan and cry out, "Oh, I long so to do something for this ailing one." Did Jesus Christ perform any healing by wishing that He had the power? No. God gave Him the power; why shouldn't He use it when all He was required to do to lay hold of it was to recognize that "I and the Father are one"?

So, dear friend, if you believe in the works of the Father, believe also in His Spirit in the midst of you, waiting to be recognized and put to practical use. Through "Christ in you" you are the "beloved Son" in whom the Father is well pleased.

All power is given unto you in all the affairs of mind and body. Exercise your God-given power, authority, and dominion and rise out of bondage to conditions of lack and discord.

There is a saying that "God helps those who help themselves." You are God's executive, and your indwelling Lord is depending on you to make His glory manifest. Then be up and doing. Do the will of Him who sent you. In so doing you are not only helping yourself but you are helping others.

Appendix B

From the Writings of Charles Fillmore

Reform Your God Thought

This is distinctly the age of reform. Never before
have there been such widespread and persistent efforts
by both men and women to right the wrongs of religion,
society, and politics.

From the hearts and souls of millions goes up the
cry, "Set us free from our burdens." Every imaginable
scheme of release is proposed, and each advocate of a
panacea for the people's ills stoutly affirms his to be the
only remedy that has virtue. It is observed that the majority of these reformers are clamorous that laws be enacted
to force their theories upon the people. In this, they are
following the same methods to cure the ills of the body
politic that they have followed in curing the body physical, and the results will surely be of like impotency.

Laws, whether natural or artificial, are but the evidence of an unseen power. They are simply effects, and
effects have no power in themselves. When man looks to
them for help in any condition of inharmony, he is de-
parting from a universally recognized principle of se-
quence. God, Spirit, or Mind—whatever you choose to
name it—is the supreme dictator, and thought is its only
mode of manifestation. Mind generates thought perpetually; all the harmonious and permanent affairs of men
and the innumerable systems of the infinite cosmos are
moved in majestic measures by its steady outflow.

All power has its birth in the silence. There is no
exception to this rule in all the evidence of life. Noise is
the dying vibration of a spent force. All the clatter of
visibility, from the harangue of the ward politician to the
thunder's roar, is but evidence of exhausted power. As
well try to control the lightning's flash by wrapping the
thunder about it as attempt to regulate men's minds by
statutory enactments.

All reforms must begin with their cause. Their cause

is mind, and mind does all its work in the realm of silence, which, in reality, is the only realm where sound and power go hand in hand. The visible outer world, with all its social, religious, and political laws, customs, and ceremonies, is but the flimsy screen upon which mind throws its incongruous opinions. God's thought is love, the inherent potentiality of the God man, which knows neither persons nor things, mine nor thine, but a universal brotherhood in which perfect equity and justice reign in joint supremacy. All philosophers and sages have recognized this silent cause, this perpetual outflow from center to circumference. Emerson says of Plato: "He was born to behold the self-evolving power of Spirit, endless generator of new ends; a power which is the key at once to the centrality and the evanescence of things." Jesus said: "The kingdom of God is within you." "Seek ye first his kingdom, and his righteousness; and all these things shall be added unto you." Elijah found God not in the whirlwind or the earthquake or the fire, but in the "still small voice."

All men who have moved the world to better things have received their inspiration from the Spirit within and have always looked to it for instruction. God is not a person who has set creation in motion and gone away and left it to run down like a clock. God is Spirit, infinite Mind, the immanent force and intelligence everywhere manifest in nature. God is the silent voice that speaks into visibility all the life there is. This power builds with hands deft beyond the comprehension of man and keeps going, with all its intricate machinery, universe upon universe, one within another, yet never conflicting. All its building is from center to circumference. The evidence for this runs from the molecule and the atom of the physicist to the mighty swing of a universe of planets around their central sun.

Every act of man has its origin in thought, which is expressed into the phenomenal world from a mental center that is but a point of radiation for an energy that lies back of it. That point of radiation is the conscious I,

which in its correct relation is one with Cause and has at
its command all the powers potential in Cause. The conscious I can look in two directions—to the outer world,
where the thoughts that rise within it give sensation and
feeling, which ultimate in a moving panorama of visibility; or to the world within, whence all its life, power, and
intelligence are derived. When the I looks wholly within,
it loses all sense of the external; it is then as the Hindu
yogi sitting under his banyan tree with his eyes riveted
on the point of his nose, denying his very existence until
his body is paralyzed. When it looks wholly without,
upon sensation and feeling, it loses its bearings in the
maze of its own thought creations. Then it builds up a
belief of separateness from, and independence of, a causing power. Man sees only form and makes his God a
personal being located in a city of dimensions. This belief of separateness leads to ignorance, because all intelligence is derived from the one Divine Mind, and when
the soul thinks itself something alone, it cuts itself off in
consciousness from the fount of inspiration. Believing
himself separate from his Source, man loses sight of the
divine harmony. He is like a musical note standing alone,
looking upon other notes but having no definite place
upon the great staff of nature, the grand symphony of life.

Life is a problem informed by a principle whose essence is intelligence, which the wise man always consults. The ignorant and headstrong trusts to his intellect
alone to carry him through and he always is in a laby-
rinth of errors.

A belief prevails that God is somewhat inaccessible,
that He can be approached only through certain religious
ordinances; that is, a man must profess religion, pray in a
formal way, and attend church in order to know God. But
these are mere opinions that have been taught and accepted by those who perceive the letter instead of the
spirit. For if God is Spirit, the principle of intelligence
and life, everywhere present at all times, He must be just
as accessible as a principle of mathematics and fully as
free from formalism. When a mathematician finds that his

answer to a problem is not correct, he consults the principle and works out the correct solution. He knows that all mathematical problems inhere in mathematical principles and that only through them can they be worked correctly. If he persistently ignored principles and blundered around in a jungle of experiments, he would be attempting to get up "some other way" and he would prove himself a "thief and a robber," for there is but one way. Jehovah God, infinite Mind in expression, is the way, and this Mind is always within reach of every man, woman, and child.

It is not necessary to go in state to God. If you had a friend at your elbow at all times who could answer your every question and who loved to serve you, you certainly would not feel it necessary to go down on your knees to him or ask a favor with fear and trembling.

God is your higher self and is in constant waiting upon you. He loves to serve and will attend faithfully to the most minute details of your daily life. If you are a man of the world, ask Him to help you to success in any line that you may choose, and He will show you what true success is. Use Him every hour of the day. If you are in doubt about a business move, no matter how trivial, close your eyes for an instant and ask the One within yourself what to do, just as you would send a mental message to one whom you know and who could catch your thought. The answer may not come instantly; it may come when you least think of it, and you will find yourself moved to do just the right thing. Never be formal with God. He cares no more for forms and ceremonies than do the principles of mathematics for fine figures or elaborate blackboards.

You cannot use God too often. He loves to be used, and the more you use Him the more easily you use Him and the more pleasant His help becomes. If you want a dress, a car, a house, or if you are thinking of driving a sharp bargain with your neighbor, going on a journey, giving a friend a present, running for office, or reforming a nation, ask God for guidance. . . .

Nothing is too wicked or unholy to ask God about. In my early experience in the study of Christian metaphysics, I was told that through the power of Divine Mind I could have anything I desired. I had a lot I wanted to sell and I asked God to dispose of it to a certain man who I thought needed it. That night I dreamed that I was a bandit holding up my customer. The dream showed me that I was asking God to do what was not right, and I thereby gained a lesson. A saloonkeeper came to me for health treatments and was helped. He said, "I also need treatments for prosperity, but, of course, you could not prosper a man in my business." I replied: "Certainly. God will help you to prosper. 'If ye shall ask anything of the Father, he will give it you in my name' does not exclude saloonkeepers." So we prayed for prosperity for the man. He afterward reported that he was out of the saloon business and had found prosperity in other lines of work.

If you are doing things that are considered wicked, you will find swift safety in asking God first, then acting or refraining, as you are moved. Some persons act as if they thought that they could hide themselves from the one omnipresent Intelligence, but this is the conclusion of thoughtlessness. God knows everything you do, and you might just as well have His advice. God does not want you to reverence Him with fear. God certainly never can get your confidence if you constantly stand in quaking fear of Him. He will do you a favor just as quickly if you ask in a jolly, laughing way as He would if you made your request in a long, melancholy prayer. God is natural and He loves the freedom of the little child. When you find yourself in His kingdom, it will be "as a little child."

God's kingdom of love and unity is now being set up in the earth. His hand will guide the only ship that will ever sail into the Arcadian port, and the contented, peaceful, and happy people who throng its decks will sing with one voice, "Glory to God in the highest."

Overcoming the Poverty Idea

Every lesson of Scripture illustrates some phase of mental action and can be applied to each individual life according to its most pressing need at the moment of its perception.

The conflicts between the children of Israel and the Philistines represent the conflicts that are always taking place in your mind and that are reflected in your body and affairs.

If you are ignorant of the laws of mental action, you get but the mere shell of the lesson in reading Scripture, and it is not of much real benefit. If, however, you consider that the characters in the narrative represent ideas in your own mind and if you follow them out in their various movements, you will solve all the problems of your life through a study of Scriptures. This does not mean that a study of the written Word alone will solve for you the problems of life, but you will see Scripture as the outward symbol of an inward condition and, through its study and its application you will come into an apprehension of the real Scripture, the Bible of the ages, the Book of Life within your own consciousness.

In everyone may be found the conflicting ideas represented by the children of Israel and the Philistines. They are pitted against each other, and the conflict goes on night and day. We call these warring thoughts Truth and error. We stand on the side of Truth and know that its thoughts are the chosen of the Lord, the Children of Israel, but the error thoughts seem so formidable that we quake and cringe in their presence.

We know that Truth must eventually prevail but we say that error is so large and strong that we cannot now cope with it—that we will do so when we have gathered more strength.

Thoughts are not all of the same importance. Some

are large and strong and some are weak and small. There
are aggressive, domineering thoughts that parade themselves and brag about their power and, with fearful
threats of disaster, keep us frightened into submission to
their unrighteous reign.

These domineering thoughts of error have one argument that they impress upon us at all times, and that is,
fear of results should we dare to meet them and to oppose
openly their reign. This fear of opposing error, although
we know it to be false, is woven into our whole mental
fabric.

This fear is portrayed by the spear of Goliath, and
the narrative most aptly states, "And the staff of his spear
was like a weaver's beam."

The first step to rid your mind of this giant bugaboo
is to get a clear perception of what your rights are as a
child of God. You know that you should not be under the
dominion of anything in the heavens above or in the
earth below. You are given dominion over all. If you are
not exercising that dominion, now is the time to begin.
You will never find a better time nor a more propitious
state of consciousness. If you are in fear of the boastings
of this brawny Philistine, seek out the way to "give the
dead bodies . . . unto the birds of the heavens." There is a
way, a righteous way, and it is the duty of every one of
God's children to find it. This way is graphically set forth
in the 17th chapter of I Samuel.

The name David means "the beloved of the Lord"
and David represents your righteous perception of your
privileges as a child of the living God. You are not a
slave to anything or to anybody. You cannot be alarmed
by the threat of this god of mammon. You have the perception of Truth and you sling it at the center of his carnal thinking, which is the forehead.

This formidable shield and armor of brass do not
intimidate you, because you know that they are empty
show, that the right idea will reach the vulnerable part in
spite of them and the braggart will go down.

Whole armies of good people, righteous people,

Christians, the children of Israel, believe that this power cannot be overcome. They are looking for something larger and stronger in a material way to be brought forth for its destruction. They forget that "the battle is Jehovah's."

Are you cringing in the sight of this Goliath? Does he come out daily and frighten you with his display of strength and his threats? It does not have to be so. There is a little idea in your mind that can slay him: the perception of your place in Divine Mind. You doubtless have not considered it of much importance. You have kept it off on the mountainside of your spirituality shepherding your innocent thoughts. You have not considered it equal to coping with the affairs of active life. Now let this David come forth. Get a clear idea of where you really belong in creation and what your privileges are. Then that boasting Philistine will cause your perception of justice and equity to say hot words of Truth. You will ask, "Who is this uncircumcised Philistine, that he should defy the armies of the living God?"

Do you think it possible that God has so ordained it that men cannot escape from the servitude of hard conditions? Verily not. This would not be justice, and who dare say that God is not just?

No, it is your privilege at any time to step boldly out and to defy the giant of the Philistines. The Lord has been with us in slaying the fear of sickness and of sin— the bear and the lion of David—and why should He not be with us in slaying this fear of poverty with which the mammon champion so unsparingly whips us?

"The battle is Jehovah's," and He will be with us, and we shall be delivered "out of the hand of this Philistine."

The weapons of the Lord's man are not carnal; he does not wage war after the manner of the world. He does not use steel, brass armor, and coats of mail. These are the protection of selfishness and the weapons of oppression.

The beloved of the Lord is the devout shepherd Da-

vid, who goes forth in the simplicity of justice, knowing
that his own innocence is his defense. His weapons are
not those accepted by the world as equal to the occasion
—the shepherd's sling and its smooth stones. These are
the words of Truth, and it is the will that sends them
forth. They are disdained by the Philistine but they do
their work, and the great mass of materiality goes down
before their sure aim. So the Lord has this day given this
financial fear in all its phases into our hands. We know
that it is not true that man is servile to the money idea.
He does not have to slave for his brother man and cringe
to him in order to obtain this universal servant of all. No,
we are not bound to this wheel of work day in and day
out that the god of mammon may be appeased on his own
terms.

We are the children of the living God. The living
Father is here today and always, right in our midst, and it
is our privilege to claim Him as our support and resource
on conditions and terms that He will reveal to us when
we have acknowledged Him and dismissed the fear of
mammon.

The five smooth stones chosen by David out of the
brook represent five irrefutable statements of Truth.
These five statements, slung from a mind confident of
itself and its cause, will suddenly crush the forehead of
Goliath, error's giant. These statements are covered by
the following affirmations and denials:

*I am the beloved of the Lord, and He will be with me
in all my righteous words, and they shall accomplish that
for which I send them forth.*

*I cannot be deprived of my own and I dissolve in my
own mind and in the minds of all men the belief that
what is mine can be withheld from me.*

*My own shall, by the sure and certain law of God,
come to me, and I now welcome it in the presence of this
clear perception of Truth.*

*I am under obligations to no one. God, my opulent
Father, has poured out to me all resource, and I am a
mighty river of affluence and abundance.*

My bounty is so great that men marvel at its sumptuous abundance. I own nothing selfishly, yet all things in existence are mine to use and, in divine wisdom, to bestow upon others.

===========

God Presence

I am now in the presence of pure Being and immersed in the holy Spirit of life, love, and wisdom.

I acknowledge Thy presence and power, O blessed Spirit. In Thy divine wisdom now erase my mortal limitations, and from Thy pure substance of love bring into manifestation my world, according to Thy perfect law.

Man knows intuitively that he is God's supreme creation and that dominion and power are his, though he does not understand fully. The I AM of him ever recognizes the one divine Source from which he sprang, and he turns to it endeavoring to fathom its wonderful secrets. Even children grope after the truths of Being.

No man knows the beginning of the query, "Who, what, and where is God?" It is dropped from the lips of the little child when he first begins to lisp the name of father and of mother, and it is repeated throughout the years.

Who made you? Who made me? Who made the earth, the moon, and the sun? God. Then who made God?

Thus, back to the cause beyond the cause ever runs the questioning mind of man. He would understand the omnipresence that caused him to be.

Does an answer ever come to these questionings? Does man ever receive satisfactory returns from this mental delving in the unfathomable? Each man and each woman must answer individually, for only the mind of

God can know God. If you have found God in your own
soul, you have found the source of health, of freedom,
and of the wisdom that answers all questions.

Language is the limitation of mind; therefore, do not
expect the unlimited to leap forth into full expression
through the limited.

Words never express that which God is. To the inner
ear of the mind awakened to its depths, words may carry
the impulses of divine energy and health that make it
conscious of what God is, but in their formulations, such
words can never bind the unbindable.

So let us remember that by describing God with
words in our human way we are but stating in the lisping
syllables of the child that which in its maturity the mind
still only faintly grasps. Yet man may know God and
become the vehicle and expression of God, the unlimited
fount of life, health, light, and love.

God is the health of His people.

Man recognizes that health is fundamental in Being
and that health is his own divine birthright. It is the orderly state of existence, but man must learn to use the
knowledge of this truth to sustain the consciousness of
health.

Health is from the Anglo-Saxon word meaning
"whole, hale, well." The one who uses the word really
implies that he has an understanding of the law of the
perfect harmony of Being. Health is the normal condition
of man and of all creation. We find that there is an omnipresent principle of health pervading all living things.
Health, real health, is from within and does not have to
be manufactured in the without. Health is the very essence of Being. It is as universal and enduring as God.

Being is the consciousness of the one Presence and
the one Power, of the one intelligence, and man stands in
the Godhead as *I will.* When man perceives his place
in the great scheme of creation and recognizes his I AM
power, he declares, "I discern that I will be that which I
will be."

Man is the vessel of God and expresses God. But there is a mighty difference between the inanimate marble, chiseled by the sculptor into a prancing steed, and the living, breathing horse consciously willing to be guided by the master's rein.

So there is a wide gap between the intelligence that moves to an appointed end under the impulse of divine energy and that which knows the thoughts and desires of Divine Mind and cooperates with it in bringing about the ends of a perfect and healthy creation.

"No longer do I call you servants; for the servant knoweth not what his Lord doeth; but I have called you friends; for all things that I have heard from my Father I have made known unto you."

It must be true that there is in man a capacity for knowing God consciously and communing with Him. This alone insures health and joy and satisfaction. It is unthinkable that the Creator could cause anything to be that is so inferior to Himself as to remove it beyond the pale of fellowship with Him.

Even in metaphysical concepts of God, the impression left us is of a Creator great in power, wisdom, and love. In one sense, this is true, but the standard by which man compares and judges these qualities in his mind determines his concept of God.

If I say that God is the almighty power of the universe and have in mind power as we see it expressed in physical energy and force, I have not set up the right standard of comparison. It is true that all power comes from God, but it does not follow that the character of the thing we term power is the same in the unexpressed as in the expressed.

God is power; man is powerful. God is the indescribable reservoir of stored-up energy which manifests no potency whatever until set in motion through the consciousness of man, yet possesses an inexhaustible capacity that is beyond words to express. When that power is manifested by man, it becomes conditioned. It is described as powerful, more powerful, most powerful, and it has its various degrees of expansion, pressure, velocity, force, and the like.

This power is used by men to oppress one another, and there has come to be an idea that God is power in the sense of great oppressing capacity. It is an ancient idea that He can and does exercise His power in punishing His creations, pouring out upon them His vengeance.

But this is not the character of divine power. If by power we mean force, energy, action, oppression, then we should say that God has no power, that God is powerless; because His power is not like the so-called power that is represented by these human activities.

God is wisdom—intelligence—but if we mean by this that God is "intelligent," that His knowledge consists of the judgments and inferences that are made in a universe of things, then we should say that God is nonintelligent.

God is substance; but if we mean by this that God is matter, a thing of time, space, condition, we should say that God is substanceless.

God is love; but if we mean by this that God is the love that loves a particular child better than all children, or that loves some particular father or mother better than all fathers and mothers, or that loves one person better than some other person, or that has a chosen people whom He loves better than some other people who are not chosen, then we should say that God is unloving.

God does not exercise power. God is that all-present and all-quiet powerlessness from which man "generates" that which he calls power.

God does not manifest intelligence. God is that unobtrusive knowing in everyone that, when acknowledged, flashes forth into intelligence.

God is not matter nor confined in any way to the idea of substance termed matter. God is that intangible essence which man has "formed" and called matter. Thus, matter is a limitation of the divine substance whose vital and inherent character is above all else limitless.

God is not loving. God is love, the great heart of the

universe and of man, from which is drawn forth all feeling, sympathy, emotion, and all that goes to make up the joys of existence.

Yet God does not love anybody or anything. God is the love in everybody and everything. God is love; man becomes loving by permitting that which God is to find expression in word and act.

The point to be clearly established is that God exercises none of His attributes except through the inner consciousness of the universe and man.

God is the "still small voice" in every soul that heals and blesses and uplifts, and it is only through the soul that He is made manifest as perfect wholeness.

Drop from your mind the idea that God is a being of majesty and power in the sense that you now interpret majesty and power.

Drop from your mind the belief that God is in any way separated from you, that He occupies form or space outside of you, or that He can be manifested to your consciousness in any way except through your own soul.

We look at the universe with its myriad forms and stupendous evidences of wisdom and power and we say: All this must be the work of one mighty in strength and understanding; I should stand in awe of such a one and realize my own insignificance in His presence. Yet when we behold the towering oak with its wide-spreading branches, we say it grew from a tiny acorn. A little stream of life and intelligence flowed into that small seed and gradually formed the giant tree. It was not created in the sense that it was made full-orbed by a single fiat of will, but it grew from the tiny slip into the towering tree through the inherent potentialities of the little seed, the acorn.

So God is in us the little seed through which is brought forth the strong, healthy Christ man.

That "still small voice" at the center of our being does not command what we shall be or what we shall do or not do. It is so gentle and still in its work that in the hurly-burly of life we overlook it entirely. We look out and, beholding the largeness of the world of things, we begin to cast about for a god corresponding in character with this world.

But we do not find such a god on the outside. We must drop the complex and find the simplicity of "the most simple One" before we can know God. We must become as a little child.

Jesus said "God is Spirit" not "a Spirit," as in the King James Version. According to Webster, the word *spirit* means "life or living substance considered independently of corporeal existence; an intelligence conceived of apart from any physical organization or embodiment; vital essence, force, or energy as distinct from matter; the intelligent, immaterial, and immortal part of man; the spirit, in distinction from the body in which it resides."

Paul says, "In him we live, and move, and have our being." If we accept the Scriptures as our source of information, there can be no higher authority than that of Jesus and Paul. They say that God is Spirit.

Spirit is not matter, and Spirit is not person. In order to perceive the essence of Being, we must drop from our mind the idea that God is circumscribed in any way or has any of the limitations usually ascribed to persons, things, or anything having form or shape. "Thou shalt not make unto thee a graven image, nor any likeness of anything that is in heaven above, or that is in the earth beneath."

God is life. Life is a principle that is made manifest in the living. Life cannot be analyzed by the senses. It is beyond their grasp; hence, it must be cognized by Spirit.

God is substance; but this does not mean matter, because matter is formed while God is the formless. This substance that God is lies back of all matter and all forms. It is that which is the basis of all form yet enters not into any form of finality. It cannot be seen, tasted, or touched. Yet it is the only "substantial" substance in the universe.

God is love: that from which all loving springs.

God is Truth: the eternal verity of the universe and man.

God is mind. Here, we touch the connecting link between God and man. The essential being of God as principle cannot be comprehended by any of the senses or faculties, but the mind of man is limitless, and through it, he may come in touch with divine principle.

It is the study of mind that reveals God. God may be inferentially known by studying the creations that spring from Him, but to speak to God face to face and mouth to mouth, to know Him as a child knows his father, man must come consciously into the place in mind that is common to both man and God.

Men have sought to find God by studying nature, but they have always fallen short. This seeking to know God by analyzing the things made is especially noticeable in this age. Materialistic science has sought to know the cause of things by dissecting them. By this mode, they have come to say: We must admit that there is a cause, but we have not found it; so we assume that God is unknowable.

To know God as health, one must take up the study of the healthy mind and make it, not physical appearance, the basis of every calculation. To study mind and its ideas as health is a departure so unusual that the world, both religious and secular, looks upon it as somehow impracticable. The man who lives in his senses cannot comprehend how anything can be got out of the study of something apparently so intangible.

The man of affairs cannot see what mind or its study has to do with matters pertaining to his department of life, and the religionist who worships God in forms and ceremonies makes no connection between the study of mind and finding out the real nature of God.

Behold, I go forward, but he is not there;
And backward, but I cannot perceive him;
On the left hand, when he doth work, but I cannot
    behold him;

He hideth himself on the right hand, that I cannot
   see him.

Thus, ever cries the man who looks for God in the external, for health from an outside source.

In mathematics, the unit enters into every problem;
and in existence, mind is common to all, above and below, within and without. The secret of existence will
never be disclosed before man takes up and masters the
science of his own mind.

Man's consciousness is formed of mind and its ideas,
and these determine whether he is healthy or sick. Thus,
to know the mysteries of his own being, he must study
mind and its laws.

Many persons in every age have come into partial
consciousness of God in their own soul and have com-
muned with Him in that inner sanctuary until their faces
shone with heavenly light; yet the mysteries of creative
law were not revealed to them, because they did not get
an understanding of its key, which is mind.

Mind is the common meeting ground of God and
man, and only through its study and the observation of all
the conditions and factors that enter into its operation can
we come into the realization of God as abiding health
and sustenance.

God is mind; and we cannot describe God with
human language, so we cannot describe mind. To describe is to limit, to circumscribe. To describe mind is to
limit it to the meaning of sense. In our talk about mind,
we are thus forced to leave the plane of things formed
and enter the realm of pure knowing.

We can only say: I am mind; I know. God is mind;
He knows. Thus, knowing is the language I use in my
intercourse with God.

If you ask me about the language I use in communi-
cating with God, I am not able to tell you; because you
are talking from the standpoint of using words to convey
ideas, while in the language of God, ideas in their original purity are the vehicles of communication.

But ideas are the original and natural agents of

communication, and everyone is in possession of this easy way of speaking to God and man. Thus, we may learn to use this divine and only true way consciously if we will but recognize it and use it on the plane of mind.

But we must recognize it. This is the one truth that we have to reveal to you: how to recognize this divine language in your own consciousness and how, through recognition, to bring it forth into visibility. It is a truth, however, that we cannot reveal to you by a series of eloquent essays on the majesty, power, and wisdom of God and on the everlasting joy that follows when you have found Him; but only by showing you in the simplest way how to come into conscious relations with the Source of omnipresent wisdom, life, and love, by taking with you in the silent inner realms the first steps in the language of the soul.

Compared with audible language, communion in mind can be said to be without sound. It is the "still small voice," the voice that is not a voice, the voice using words that are not words. Yet its language is more definite and certain than that of words and sounds, because it has none of their limitations. Words and sounds are attempts to convey a description of emotions and feelings, while by the language of mind, emotions and feelings are conveyed direct. But again, you must transcend what you understand as emotion and feeling in order to interpret the language of God. This is not hard. It is your natural language, and you need only return to your pristine state of purity to achieve it entirely.

You are mind. Your consciousness is formed of thoughts. Thoughts form barriers about the thinker, and when contended for as true, they are impregnable to other thoughts. So you are compassed about with thought barriers, the result of your heredity, your education, and your own thinking. Likewise, your degree of health is determined by your thoughts, past and present.

These thoughts may be true or false, depending on your understanding and use of divine law. You must open the walls of your mental house by a willingness to receive and weigh these thoughts in the balance of good judgment and to drop out of your mind everything except this one powerful idea: I want to know God's Truth; I am now willing to learn.

If there is not in your consciousness a demonstration that mind has a language on its own silent plane and that it can manifest itself in your mind, body, and affairs, then you can go back to your old convictions.

The fundamental basis and starting point of practical Christianity is that God is principle. By principle is meant definite, exact, and unchangeable rules of action. That the word principle is used by materialistic schools of thought to describe what they term the "blind forces of nature" is no reason why it should convey to our mind the idea of an unloving and unfeeling God. It is used because it best describes the unchangeableness that is an inherent law of Being.

From the teaching that the Deity is a person, we have come to believe that God is changeable; that He gets angry with His people and condemns them; that some are chosen or favored above others; that in His sight good and evil are verities, and that He defends the one and deplores the other. We must relieve our mind of these ideas of a personal God ruling over us in an arbitrary, manlike manner.

God is mind. Mind evolves ideas. These ideas are evolved in an orderly way. The laws of mind are just as exact and undeviating as the laws of mathematics or music. To recognize this is the starting point in finding God.

God loves spiritual man, and that love is expressed according to exact law. It is not emotional or variable, nor is there any taint of partiality in it. You are primarily a spiritual being, the expression of God's perfection, the receptacle of His love; and when you think and act in the consciousness of perfection and love, you cannot help being open to the influx of God's love and to the fulfillment of His divine purpose. This is the exact and undeviating law that inheres in the principle that God is.

God is wisdom, and wisdom is made manifest in an orderly manner through your consciousness.

God is substance—unchangeable, incorruptible, imperishable—to the spiritual mind and body of man.

This substance of mind—faith—does not happen to be here today and there tomorrow, but it is moved upon by ideas, which are as unchanging as Spirit.

In Spirit, you never had a beginning, and your I AM will never have an ending. The world never had a beginning and will never have an ending. All things that are always were and always will be, yesterday, today, and forever the same.

But things formed have a beginning and may have an ending.

But God does not form things. God calls from the depths of His own being the ideas that are already there, and they move forth and clothe themselves with the habiliments of time and circumstance in man's consciousness. We must have firmly fixed in our understanding the verity that we shall have to square all the acts of our life.

God is never absent from His creations, and His creations are never absent from their habiliments; hence, wherever you see the evidences of life, there you may know that God is.

If you are manifesting health, that health has a source that is perpetually giving itself forth. A perpetual giving forth implies a perpetual presence.

There is no absence or separation in God. His omnipresence is your omnipresence, because there can be no absence in Mind. If God were for one instant separated from His creations, they would immediately fall into dissolution. But absence in Mind is unthinkable. Mind is far removed from the realm where time and distance prevail. Mind is without metes or bounds; it is within all metes and bounds; it does not exist but inheres in all that is. Hence, in Spirit and in Truth you can never for one instant be separated from the life activity of God even though you may not externally feel or know of His presence.

God lives in you, and you depend on Him for every breath you draw. The understanding you have, be it ever so meager, is from Him, and you could not think a thought or speak a word or make a movement were He not in it. Your body is the soil in which God's life is planted. Your mind is the light for which He supplies the oil. "I am the light of the world," said Jesus. "Ye are the light of the world."

Intelligence is the light of the world. "Let your light shine." How? By increasing the supply of oil, by increasing your consciousness of life, and by learning how to draw upon the omnipresent God for every need.

———————

A Sure Remedy

Here is a mental treatment that is guaranteed to cure every ill that flesh is heir to: Sit for a half-hour every night and mentally forgive everyone against whom you have any ill will or antipathy. If you fear or if you are prejudiced against even an animal, mentally ask forgiveness of it and send it thoughts of love. If you have accused anyone of injustice, if you have discussed anyone unkindly, if you have criticized or gossiped about anyone, withdraw your words by asking him, in the silence, to forgive you. If you have had a falling out with friends or relatives, if you are at law or engaged in contention with anyone, do everything in your power to end the separation. See all things and all persons as they really are—pure Spirit—and send them your strongest thoughts of love. Do not go to bed any night feeling that you have an enemy in the world.

Be careful not to think a thought or to say a word that will offend. Be patient, loving, and kind under all circumstances. You can do this if you are faithful to the silent hour, because there you will be helped to overcome the selfishness of the carnal sense.

There is an immutable law lying back of this healing method. God is love, and love is manifest as life. God is thus manifest in and through all His creations. If we do aught to cut off the love of any person, we are cutting off the love of God; hence, we are cutting off the life that flows through all. When we, by withdrawal from our fellows, in any way cut the cords of love that bind us together as men and women, we, at the same time, sever the arteries and veins through which the universal life flows. We then find ourselves mere bundles of strained nerves, trembling and shaking with fear and weakness, and finally dying for the lack of God's love. But omnipresent Spirit ever seeks to flow into us and to stimulate us in every faculty. We must, however, by our words and acts acknowledge this all-powerful Presence as the moving factor in our life, because each of us has inherent free will, which welcomes or rejects all, even God not being excepted.

Self-condemnation is also a great error, leading to dire results. If you have accused yourself of ignorance, foolishness, fear, sickness, anxiety, poverty, anger, jealousy, stinginess, ambition, weakness, or if you are melancholy and indulge in the "blues," ask forgiveness for each of the loving Father in whose image and likeness you spiritually have perfect life. Say often to this omnipresence:

I do now sacrifice these human limitations unto Thee, O Father! I am obedient unto the law of my being and I know that in Thee I am brave, true, energetic, wise, pure, perfect, strong, rich, and courageous. Thou art my almighty resource, and I do trust in Thee utterly.

Appendix C

Unity Chronology Since 1975

1975 Dedication of the new Unity World Headquarters Activities Center and Unity Inn was held.

1977 The International New Thought Alliance Archives was added to the Unity Library. The Lowell Fillmore Memorial Garden was dedicated. The birthplace of Myrtle Page Fillmore was honored by a historical marker in a dedication held at Pagetown, Ohio.

1978 The Unity Village Community and Visitors Center was completed.

1979 Unity School for Ministerial and Religious Studies was renamed Unity Ministerial School.

1980 Unity School for Religious Studies was established by the Education Department.

1982 Wee Wisdom School was discontinued.

1983 John A.V. Strickland succeeded James Dillet Freeman as director of Silent Unity. Unity School resumed responsibility for ministerial education as USRS expanded to include the Ministerial Education Program.

1984 Connie Fillmore was appointed executive vice president of Unity School.

1987 Connie Fillmore succeeded Charles R. Fillmore as president of Unity School. The Development Department was formed.

1989 Celebration of Unity's Centennial. New Silent Unity building and the Unity School of Christianity Historical District were dedicated. Chris Jackson was named an executive vice president.

1990   Jim Rosemergy was named an executive vice president. USRS offered the Spanish Continuing Education Program.

1991   Mary-Alice and Richard Jafolla succeeded John A.V. Strickland as directors of Silent Unity. *Wee Wisdom* magazine ceased publication.

1992   *The Word* public service announcement television program ceased airing.

1994   Silent Unity satellite ministries were established in Germany, New Zealand, Australia, France, Ghana, Great Britain, and Mexico. The first annual World Day of Prayer was organized.

1995   The first Unity World Conference was held in Birmingham, England. The Outreach Department was formed.

1996   The Unity Rose Garden was accredited by All-America Rose Selections, Inc. (AARS). Unity World Headquarters established a home page on the Internet: (http://www.unityworldhq.org).

1998   Lynne Brown succeeded Mary-Alice and Richard Jafolla as director of Silent Unity.

1999   Unity School premiered its new publishing imprint, Unity House, at Book Expo America in Los Angeles.

About the Author

Born in Wilmington, Delaware, in 1912, James Dillet Freeman moved to Kansas City with his family when he was ten years old. He attended Kansas City public schools and the University of Missouri, where he graduated with honors in 1932. He began writing verse at the age of ten and by the time he finished college, his poems had been published in national publications.

While still in college, Jim was given summer work in 1929 at Unity School by invitation of Unity's cofounder Myrtle Fillmore. After a year of postgraduate work at the University, he joined the Unity staff on a permanent basis in 1933, serving in the School's prayer ministry as a letter writer.

As the need for trained Unity ministers developed, Jim was ordained and led in 1946 to organize a training program, which has now become the Unity School for Religious Studies. He served as director of Unity's ministerial program for twenty years. In 1971, Rev. Freeman became director of Silent Unity, the worldwide prayer ministry that responds to more than two million people annually. Shortly after that, he became a member of the Board of Trustees and first vice president of Unity School. In 1984, Jim retired from these last three positions in order to devote more time to writing and speaking on behalf of the Unity movement.

However, it is as a poet and author that James Dillet Freeman is best known. He has inspired literally millions. He has been called "a modern day transcendentalist" who writes in the tradition of Emerson, Thoreau, and Whitman. His work has been translated into thirteen languages and he has been published in *The New Yorker, Saturday Review,*

Scientific Monthly, Christian Herald, The New York Times, Reader's Digest, and many other publications.

It is estimated that published copies of Jim Freeman's poems exceed 500 million. His work has been taken to the moon twice, a distinction he shares with no other author. His 1941 "Prayer for Protection" was taken aboard Apollo 11 in July 1969 by Lunar Module pilot Edwin E. Aldrin, Jr. Aldrin had the poem with him when he made his historic moonwalk! Two years later, Jim's 1947 poem "I Am There" went to the moon with Colonel James B. Irwin on Apollo 15. Irwin left a microfilm copy of the poem on the moon!

In 1995, "I Am There" was featured on the television program *Angels II: Beyond the Light* on NBC. In talking about the poem, which is probably his best-known work, Jim says: "Of all the things I have ever written, 'I Am There' has meant the most to the most people. I wrote it in great anguish of spirit, out of a deep personal need. It has been reprinted many times and people have written from all over the world to tell me how much it has meant to them."

Jim has published twelve books, some by Doubleday, Harper & Row and some by Unity Books, including *The Case for Reincarnation, The Hilltop Heart, Love Is Strong as Death,* and *Once Upon a Christmas.* He also contributed a chapter in the Unity anthology *New Thought for a New Millennium.*

Printed in the U.S.A.

107-1917-75C-2-00